TABLOID JUSTICE

TABLOID JUSTICE

Criminal Justice
in an Age of Media Frenzy

Richard L. Fox
Robert W. Van Sickel

LYNNE
RIENNER
PUBLISHERS

BOULDER
LONDON

Published in the United States of America in 2001 by
Lynne Rienner Publishers, Inc.
1800 30th Street, Boulder, Colorado 80301
www.rienner.com

and in the United Kingdom by
Lynne Rienner Publishers, Inc.
3 Henrietta Street, Covent Garden, London WC2E 8LU

Library of Congress Cataloging-in-Publication Data
Fox, Richard L., 1967–
    Tabloid justice : criminal justice in an age of media frenzy / Richard L. Fox, Robert W. Van Sickel.
        p.   cm.
    Includes bibliographical references and index.
    ISBN 1-55587-913-6 (alk. paper)
    ISBN 1-55587-938-1 (pbk. : alk. paper)
    1. Mass media and criminal justice—United States. 2. Criminal justice, Administration of—United States.   I. Van Sickel, Robert W., 1956–   II. Title.
P96.C742 U63 2000
070.4'49364973—dc21

                                                                                00-042505

British Cataloguing in Publication Data
A Cataloguing in Publication record for this book
is available from the British Library.

Printed and bound in the United States of America

∞   The paper used in this publication meets the requirements
     of the American National Standard for Permanence of
     Paper for Printed Library Materials Z39.48-1984.

5   4   3   2   1

Contents

PART 3 CONCLUSION

Tables and Figures

FIGURE

Preface

During the 1990s, we had literally hundreds of conversations about the U.S. media's coverage of politics and law. In a basic sense, this book is the result of those conversations. We have long been alternately amused and repulsed by the media's presentation of the criminal justice system and what we have increasingly come to see as the trivialization of legal news. As a couple of dedicated law and politics "news junkies," we have found the rancorous debate on the news-talk and commentary programs to be eminently entertaining. But the increasingly sensationalistic nature of such programs has fostered a concern about the possible negative effects that such programming may have on public attitudes about the judicial process.

After witnessing thousands of hours of programming devoted to the O.J. Simpson trials and to the still-unsolved murder of JonBenet Ramsey, we felt that an examination of the media effects of such programming was called for. Thus, our goals here are to present a systematic exploration of the ways that the media have covered high-profile cases throughout the1990s and to assess the impact of such coverage on public attitudes toward the U.S. justice system.

Hidden within the pages of any scholarly study are the efforts of numerous individuals, and our list of debts in this regard is particularly long. Accordingly, we would like to express our gratitude to a number of people who have offered invaluable assistance in the completion of this book. Richard Niemi's support of our original proposal helped to keep this project alive, and although the final product is much different from the prospectus he originally reviewed, his early support was essential. We are perhaps most deeply indebted to Steven Wasby, who was instrumental in helping to shape the final draft. He reviewed several versions of the manuscript, and his comments were uniformly helpful, expediently delivered, and relentlessly candid. Jennifer Lawless was also a critical source of help and friendship as she meticulously edited and commented on the manuscript. A number of other friends and colleagues read all or parts of the manuscript. In this regard, we would like to thank Zoe Oxley, Eric R. A. N. Smith, and James Underwood. We would like to express our gratitude to Lynne Rienner's anonymous reviewer, whose two detailed evaluations were enormously helpful in our revising and reformulating of the final manuscript. Several other friends and colleagues helped craft our survey, including M. Kent Jennings, Theodore Gilman, Clifford Brown, and Terry Wiener. Liam Joynt, Andrew Wininger, and Mathew Barry, students at Union College, helped to gather and compile data, usually for little or no pay, and their devotion to the project has been greatly appreciated.

We are also indebted to Dean Christina Sorum and the Union College Faculty Research Fund for their generous assistance in funding our study. The staffs at Nielsen Media Research and the Pew Research Center were very supportive in helping us gather some of our data. Finally, we would like to thank the Brentwood Group, which offered us special consideration in conducting our national survey in an efficient and cost-effective manner.

Finally, our families and friends were a constant source of support, encouragement, perspective, and friendly criticism. We simply couldn't have done it without them, and we thus offer our deepest appreciation to Dominique, Stephanie, Eli, Naomi, Bill and Anita Kaplan, Robert Schuhmann, Olutumininu Coker, Lori Marso, and the indispensable Richard E. Rupp.

TABLOID JUSTICE

Introduction:
A Time of Tabloid Justice

This trial . . . is the most significant legal event ever to confront
America's direct understanding of the legal process.

—Law professor Frank Macchiarola,
discussing the O.J. Simpson case[1]

Throughout the 1990s, the U.S. public repeatedly focused on a series of
high-profile, often celebrity-centered criminal trials and investigations.
Each of these cases became something of a national obsession and was
associated with extraordinary levels of mass media coverage. Although
such "media trials" have occurred episodically at least since the 1920s,
the past decade has witnessed an enormous increase in their number.
Arguably beginning with the William Kennedy Smith trial in 1991, and
reaching a fever pitch during the O.J. Simpson criminal trial in 1995,
the public's apparently insatiable appetite for such events has steadily
risen, as has the media's devotion to their presentation. The coverage of
the Simpson saga has only recently been exceeded by the attention
devoted to the scandal and impeachment proceedings involving
President Bill Clinton and Monica Lewinsky.

Some of the past decade's other notable cases have involved such
figures as Lorena Bobbitt, Lyle and Erik Menendez, Susan Smith, Marv
Albert, Timothy McVeigh, Louise Woodward, the Los Angeles Police

Department officers who beat Rodney King, and Jack Kevorkian.[2] Even criminal cases that have never actually made it to the trial stage of the judicial process, such as those involving the seventeen-year hunt for the Unabomber or the murder of six-year-old beauty queen JonBenet Ramsey, have also been major, sustained media stories.[3] And the Clinton-Lewinsky matter, which was not even an expressly criminal case as the preceding cases were, nevertheless seemed to push aside most other political and legal news for all of 1998. This scandal was a sort of inevitable culmination of the decade's previous media cases, in that it involved most of the elements that seem to be predictors of both media attention and public titillation: politics, sex, law, crime, gender dynamics, and celebrity participants. As a final twist, once the Clinton-Lewinsky scandal evolved into the Clinton impeachment investigation and Senate trial, the mainstream press seemed ready to assure itself that it was, after all, only covering a profoundly important political development and not merely a tawdry saga of sexual misjudgment by the highest official in the land. Yet throughout 1998, the press often covered this high-level legal battle in the very same manner to which it had become accustomed in its coverage of the more tabloid-like cases mentioned above.

As evidence of the centrality of these events in the lives of U.S. citizens, recent polls indicate that more citizens can identify JonBenet Ramsey, a child generally unknown before her death at the end of 1996, than the vice president of the United States. Results from a similar survey reveal that roughly six times as many Americans know the name of the judge who presided in the Simpson murder trial than can identify William Rehnquist, the Chief Justice of the United States (see Table 4.2). Comparable levels of public awareness exist for acquitted rape suspect William Kennedy Smith.[4] These names, and the alleged or actual criminal conduct associated with them, have become cultural reference points for many Americans. Public knowledge and awareness of these events far exceed those of subjects that many commentators would deem much more important and worthy of a national focus.[5]

Media organizations have now become the willing transmitters of extensive and in-depth coverage of these events. Although stories about tawdry criminal trials and detailed accounts of the personal lives of trial participants have historically been the stuff of the tabloid press, the mainstream print and television media have now joined the act. For instance, *Time* and *Newsweek*, the two highest-circulation news-magazines in the United States, covered most of the aforementioned cases in great detail. Even the nightly network news broadcasts on ABC,

CBS, and NBC, which ostensibly have as their mission the reporting of the most important news in the nation,[6] gave these tabloid-like stories considerable airtime. An increasing number of television network news-magazines, such as ABC's *20/20* and NBC's *Dateline*, also pay frequent attention to criminal trials and investigations around the country. Additionally, the recent explosion of cable television talk and news stations, such as CNN, MSNBC, CNBC, the Fox News Channel, and Court TV, has led to many programs devoted to analyzing the trials and investigations of the day. Even more general cable channels, such as Discovery, the Learning Channel, Arts & Entertainment, and the History Channel, now regularly broadcast shows that deal with crime, criminal justice, and the legal system.

Further, the phenomenal growth of the Internet has resulted in numerous websites that offer coverage and discussion of criminal trials. At the end of 1998, for example, there remained about 100 websites dedicated to various O.J. Simpson matters, even though Simpson's civil trial ended in early 1997. These sites included a wide array of straightforward news, parodies, discussion groups, jokes, photographs, and games. Similarly, there were more than fifty websites that focused on the investigation of JonBenet Ramsey's death, as well as another 27,000 individual JonBenet-related webpages. In late 1998, a cursory search of the key words "Monica Lewinsky" on Yahoo!, a leading Web search engine, resulted in the listing of over fifty dedicated websites, and an additional 94,000 individual references, including everything from fan clubs to pornographic satire.[7]

DEFINING TABLOID JUSTICE

Aside from the enormous increase in the amount of mass media and independent coverage of the criminal justice process and the legal system, it is perhaps the fundamental shift in the style of this coverage that is most interesting—and perhaps most alarming. In this book, we argue that the United States has entered an era of *tabloid justice*, in which the mass media, in both their traditional and emerging forms, now tend to focus on the sensationalistic, personal, lurid, and tawdry details of unusual and high-profile trials and investigations. Throughout this book, we employ the phrase "tabloid justice," often referring to tabloid justice cases or tabloid justice coverage. This phrase embodies three important elements.

First, in an era of tabloid justice, the educational function of the press is undermined by its entertainment role.[8] The media focus on criminal trials and investigations as sources of entertainment, as opposed to civic education. In covering the most titillating or shocking aspects of a story, present-day coverage often trivializes more important structural and procedural issues. For example, during the period of January through October 1998, the *New York Times* ran at least eighteen stories that mentioned Monica Lewinsky's infamous blue dress, which was found to be stained with the president's "genetic material." In contrast, the *Times* presented only eleven stories that referenced the details of the independent counsel statute under which former judge Kenneth Starr actually derived his power and authority to investigate the scandal. *Newsweek* magazine's coverage shows a similar disparity, with six stories mentioning the blue dress but no articles focusing explicitly on the details of Starr's statutory authority.[9]

The second component of the tabloid justice atmosphere is a frenzy of media activity that envelops a given legal proceeding. The more respected media outlets, as well as the many acknowledged tabloid sources, are deeply involved in the coverage. The story is discussed, dissected, and analyzed by all forms of media. This media frenzy is perhaps best illustrated by the emergence of a veritable army of professional legal commentators. Each of these pundits is presented as a source of instantaneous expert opinion on everything from police behavior, prosecutors, the criminal mind, and defense strategies to impeachment, the separation of powers, and the inner workings of Congress. Yesterday's expert on race and the criminal justice system becomes today's authority on constitutional interpretation and the history of presidential scandal. For instance, in 1998, MSNBC's television program *Internight* offered the same panel of guests as experts on both presidential impeachment and the JonBenet Ramsey murder investigation. In both cases, the experts offered little historical, legal, or political background. Rather, the pundits focused overwhelmingly on the personal aspects of each issue, offering unfounded speculation about the extent of the relationship between President Clinton and Monica Lewinsky, and the possibility that JonBenet's brother might be the real murderer. Similarly, when Speaker of the U.S. House of Representatives Newt Gingrich announced his resignation in November 1998, *Rivera Live* featured a panel of "congressional experts," which consisted of a criminal defense attorney, a law professor, and a former federal prosecutor. The time of tabloid justice is a time when important legal and political issues—not to mention news stories not related to criminal proceedings—become lost in a cacophony of commentary, prognostication, and confrontation.

The third characteristic of the tabloid justice environment is the presence of an attentive public that witnesses these legal travails and uses them as a means by which to understand and assess the criminal justice process. Public interest, as measured through increased television ratings and publication sales, spurs continued media focus on the legal proceedings. On the one hand, this new era has resulted in an enormous increase in the public's basic awareness of the criminal justice system. On the other hand, the tabloid nature of contemporary media coverage may result in higher levels of public misinformation about the workings of the system and a corresponding drop in the public's faith in criminal justice in the United States.[10] Further, the polarizing manner in which the media now cover criminal trials, often in terms of blacks versus whites or men versus women, has potentially aggravated some of the most troubling social divisions in U.S. society.

When all three dynamics—a legal proceeding presented largely as entertainment, an obsessive media establishment, and an intensely attentive public—converge, the environment of tabloid justice emerges. Within this context, the idealized priorities of the criminal justice system, such as justice and fairness, have become secondary to the press's interest in attracting large audiences by presenting shocking images. This is the atmosphere of the tabloid justice era that we examine in this book.

▪ MASS MEDIA EFFECTS ON PUBLIC ATTITUDES

Central to our argument that tabloid-style coverage of these trials has important consequences for U.S. society is the question of whether mass media presentations have important effects on public attitudes. Most observers fully accept that both factual and fictional media stories help shape the thinking and behavior of the mass public.[11] Scholars also offer propositions about the mass media's ability to influence public opinion and behavior. Many of these academic theories proceed from a *social constructionism* perspective, or a belief that our reality is composed entirely of the information we gather from social interactions, rather than from any actual objective, empirical, or socially transcendent knowledge or insight.[12] Intense exposure to media images alters our views of reality. Many theories of mass media effects assert that heavy exposure to media-generated images may eventually convince consumers that the symbolic reality presented is an accurate reflection of objective social conditions.[13] But to see the world as it is portrayed in the mass media would be to embrace numerous incorrect views. Research shows that many shared misconceptions about occupational pursuits, ethnic groups, racial minorities, the elderly, social and gender roles, and crime and crime rates are at least partly cultivated through exposure to the mass media.[14] It is important to note, however, that such misconceptions may vary widely depending on both the audience and the particular medium conveying the message.

Assuming that the mass media do affect public attitudes and beliefs,[15] it is important to make distinctions among these media, as many of the differences hinder the construction of a general theory of media effects. For instance, television is a powerful medium for transmitting a sense of realism and emotional appeal.[16] Television's greatest impact is probably derived from its ability to reach millions of viewers simultaneously with the same powerful images. Because of the immediate and noncontextual nature of such images, however, research has shown that more than 75 percent of average viewers cannot identify either the specific major facts or the general theses of many television news stories.[17] In contrast, newspapers and magazines do a better job of providing readers with facts than either audio (radio) or visual (television) forms of media.[18] The advent of cable and satellite television and the presence of video images on the Internet have complicated matters further by making it difficult to determine what media have what impact.

Despite the various conceptual problems outlined above, three basic models tend to dominate the academic debate about media effects. Each of these models offers an account of the mass media's effects on the public's notions of social reality.[19]

The first of these approaches has been termed the *hypodermic needle* model.[20] As the term suggests, this perspective assumes that the mass media have a direct and significant effect on the way people perceive social conditions. The public imbibes media coverage like a drug, and the effects are powerful and long lasting.[21] Citizens are thought to be autonomous consumers of media-generated news, to which they turn for answers and from which they adopt beliefs about society and "acceptable" opinions about its various aspects.[22]

A second perspective, standing in contrast to the hypodermic needle model, has been called the *limited effects* model.[23] As with the hypodermic needle model, this theory posits that a person turns to the media for information and answers. But this perspective also holds that individuals do far more than simply take in and adopt the "reality messages" conveyed by the media. Rather, individuals assess the accuracy of that information in light of what they already know from other sources such as family, school, associations, church, and so on. Thus, although this model is also based on a notion of social constructionism, there is recognition that citizens have preexisting, relatively independent perceptions that condition or blunt the power of new information, such as that emanating from mass media sources. What is more, people from similar backgrounds and experiences are thought to see the world and react to media images in a way that is more alike than different. In effect, they share both the same "symbolic reality" and "experienced reality."[24]

A third perspective has been called *subtle* or *minimal effects*.[25] This model posits that the impact of the mass media is neither total (hypodermic needle) nor significantly mitigated by other factors (limited effects) but somewhere in between. From this perspective, the media's influence can be seen especially in the areas of "agenda-setting," "priming," and "framing," and each of these aspects is briefly described here.

"Agenda-setting" acknowledges that the media choose, for a variety of reasons, to cover a limited and rather predictable range of topics, persons, and organizations in their newscasts and stories.[26] Thus, the mainstream press, in effect, tells us "what to think about."[27] For example, when coverage of crime so saturates local newscasts that other important topics are pushed to the side, the public will perceive crime to be more important than U.S. relations with Iraq, poverty, or ethnic violence in the Balkans, for instance. The agenda-setting function of the media helps determine what citizens perceive as the most important issues of the day.

Closely related to agenda-setting, "priming" refers to the idea that when citizens think about people in the news, they will consider individuals in light of the issues and topics covered in the news. Most priming-effect research examines how people assess presidents.[28] In continuing with our example of crime, if crime is covered extensively in the news, then the priming effect would dictate that citizens evaluate the president in terms of how they feel the "crime problem" is being addressed.

A third component of this approach, "framing," embodies the notion that the content and format of news coverage may result in citizens adopting particular political attitudes. In the area of crime news, Shanto Iyengar has differentiated between "thematic" coverage, which employs statistics and discusses general trends, and "episodic" coverage, which employs anecdotal individual crime stories.[29] Iyengar and others have found that the framing of crime news, either in episodic or thematic terms, has led citizens to draw different conclusions about the appropriate response to crime policy.[30] This finding is particularly important in our analysis as all of the tabloid justice cases are examples of episodic coverage.

Importantly, all of the foregoing theories hold, albeit with significant variations, that mass media images do in fact influence the public's general and specific perceptions of society.[31] Thus, if we accept the premise that media exposure affects how people view the world, then we must explore the question of how the media choose what to cover, as well as the style of that coverage.

WHAT EVENTS ARE DEEMED NEWSWORTHY?

On the most basic level, we might posit that the news simply exists, it simply happens, in some objective sense, and that the mass media cover as much of it as possible given their resources. But *is* the news already "out there," with reporters and news organizations simply going out and "getting the story"? Most scholars of the media would find this too simplistic an assertion. In contrast, perhaps the news is quite simply what the press says it is. In other words, reporters, editors, and producers quite literally decide what news *is*.[32] Thus, as previously mentioned, a number of scholars have ascribed a substantial agenda-setting function to the mass media.[33] A substantial body of scholarly research has concluded that the media do enjoy the power of agenda-setting at least to some degree.[34] This makes the focus of the following paragraphs particularly important, as we consider the manner in which the media determine both who and what are worthy of their attention.

In considering what the media cover, it is important to think about the theoretical role the press should play in a democratic society. In the idealized conception of a democratic press, newsworthiness would be determined by the objective importance of a story. For the national news media, this might require a focus on major questions of public policy, foreign policy, and serious national developments. The media would serve as public educators on issues and stories that are significant to a large number of citizens. Additionally, the media would serve as watchdogs, holding government and other powerful institutions accountable for the exercise of their power. Finally, an idealized conception of mass media would allow for the free exchange of a myriad of perspectives and ideas.[35]

When we contrast these idealized notions with the actual workings of the mass media, it becomes apparent that these democratic imperatives are strikingly absent in the present news environment. Obviously, the extent to which the media ever conformed to these idealized notions is debatable. Nevertheless, in the contemporary world of journalism, newsworthiness appears to be determined by the interaction of two factors: the "objective" importance of an event and the goals of media organizations, which are often linked to the existence and perceived desires of a specific target audience or market. Portrayals of social reality reflect the subjective judgments of news organizations in their representations of human nature, social relations, and the norms and structure of society.[36] Not surprisingly, in deciding what news is, the activities and goals of the mass media themselves become nearly as determinative as the actual real-world events that they cover.

Mainstream news organizations consistently offer predictable coverage of certain actors and events. In his classic study *Deciding What's News*, Herbert Gans identified three subjects that dominate news coverage: known people, unknown people in unusual circumstances, and a prescribed set of activities.[37] Known people include all public figures, whether they occupy positions of influence or not. Unknown people include protesters, victims (mostly of crime), lawbreakers, voters, and those engaged in highly unusual behaviors. The third category, activities, involves the kinds of events on which the media focus—government conflicts and disagreements, government decisions, proposals, government personnel changes, protests, crimes, scandals, natural and other disasters, technological innovation, and national ceremonies.[38]

Published in 1979, Gans's study is based on media coverage during the late 1960s and early 1970s. Thus, one might assume this to be an outdated set of characteristics of newsworthiness. Gans's assessment, however, established a framework that still applies today. Writing more recently, media scholar Richard Davis identifies eight factors that journalists and media outlets use to determine newsworthiness: major events, timeliness, drama, conflict, unusual elements, unpredictable elements, famous names, and visual appeal.[39] In comparing the lists of Gans and Davis, we see a great deal of overlap. Importantly, though, Davis asserts that in the 1990s a new media culture took shape, and standards of newsworthiness evolved accordingly. Similarly, Davis and Diana Owen argue that "entertainment value" is now a central feature in the determination of newsworthiness, as news outlets find themselves in an increasingly more competitive struggle for viewers, readers, and listeners.[40] This competition contributes to the mainstream media's willingness to cover tabloid stories with much more vigor and detail than previously.

Since the 1960s, the style, format, and level of commercial competition have altered the relative balance and mix of hard news and entertainment that the press presents. For instance, although there has never been a time in U.S. history when a murder case involving a celebrity as well-known as O.J. Simpson would not have been a major media story, past coverage could not have compared to that of today in terms of its sheer volume, immediacy, and pervasiveness.[41] In the 1950s or 1960s, it would have been hard to imagine a scene, such as that which occurred the morning after the murders of Nicole Brown Simpson and Ronald Goldman, in which local network-affiliated news crews jostled one another to broadcast live, graphic video images from the blood-splattered front yard of the infamous Bundy Avenue condominium in California.[42] What has changed since the Gans study is simply the intensity and pervasive nature of today's media coverage.[43] In search of any unique angle, journalists and media organizations today are more likely to flock to a sensational story and cover almost any imaginable detail, including the most trivial.

Beyond the general standards of newsworthiness identified above, the selection of stories is strongly conditioned by the internal goals of the various media outlets themselves. National network news broadcasts, local news broadcasts, and cable news outlets all have different goals and imperatives, and all of them are ultimately beholden to a corporate bottom line. News events are packaged in ways that particular media outlets believe will be of interest to their specific targeted market or audience. Programs such as CNBC's *Rivera Live* and MSNBC's *Internight* cater to a group of "scandal junkies," who apparently never tire of repetitive coverage of the latest trial or legal controversy. Programs certainly determine newsworthiness based on the niche of consumers they wish to attract.

PURPOSE AND GOALS

The effects of media coverage and the decisions news organizations make about what to cover provide a critical foundation in helping to carry out our general aim of explicating and explaining the dynamics of the era of tabloid justice. Throughout this book, two central questions guide our analysis: How are high-profile legal proceedings covered in the media culture of the 1990s? And what impact has this coverage had on the public's knowledge of and attitudes about the criminal justice system? Generally, the answers to these questions are necessarily complex and depend on the particular cases and contexts. However, when viewed as a group, they have an importance far beyond their existence simply as a new form of entertainment. Because of the public attention they have received, as well as the public reaction to many of their outcomes, these cases have potentially broad and important ramifications for the functioning of the criminal justice system in the United States.

In some instances, these cases have highlighted legitimately troubling and controversial aspects of the criminal justice system. At other times, they (arguably) demonstrate that the criminal justice system is functioning as intended. But most important, we believe that these cases, and particularly the media's portrayal of them, have played a substantial role not only in exposing a new and irresponsible era of journalistic standards but also in undermining public faith in the criminal justice system in contemporary America. Of course, one could argue that the public would be entirely justified in being skeptical about the criminal justice system. However, we believe that weaknesses in the system are exploited and sensationalized by tabloid-style coverage. The media emphasis on highly anomalous cases, presented as though they illustrate the everyday workings of the system, presents an inaccurate picture of criminal justice in the United States.

Our central contentions attempt to answer questions posed by a number of scholars, journalists, and legal professionals such as Susanna Barber, Ronald Goldfarb, Burton Katz, Alan Dershowitz, and Anna Quindlen, who have grappled with assessing the benefits of extensive televised coverage of the legal system.[44] Most such writers focus on the need to protect the rights of defendants and suggest that increasing the presence of cameras in the courtroom may have the effect of improving the behavior of legal professionals and juries, by making certain that they are held publicly accountable for their actions.[45] In considering wider public benefits from increased coverage of the justice system, three possible benefits emerge: civic education about the inner workings of the legal system, greater public assurance of due process (as the media's coverage forces the courts to behave in a fair manner), and increased public confidence in the legal system.

While commentators are skeptical about these public benefits, especially Barber, Dershowitz, and Quindlen, they tend to assert that any
coverage is at least better than no coverage. What is missing in these
assessments, as Barber notes, is any broad empirical evidence about the
positive effects of trial coverage on public attitudes.[46]

Although the increased media coverage of the 1990s did provide
an opportunity for the public to learn about the courts, we will contend
that the tabloid-like nature of even mainstream press behavior undermined the possibility of broader public benefits. We will argue that this
style of media coverage in the 1990s has resulted in lower levels of
public confidence, while at the same time doing little to increase factual, substantive knowledge of the judicial process. In sum, observers of
the legal system may make accurate predictions about the benefits of
television coverage in modifying the behavior of lawyers and judges,
but for the most part they have underestimated the negative effects of
contemporary media coverage on wider public attitudes.

Throughout this book, we seek to demonstrate that the media's
coverage of various high-profile criminal cases has had a negative
effect on the way in which Americans perceive the criminal justice system, largely in terms of public confidence toward the everyday workings of the system. We contend that this coverage has led us to a troubling intersection of mass media agenda-setting and entertainment
programming. The agenda that the media have adopted is now heavily
skewed toward a series of legal proceedings that often have little objective importance to the lives of a vast majority of Americans. Here, we
freely admit a basic bias that we harbor. We believe that regular,
detailed, factual coverage of public policy, government, and the legal
system is simply more important than stories about individual criminal
trials, let alone stories about the personality quirks of defense lawyers,
the hairstyles of attorneys, the analyses of the president's phone sex
preferences, or extensive video footage of JonBenet Ramsey's beauty
contests.

Ultimately, tabloid justice–style coverage has distorted the public's
perception of the criminal justice system. For instance, during the coverage of most of these cases, the news media tend to give the impression that the majority of defendants actually *have* trials and that they
are either found guilty or acquitted after a jury has considered all relevant evidence.[47] In contrast, relatively little attention has been devoted
to the more prevalent problems of plea bargaining, court bureaucracy,
and courtroom subcultures. Thus, the agenda that is set by the media in

legal coverage often ignores broader, substantive public issues. The style of media coverage that emerges from these legal proceedings presents a missed opportunity to inform the public about the criminal justice system.

ORGANIZATION OF THE BOOK

In presenting our argument, we divide this book into three parts. Part 1 presents an account of the rise of the media's current obsession with covering high-profile criminal cases and of the mainstream media's adoption of a tabloid mode of coverage with regard to criminal cases and legal issues. In Chapter 1, we argue that the 1990s were a unique period, both in terms of the amount of media coverage that criminal cases received, and the public's interest in criminal justice proceedings. We introduce some of the decade's major media cases and offer brief summaries of those involving William Kennedy Smith, Rodney King, the Menendez brothers, Louise Woodward, O.J. Simpson, JonBenet Ramsey, and President Bill Clinton and Monica Lewinsky. We assert that these cases have been the most important, both in the levels of media attention and in the public interest paid to them. These are also the cases that best illustrate the mass media's behavior in the era of tabloid justice.

In addition, Chapter 1 considers the characteristics that seem to elevate a given legal proceeding to a very high level of national interest. Clearly, an urgent sense of human intrigue is important, but this can take many forms. Violence, especially murder, has always been a predictable draw. In fact, murder accompanied by sex has traditionally been seen as the most titillating of all crime stories. But other factors, such as race, gender, celebrity, and social class, also appear to be good predictors of the public's (or media's) interest in particular legal proceedings. In sum, Chapter 1 addresses the media's constant search for the next "trial of the century."

In Chapter 2, we argue that although the mainstream media's attention to such trials began at least as early as the celebrated Lindbergh baby case of the 1930s, and has continued through the ensuing decades, the 1990s definitely witnessed an exponential increase in both the amount and immediacy of such coverage. We offer empirical evidence of the overall increase in the media's coverage of U.S. courts and criminal justice issues. Also in Chapter 2, we revisit Chapter 1's discussion of newsworthiness by drawing a distinction between the ways in which the traditional mainstream media and the so-called tabloid or entertainment media have historically defined a good story. We suggest that there have been important changes in the news business since about 1990 and that the emergence of television newsmagazines and the Internet has been accompanied by an extraordinary increase in media coverage of the judicial process. Perhaps even more significant, the 1990s also have seen a blurring of the general lines that have traditionally divided the mainstream and tabloid presses.

In Chapter 3, we discuss the rise of the so-called new media, considering phenomena such as cable television news, talk programs, and the Internet. These media have contributed greatly to the increasing entertainment flavor of political and legal news. In addition, they have blurred the line between the reporting of, and the consuming of, political and legal news. In effect, cable news-talk shows and Internet chat groups allow the public an opportunity to participate in, as well as to consume, the news. It is also worth noting that it is not at all unusual nowadays for cable news shows, in particular, to devote considerable time to journalists discussing how other journalists are covering a particular story. Mass media coverage of a story, in some sense, becomes the story itself. This new self-referential mode of coverage comprises yet another aspect of this new era of media behavior.

Part 2 of the book assesses the impact of the new tabloid justice media culture. We emphasize here that our primary concern is that the era of tabloid justice represents an important missed opportunity, in which the press has squandered the chance to truly educate the public about the criminal justice system and has instead left citizens with little more than a detailed memory of the personalities involved in these cases. The chapters in Part 2 present the findings from our 1999 national poll of more than 1,000 respondents. The poll focused on seven of the most prominent cases in the 1990s. (For a full description of our survey methods and a copy of the survey instrument, see Appendix B.)

In presenting our results, we examine public attitudes toward specific actors and features of the judicial process, including the jury system, defense attorneys, prosecutors, judges, and the police. We demonstrate that although citizens may now possess more familiarity with some of the structural and procedural components of the judicial process, the era's tabloid-style legal coverage has led to unduly negative assessments of the criminal justice system. Ultimately, we conclude that the tabloid-like coverage of criminal justice works to undermine the legitimacy of the system. Indeed, a significant number of citizens have begun to worry about their own possible treatment in the legal process as a result of what they have learned from these tabloid cases.

Chapter 5 considers whether the new media culture has had different impacts on the public attitudes of members of different races, education levels, income levels, and men and women. Because divisions among these groups have been central features in many of the cases in this analysis, our goal here is to examine how the media coverage of these issues affects the public's views about them. For instance, did the Simpson and Rodney King cases change or inflame racial attitudes? Did the outcomes of the cases involving William Kennedy Smith and President Clinton have different effects on the views of men and women? We attempt to answer these questions by examining how blacks and whites, women and men, and the rich and poor view the criminal justice system and the tabloid justice cases. Ultimately, we conclude that tabloid justice coverage has simply reinforced different social groups' existing attitudes about the system, rather than teaching them about the real everyday workings of justice in the United States.

Finally, in Part 3, we summarize our central argument and findings. We then draw some broad conclusions about what the past decade has meant not only for the future of the criminal justice system but also for the mass media's relationship with that system. We conclude by speculating about what the future holds in terms of this relationship.

NOTES

1. Frank Macchiarola, "Finding the Truth in an American Criminal Trial: Some Observations," *Cardozo Journal of International Comparative Law* 5 (spring 1997): 97.

2. For a discussion of these and other notable trials in U.S. history, see Edward W. Knappman, ed., *American Trials of the 20th Century* (Detroit, Mich.: Visible Ink Press, 1995); and Gilbert Geis and Leigh B. Bienen, *Crimes of the Century* (Boston: Northeastern University Press, 1998).

3. For an analysis of the Unabomber case, see Robert Graysmith, *Unabomber: A Desire to Kill* (Washington, D.C.: Regnery Publishing, 1997). We discuss the Ramsey case further in Chapter 1.

4. Polling information about the public's knowledge of well-known criminal cases was provided by the Pew Research Center. Questions were asked between 1991 and the end of 1997.

5. Although we would ideally hope for expanded coverage of important domestic and international political and social issues, those who have studied

the media's portrayal of the electoral process have found that "issue coverage" has been rare and episodic. See Thomas Patterson, *The Mass Media Election: How Americans Choose Their President,* 3d ed. (Westport, Conn.: Praeger, 1988); and Eric R. A. N. Smith, *The Unchanging American Voter* (Berkeley: University of California Press, 1989).

6. For a discussion of how the networks have historically determined what stories to cover, see Herbert Gans, *Deciding What's News: A Study of CBS Evening News, NBC Nightly News, Newsweek, and Time* (New York: Vintage Books, 1979), chapter 3.

7. Our Web searches for each of these cases were conducted on November 3, 1998.

8. Historically, one of the primary arguments made in favor of increased electronic media access to the courts has been the supposed educational function of such coverage. For an effective summary of these arguments, see Susanna Barber, *News Cameras in the Courtroom: A Free Press–Fair Trial Debate* (Norwood, N.J.: Ablex, 1987), pp. 54, 94–95.

9. These figures are based on a Lexis-Nexis search conducted on October 6, 1998.

10. Another major argument in favor of increased media coverage of the courts has been that press attention fosters an increased confidence in the system. (See, for instance, Barber, *News Cameras in the Courtroom*, p. 54 ff.) As we shall see, this has not been a result of the tabloid era of media coverage of criminal trials.

11. Doris Graber, *Mass Media and American Politics,* 5th ed. (Washington, D.C.: Congressional Quarterly Press, 1997), p. 188.

12. Ray Surette, *Media, Crime, and Criminal Justice: Images and Realities,* 2d ed. (Belmont, Calif.: Wadsworth Publishing, 1998), p. 5.

13. There are considerable methodological problems involved in attempting to measure the effects of media exposure on people's attitudes and perceptions. For good discussions of these difficulties, at least as applied to the study of politics, see Graber, *Mass Media and American Politics*, pp. 205–207; Benjamin R. Page, Robert Y. Shapiro, and Glenn R. Dempsey, "What Moves Public Opinion," *American Political Science Review* 81 (March 1987): 23–43; and Thomas Dye, L. Harmon Zeigler, and S. Robert Lichter, *American Politics in the Media Age,* 4th ed. (Fort Worth, Tex.: Harcourt Brace, 1992), p. 106.

14. Albert Bandura, "Social Cognitive Theory of Mass Communication," in Jennings Bryant and Dolf Zimmerman, eds., *Media Effects: Advances in Theory and Research* (Hillsdale, N.J.: Lawrence Erlbaum, 1994), p. 76.

15. Assessing such effects is made yet more difficult when one considers the wealth of research that indicates Americans possess very little real knowledge about politics or the judicial process. See, for instance, John P. Robinson and Dennis K. Davis, "Television News and the Informed Public: An Information-Processing Approach," *Journal of Communication* 40 (summer 1990): 106–109; L. Harmon Zeigler and William Haltom, "More Bad News About the News," *Public Opinion* (May/June 1989): 50–52; Michael Robinson, "Public Affairs Television and the Growth of Malaise," *American Political Science Review* 70 (1976): 425–430; Dye, Zeigler, and Lichter,

American Politics in the Media Age, pp. 104–108; and Richard Davis and Diana Owen, *New Media and American Politics* (New York: Oxford University Press, 1998), pp. 165–166.

16. Graber, *Mass Media and American Politics*, p. 189.

17. See Jacob Jacoby and Wayne D. Hoyer, "Viewer Miscomprehension of Televised Communications: Selected Findings," *Journal of Marketing* 46 (fall 1982): 12–26.

18. Robinson and Davis, "Television News and the Informed Public, pp. 106–119; and Graber, *Mass Media and American Politics*, pp. 189–190.

19. This discussion is adapted, in part, from Maxwell McCombs, "News Influence on Our Pictures of the World," in Bryant and Zimmerman, *Media Effects*, pp. 1–16; and John R. Zaller, *The Nature and Origins of Mass Opinion* (New York: Cambridge University Press, 1992).

20. Roy Edward Lotz, *Crime and the American Press* (Westport, Conn.: Praeger, 1991), pp. 40–41.

21. Cecil Greek, "Crime and the Media Course Syllabus and Lectures," www.fsu.edu/~crimdo/grade&m.html#lectures, online without pagination.

22. Greek, "Crime and the Media," online without pagination; Lotz, *Crime and the American Press*, pp. 37–48; and Surette, *Media, Crime, and Criminal Justice*, pp. 11–12.

23. The foundation for this approach is laid out in Shanto Iyengar and Donald Kinder, *News that Matters* (Chicago: University of Chicago Press, 1987), pp. 112–120.

24. Surette, *Media, Crime, and Criminal Justice*, pp. 11–12.

25. The "minimal effects" conceptualization is presented in Iyengar and Kinder, *News that Matters*, pp. 19–33, 116–120.

26. For an overview of agenda-setting research, see Everett M. Rogers, William B. Hart, and James W. Dearing, "A Paradigmatic History of Agenda-Setting Research," in Shanto Iyengar and Richard Reeves, eds., *Do the Media Govern?* (Thousand Oaks, Calif.: Sage, 1997), pp. 225–236.

27. Iyengar and Kinder, *News That Matters,* pp. 2–4.

28. For an assessment of how the priming effect influenced voter assessments of President George Bush, see Joanne Miller and Jon A. Krosnick, "Anatomy of News Media Priming," in Iyengar and Reeves, *Do the Media Govern?* pp. 258–275.

29. Shanto Iyengar, *Is Anyone Responsible? How Television Frames Political Issues* (Chicago: University of Chicago Press, 1991), pp. 13–16, 26–31, 39–45. This is generally considered the authoritative work on "framing."

30. For sources on how the media frames crime issues, see Robert Entman, "Modern Racism and Images of Blacks in Local Television News," in Iyengar and Reeves, *Do the Media Govern?* pp. 283–286; and Franklin D. Gilliam, Jr., Shanto Iyengar, Adam Simon, and Oliver Wright, "Crime in Black and White: The Violent, Scary World of Local News," in Iyengar and Reeves, *Do the Media Govern?* pp. 287–295.

31. Other theories of media effects include the "bandwagon effect," which posits that people simply want to be on the winning side. For a discussion of

this approach, see Albert H. Cantril, *The Opinion Connection* (Washington, D.C.: Congressional Quarterly Press, 1991). Another approach examines the "third-person effect" (in which people perceive broad media effects on everyone but themselves). A description of this idea is contained in W. Phillips Davison, "The Third-Person Effect in Communication," *Public Opinion Quarterly* 47 (spring 1983): 1–15. However, we believe that we have presented the most widely discussed theories here.

32. Kathleen Hall Jamieson and Karlyn Kohrs Campbell, *Interplay of Influence: News, Advertising, Politics, and the Mass Media,* 4th ed. (Belmont, Calif.: Wadsworth Publishing, 1998), p. 19; and Greek, "Crime and the Media," online without pagination.

33. See, generally, Donald Shaw and Maxwell McCombs, *The Emergence of American Political Issues* (St. Paul, Minn.: West Publishing, 1977), chapter 1; and Iyengar and Kinder, *News that Matters.*

34. For a wide range of works that examine the role of agenda-setting, see David L. Protess and Maxwell E. McCombs, ed., *Agenda Setting* (Hillsdale, N.J.: Lawrence Erlbaum, 1991); and Bryant and Zimmerman, *Media Effects.*

35. The political functions and idealized role of the mass media are summarized in Dye, Zeigler, and Lichter, *American Politics in the Media Age*, pp. 6–19; Graber, *Mass Media and American Politics*, pp. 98–102; and Kenneth Dautrich and Thomas H. Hartley, *How the News Media Fail American Voters: Causes, Consequences, and Remedies* (New York: Columbia University Press, 1999), pp. 102–104.

36. Bandura, "Social Cognitive Theory of Mass Communication," p. 75.

37. Gans, *Deciding What's News*, pp. 8–18.

38. Ibid., pp. 16–18.

39. Richard Davis, *The Press and American Politics,* 2d ed. (Upper Saddle River, N.J.: Prentice-Hall, 1996), p. 129.

40. Davis and Owen, *New Media and American Politics*, chapter 1.

41. Gans, *Deciding What's News*, pp. 8–18.

42. Jeffrey Toobin, *The Run of His Life: The People v. O.J. Simpson* (New York: Touchstone, 1997), p. 68. Toobin's book effectively recounts the media's often offensive behavior both before and during the Simpson criminal trial.

43. For good general accounts of the modern media environment, see Larry J. Sabato, *Feeding Frenzy* (New York: The Free Press, 1993); and Thomas Patterson, *Out of Order* (New York: Knopf, 1993).

44. For works that have assessed broader public impact of media coverage of the criminal justice system, see Barber, *Cameras in the Courtroom,* pp. 95–98; Burton Katz, *Justice Overruled: Unmasking the Criminal Justice System* (New York: Warner Books, 1997), pp. 260–262; Ronald Goldfarb, *TV or Not TV: Television, Justice, and the Courts* (New York: New York University Press, 1998), especially pp. 160–166; Alan M. Dershowitz, *Reasonable Doubts: The Criminal Justice System and the O.J. Simpson Case* (New York: Simon and Schuster, 1997), pp. 129–134, 146–148, 203–204; Anna Quindlen, "Order in the Court," *New York Times*, July 25, 1994; Eileen Libby, "Court TV: Are We Being Fed a Steady Diet of Tabloid Television? No: Tacky or Not, It Helps Bring the Law to Life," *ABA Journal* (May 1994): 47;

Ruth Ann Strickland and Richter H. Moore Jr., "Cameras in State Courts: A Historical Perspective," *Judicature* 78 (November/December 1994): 128–135; and Alan M. Dershowitz, "Court TV: Are We Being Fed a Steady Diet? Yes: Its Commercialism Hides Its Potential," *ABA Journal* (May 1994): 46.

45. For a work in this area that focuses on the fair treatment of defendants, see Marjorie Cohn and David Dow, *Cameras in the Courtroom: Television and the Pursuit of Justice* (Jefferson, N.C.: McFarland, 1998).

46. Barber, *News Cameras in the Courtroom,* pp. 122–123.

47. See Greek, "Crime and the Media," online without pagination.

PART I

From Journalism to Sensationalism

1

Looking for This Week's "Trial of the Century"

These days, it's hard to tell when you're watching *Inside Politics* and when you've tuned in to *Melrose Place*. Both feature unhealthy quantities of lust, lies, betrayal and adultery, though the latter has more believable scripts.

—Steve Chapman, *Chicago Tribune* columnist[1]

In March 1997, the prime time announcement of O.J. Simpson's civil trial verdict came at the same moment that President Bill Clinton was delivering his State of the Union message to Congress and the American people. Both the mainstream television networks and many cable news channels extensively covered the Simpson drama for more than two years. Would they break into the president's speech to report the jury's verdict? Although CBS and NBC managed to restrain themselves in deference to the state of the nation, ABC printed the verdict along the bottom third of the screen. CNN and MSNBC actually chose O.J. Simpson over the president's speech.[2] In all, nine national cable networks, including the sports channels ESPN and ESPN2, offered live coverage of the verdict's announcement. ABC altered its schedule to broadcast a two-hour special on the verdict.[3]

At times, it seems as though the latest U.S. pastime is watching criminal trials and investigations on television, especially those involving

23

celebrities, murder, sex, racism, or police misconduct. And media coverage of such stories is not confined to any particular journalistic style or media outlet. Crime, criminal justice, and the judicial process now occupy the attention of national network news organizations, prestigious daily newspapers, tabloid weeklies, talk radio, cable television, and even daytime talk programs such as *Jerry Springer*, *Oprah*, and the *Ricki Lake* show.[4] The participants in these dramas also behave in ways that would have seemed extraordinary just a few decades ago. For instance, it is now increasingly common for defense attorneys to hold daily news conferences, for defendants to hire public relations specialists to represent them to the press and the public, and for police departments to maintain elaborate in-house staffs charged with "image management."[5]

In this chapter, we begin by discussing the practices and principles that seem to govern media coverage of crime and the judicial system. We then provide brief summaries of seven of the most prominent tabloid cases of the 1990s. In presenting these summaries, we focus on the actual facts of each case and less on the media coverage itself. In the ensuing chapters, we fully explore the media culture that has enveloped—and in some cases continues to envelop—these cases. However, we believe that an overview of the specific facts surrounding the cases is important because it reveals what the media deemed newsworthy in the 1990s, and it allows us to consider whether these cases warranted the high levels of media attention that they received.

MEDIA COVERAGE OF THE U.S. JUDICIAL PROCESS

Historically, U.S. trial courts have been the source of significant media coverage, especially fictionalized stories in both film and print. This attention, however, has always been episodic and often superficial. And though local television news has always devoted significant attention to crime stories, both the public and the mass media have typically ignored everyday trials.[6] For the press to report on a given criminal investigation or trial, there needs to be some factor present that is unusual or out of the ordinary, a prerequisite of newsworthiness identified by both Richard Davis and Herbert Gans, among others.[7] For instance, although hundreds of children in the United States are murdered or abducted each year, the JonBenet Ramsey investigation drew massive attention partly because it involved a six-year-old beauty queen from an extremely wealthy and prominent family.

In their book *Crimes of the Century*, Gilbert Geis and Leigh B. Bienen assert that many of the high-profile trials in the twentieth century have certain common features, such as the geographic setting of the events, the nature of the offenders and victims, and the details of the offense itself. Crimes that rise to the level of media obsession have tended to occur in the three major media markets of New York (the Charles Lindbergh baby trial, Alger Hiss, Son of Sam, Marv Albert), Chicago (Leopold and Loeb), and Los Angeles (Fatty Arbuckle, Charles Manson, the Rodney King case, O.J. Simpson). However, the increasing news homogenization, engendered by the growth of the Internet and twenty-four-hour cable news, seems to have altered this pattern, as recent tabloid-type cases have originated variously in Miami, Boston, Denver, South Carolina, and Montana.

Criminal cases that receive high volumes of media coverage normally involve provocative or shocking offenses, particularly murder (especially multiple homicides, sexual brutality, or the killing of children), although cases such as that of Alger Hiss (peacetime espionage) and Bill Clinton (perjury and obstruction of justice) do not fit neatly into such categories. As far as the identities of the perpetrators and victims go, the mass media stakes are often raised when the perpetrator is a prominent celebrity or public figure (1920s film star Fatty Arbuckle, William Kennedy Smith, O.J. Simpson, Marv Albert, President Clinton), or when the victim is a particularly unusual, intriguing, or sympathetic personality (Leopold and Loeb's alleged murder of a teenage girl, Louise Woodward's killing of an infant in her care, and JonBenet Ramsey, the six-year-old beauty queen). Sometimes the offender may not have previously been prominent or well-known but comes to represent or illustrate the public's dissatisfaction with particular institutions within the criminal justice system, as in the case of Rodney King and the Los Angeles Police Department (LAPD) and the LAPD again in the Simpson criminal trial.

In any event, we would argue that it is the nature of the media coverage, rather than the circumstances of the particular case, that characterizes the tabloid justice era. The media's emphasis on the extraordinary and sensational fosters a number of public misconceptions and may lead citizens away from considering more important issues such as plea bargaining, courtroom subcultures, attorney and judge interaction, and court bureaucracies.[8] But rather than present these structural and procedural complexities, the media tend to focus on the personal and dramatic aspects of criminal trials and investigations. Plea bargains do not involve the conflict, tension, or visual images that apparently make a story interesting enough to merit significant press attention.

On balance, the mass media offer an inaccurate—or at least incomplete—picture of the daily workings of the criminal courts. This state of affairs is worsened when we recognize that the types of trials that do receive extended coverage are what criminal justice scholar Ray Surette has called "media trials" and what we term tabloid justice cases. Surette effectively characterizes such trials as "court news as miniseries."[9] High-profile media trials are presented largely as sources of high drama and entertainment, as opposed to opportunities to educate and inform the public on the inner workings of the judicial system. They become the foci of intense public exposure and public interest, and ultimately they become part of the lore of popular culture. Many older Americans can recall the names and faces of the trial participants from previous "trials of the century," such as those involving Fatty Arbuckle, Sacco and Vanzetti, Julius and Ethel Rosenberg, Sam Shepherd, Charles Manson, and Patty Hearst.[10]

Tabloid justice–type criminal cases, with their potential for drama and pathos, can be seen as the quintessential vehicles for the melding of the previously distinct news and entertainment aspects of the mass media. During the past ten to fifteen years, patterns of development in the news business, analyzed extensively in Chapters 2 and 3, have resulted in far more competition for ratings. As the mainstream flagship institutions of the press have sought to maintain their dominance in such a marketplace, they have increasingly tended to present hard news within a structure formerly reserved for entertainment and features. In Surette's words, "fast-paced, dramatic, superficial presentations and simplistic explanations [have become] the norm."[11] William Haltom, in a study of how the press covers judicial actions, refers to this as *dramatized normality*. He hypothesizes that the "news media dramatize abnormal cases until, over time, they have normalized dramatic cases."[12]

The increasing visibility of criminal trials and investigations, when combined with the entertainment-based style in which they are presented, has given such events a symbolic importance far out of proportion with their actual number and objective significance. Because of their prominence, tabloid justice cases have become central to the social construction of "crime and justice reality"—that is, to the formation of public opinion with regard to important legal and political questions.[13] Competing visions of law, justice, and social reality are debated before the citizenry, with greater ramifications than when a very small percentage of the public tunes into a presidential speech or congressional debate.

Further, the fact that television exposes most Americans to such events holds enormous importance for their effect on the public's legal and political attitudes. Television possesses its own set of imperatives, which encourage the repetitive showing of striking images and the presentation of news in short and dramatic segments. Neither of these television-specific characteristics leads to the presentation of legal proceedings in a manner that is conducive to civic education. More important, though, the three characteristics of *serialization*, *personification*, and *commodification* appear to dominate how the criminal justice system and tabloid trials are covered by television.[14]

Criminal trials lend themselves to serialization, or the presentation of news as a series of short dramatic events (involving a relatively small number of recurring characters with specific roles) over an extended period of time. Each day's events in a trial or investigation can be presented in a short, simplified, and catchy news segment. As in the trials of O.J. Simpson and the Rodney King officers, the media received assistance from defense attorneys who, in order to influence that day's news coverage, held daily press conferences. On days in which little activity took place in the courtroom, coverage often consisted solely of information disseminated by the lawyers in these cases.

Personification refers to the presentation of events through a focus on the emotional, personal, human aspects of a story, often at the expense of context, background, structure, and analysis. This is the manner in which television presents virtually all news, but we believe that it is particularly problematic when this style of coverage is used to present images of the judicial process. After all, law is ideally intended to ensure objectivity, procedure, stability, predictability, and equality; the emotional states, biases, and personal backgrounds of the participants are not, in theory, supposed to influence the outcome of criminal investigations and trials. And yet, national newsmagazines reported on such things as the changing hairstyle of O.J. Simpson prosecutor Marcia Clark.[15] In the JonBenet Ramsey investigation, the media reported on the cost of JonBenet's beauty pageant outfits.[16] And in covering the investigation of President Clinton, ABC National News radio reported that Monica Lewinsky had two blueberry pancakes for breakfast the day independent counsel Ken Starr and members of the House of Representatives questioned her.[17] In sum, presenting the legal system through the lens of individual portraits of idiosyncratic participants undermines the educational function of the media.

The commercial imperatives of television also contribute to the commodification of criminal trials, as these events are packaged, promoted, and sold much like any other media program.[18] Coverage in cases such as those of Louise Woodward, O.J. Simpson, and, more recently, the impeachment and trial of President Clinton, serve as evidence. For instance, *E! Entertainment Television*, a cable station that does not even present any hard news programs, offered daily coverage of the Simpson criminal trial, utilizing its normal entertainment anchorpersons. Tabloid programs such as *A Current Affair*, *Hard Copy*, and *Inside Edition* mounted similar efforts.[19] All of the networks and major cable news stations have presented the Clinton-Lewinsky saga much like a dramatic miniseries, often including a musical theme, logo, and graphic introductory material. This aspect of television coverage affects the public's perception of the occasional tabloid justice case that does, in fact, have important legal or political ramifications. Examples drawn from the cases involving Rodney King, as well as the presidential impeachment and Senate trial, are instructive. But if undeniably important legal events such as these are presented in a fashion identical to the more publicly trivial cases of JonBenet Ramsey, William Kennedy Smith, Marv Albert, and O.J. Simpson, it is not surprising that the public interprets all such events simply as undifferentiated human entertainment pieces, to be viewed or ignored as one pleases.

The decision by consumers whether to follow coverage of the Clinton impeachment and Senate trial simply becomes another in an undifferentiated range of choices, which are not perceived by the viewer as being related to citizenship or the well-being of the nation. Even though such events offer valuable opportunities for public education about the legal and political systems, the mode of media coverage, combined with the public's apparently uncritical reception of that coverage, undermines the opportunity for substantive civic education.

TOP TABLOID JUSTICE CASES OF THE 1990s

The rules and norms of media coverage, especially regarding the judicial system, evolved greatly in the 1990s. As a result of the tremendous increase in the mainstream media's coverage of the justice system, a significant portion of the American public has formed, or perhaps reformed, its basic opinions about the judicial system and the role of law in society. It is problematic that anomalous yet highly visible cases have been relied upon by citizens in assessing the criminal law. In recent years, we have unquestionably witnessed a sea change in the amount and style of legal news in the mass media, as well as a corresponding increase in the public's appetite for criminal justice "infotainment." In fact, as previously stated, the merging of the previously distinct media categories of news and entertainment, as applied to coverage of the legal system, is what marks the advent of the era of tabloid justice. These trials and investigations, most of which do not involve any overarching issues of public policy, international affairs, or, at least overtly, broad social questions, have overshadowed interest in events with obvious and profound international and domestic consequences, such as Medicare, the breakup of the Soviet Union, campaign finance reform, and the extraordinary 1994 midterm elections.

The numerous trials and criminal proceedings that have captivated the public have been tabloid in nature in that they have involved personal and intimate details about often bizarre and shocking events. For instance, there was the 1994 case of Susan Smith, the South Carolina mother who drowned her own children. Before the bodies were recovered, Smith maintained her innocence, suggesting on national television that a black man had abducted her two sons at gunpoint. A national outpouring of support came her way, but when the true circumstances of the crime were revealed, she was ultimately convicted of murder and sentenced to life in prison.

Or consider the now infamous case of *Bobbitt* v. *Bobbitt*. In 1993, Lorena Bobbitt was charged with malicious wounding and assault for the "dismembering" of her husband, John Bobbitt. She claimed that she attacked him after he raped her and should not be held legally responsible for her actions due to a condition of temporary insanity. The defense presented a detailed account of the years of domestic violence and sexual abuse Lorena Bobbitt allegedly suffered. On January 21, 1994, a jury found her not guilty by reason of insanity. She was committed to a mental health facility for observation and treatment for a period of forty-five days and was then released from custody. This case gained widespread notoriety both for its graphic nature (Lorena Bobbitt, as many readers will recall, had severed her husband's penis) and for the example it provided for discussion of the increasingly widespread use of the so-called battered wife syndrome as a defense in domestic violence cases.

Table 1.1   Top Tabloid Justice Cases of the 1990s

Trial or Investigation	Year the Main Proceeding Concluded
Trial of William Kennedy Smith	1991
Trial of the officers in the Rodney King beating	1992
Trial of Lyle and Erik Menendez	1993
Trial of O.J. Simpson (criminal)	1995
Trial of Louise Woodward	1997
Trial of O.J. Simpson (civil)	1997
Investigation of President Bill Clinton and Monica Lewinsky	1999
Investigation of the murder of JonBenet Ramsey	ongoing

Note: The JonBenet Ramsey investigation began in December 1996.

Then there was the investigation of child sexual abuse charges lev-eled against pop music star Michael Jackson. A nightly news staple for weeks, the case faded from the public eye when the alleged victim accepted a large cash payment from Jackson. The list of high-profile tabloid cases might also include the rape trial of heavyweight boxer Mike Tyson, the sexual assault case brought against nationally known sportscaster Marv Albert, the investigation into the murder of fashion designer Gianni Versace, the murder trial of the killer of Ennis Cosby (son of entertainer Bill Cosby), the investigation of the assault of fig-ure skater Nancy Kerrigan (allegedly orchestrated by rival skater Tonya Harding), and the conclusion to the seventeen-year search for the so-called Unabomber, who stood accused of sending a series of mail bombs to scientists and business leaders. These and other cases have been the source of intensive media coverage.

For the purposes of our investigation, we chose to focus on seven cases (we count the criminal and civil trials of O.J. Simpson as one case) that we believe most effectively illustrate the approach of the mass media in the era of tabloid justice. Table 1.1 displays the primary indi-vidual or individuals in the proceeding and the year the trial ended. Four of the cases involve murder allegations (Menendez, Simpson, Ramsey, and Woodward), one focuses on a rape charge (Kennedy Smith), one involves police brutality (King), and one encompasses a morass of alleged sexual misconduct and perjury (Clinton-Lewinsky). In referring to these cases as episodes of tabloid justice, we do not mean to trivial-ize any of the disturbing realities of the facts alleged in each of them. We chose these cases because of the volume and style of media coverage devoted to them, the public's interest in them, and the degree to which they displayed the workings of the legal system.

Because we refer to them extensively throughout this book, the cases identified in Table 1.1 warrant a more complete presentation. As we move through the cases a number of questions must be considered. Are there issues of national importance at stake in each of them? Does the case help to educate the public about the legal system? Is the case representative of a normal judicial proceeding? Is it necessary for the public to be informed about many of the details about the participants of the cases? The answers to these questions will vary depending upon the case. However, for the majority of them we would answer no to each of these questions.

▪ William Kennedy Smith: A Kennedy Family Member Goes on Trial for Rape

It is reasonable to conclude that the trial of William Kennedy Smith, along with the Rodney King case discussed next, ushered in the tabloid justice era of the early 1990s.[20] In many ways, Smith's was the quintessential tabloid justice case. It contained almost all of the typical necessary elements: a wealthy defendant from a famous family, allegations of a violent crime with strong sexual overtones, and a trial certain to involve famous witnesses. Although it was essentially a rape case with little potential impact on public policy or legal reform, it generated unprecedented attention throughout both the mainstream and tabloid media.

The origins of the case involved something of a "he said, she said" scenario, as each side had trouble corroborating its version of the relevant events. Sometime after midnight on a Friday evening, Patricia Bowman, a twenty-nine-year-old Florida woman, met Smith, his cousin Patrick Kennedy, and his uncle, U.S. senator Edward Kennedy, at a Palm Beach nightclub. Bowman agreed to drive Smith back to the Kennedy estate, where she eventually accepted Smith's invitation to stay for drinks and tour the extravagant compound. She claimed that as the evening came to an end, she headed for a set of stairs leading to the swimming pool area. Bowman alleged that Smith essentially tackled and raped her on the lawn near the pool. She then called a friend to take her home, recounted the rape, and telephoned the police soon after. William Kennedy Smith countered that the two merely had consensual sex on the beach.

Prosecutors charged Smith with second-degree sexual battery and first-degree sexual assault. The trial, however, was repeatedly postponed in the wake of extraordinary levels of publicity. Throughout 1991, the media treated the public to virtually daily updates about the case. Because Smith was a member of the famous Kennedy family, albeit previously a very low-profile one, his trial drew an enormous number of reporters to south Florida, including journalists ranging from the *National Enquirer* to the *New York Times*. Many news organizations attempted to portray the trial as a referendum on everything from cameras in the courtroom to the then-emerging issue of date rape to the influence of wealth and celebrity on equal justice to the general state of gender relations. The fact that Senator Edward Kennedy of Massachusetts was slated to testify (former first lady Jacqueline Kennedy Onassis was also rumored to be traveling to Florida for the trial) further sparked media and public interest. The media created what some termed a circus-like atmosphere, made worse when news outlets reported that three other women were prepared to testify that Smith sexually assaulted them in the previous year. The defense then made the first of many claims that the level of pretrial publicity had hopelessly tainted the jury pool. Eventually, a six-person jury was seated, and the long-awaited trial began on December 2, 1991.

Smith's attorney, the well-known defense lawyer Roy E. Black, asserted that Bowman had lied about the encounter because of her fear of becoming pregnant, her anger at Smith when he had called her by the wrong name, and his lack of interest in developing a more serious relationship.[21] Smith's attorneys attacked the woman's credibility, while the prosecution sought to taint the defendant's story by raising the other alleged rapes. Public and media interest intensified. The then-new Court TV offered gavel-to-gavel coverage, CNN devoted large blocks of time to the case, and all three major television networks assigned reporters around the clock.[22] The local NBC affiliate offered daily commentary from famed defense attorney F. Lee Bailey, and most outlets offered insights from a wide variety of legal luminaries, feminist activists, and academic experts on rape and sexual harassment. Local entrepreneurs offered T-shirts featuring caricatures of the Kennedys in a frying pan, as well as ice cream flavors named after each of the major trial participants (the "Teddy" flavor was spiced with Chivas Regal scotch).[23] The William Kennedy Smith matter became what was probably the trial most widely covered by television up to that point in history.

Eventually, Smith was acquitted on all counts. Following a twelve-day trial, the jury deliberated for a total of one hour. Most commentators expressed little surprise at the verdict, noting the largely circumstantial and uncorroborated evidence against Smith. Some observers, however, openly feared that the acquittal would "send the wrong message to the country," symbolizing that women who accused acquaintances of rape exposed their personal lives to detailed scrutiny by the mass media, and risked destroying their reputations.[24] But most experts on rape issues, such as Susan Estrich, Susan Brownmiller, and Vivian Berger, considered this a case in which the evidence to convict was not presented. According to Brownmiller, the author of a book on the history of rape, the case had been weak all along.[25]

Rodney King: Race, Police Conduct, and Justice in Los Angeles

Although the central incident precipitating the Rodney King trials occurred prior to the alleged crime in the Kennedy Smith case, the trial and ensuing trauma occurred several months later.[26] In retrospect, this event may have signaled the beginning of the tabloid justice decade of the 1990s. On March 3, 1991, a late-breaking story interrupted the popular *KTLA News at Ten* broadcast in Los Angeles. Anchorman Hal Fishman introduced what he described as a videotape by amateur cameraman George Holliday, a resident of the nearby suburban San Fernando Valley. Shot the previous evening around midnight, the eighty-one-second tape showed what appeared to be several officers of the LAPD savagely beating a black motorist, later identified as Rodney King, next to his vehicle. The officers could be seen delivering repeated baton blows and kicks as King rolled on the ground, attempting to shield his head with his hands.

In the ensuing days, weeks, and months, these images would be seared into the minds of the nation's—and the world's—television viewers, as edited versions of the videotape were repeatedly broadcast in both real time and slow motion.[27] Legal historian Alfred Knight has called the video the "most widely viewed and evaluated piece of evidence in the history of criminal justice." Knight further notes that the tape made people "certain that the cops were guilty because they had seen the crime itself."[28] Outraged groups in Los Angeles called for the dismissal of the officers, as well as the resignation of Los Angeles Police chief Daryl F. Gates. In time, four of the officers, who eventually became the defendants in a criminal trial brought by the city, were removed from duty without pay. The city council appointed a blue ribbon panel to investigate the incident and report to the police commission. Headed by prominent attorney and later secretary of state Warren Christopher, the Christopher Commission eventually concluded that the LAPD was guilty of tolerating racism and rogue cops and called for the resignation of Chief Gates. As tensions mounted and political rhetoric reached a fever pitch, concerns were raised that the pool of potential jurors would be tainted. Still, many were surprised when a state appellate court judge, fearing a biased jury, ordered the trial moved to a new jurisdiction, the conservative white community of Simi Valley in nearby Ventura County.

A lengthy criminal trial followed in which the four officers stood accused of a number of charges including use of excessive force and failing to follow police procedure. The prosecutors argued that the officers violated codes of police conduct by using excessive, racially motivated force. They played tapes that included racial epithets and attempted to demonstrate that racism motivated the police brutality. The defense strategy attempted to persuade the jury that King had been a combative, dangerous suspect who did not comply with the officers' repeated commands. The defense offered into evidence the entire videotape, rather than the roughly nineteen-second edit that had been widely broadcast on television, which showed a more belligerent, uncooperative King. The defense also emphasized that prior to the incident, King, while highly intoxicated, had led the police on an eight-mile, high-speed chase through crowded city streets.

After hearing twenty-nine days of testimony and deliberating for one week, the all-white jury acquitted all four officers on all but one count, on which the jury deadlocked. Within hours of the verdict, angry demonstrators burned buildings, looted stores, and assaulted passersby; civic leaders called for calm and restraint. Mayor Tom Bradley announced a curfew and ordered citizens "off the streets," and California governor Pete Wilson dispatched the National Guard. In the worst urban riots since the Civil War, fifty-four people lay dead, 2,000 were wounded, and property damage in Los Angeles exceeded tens of millions of dollars.

Months after the riots, in what seemed to be an insufficient afterthought, federal prosecutors brought a second suit against the officers, charging that they violated the federal civil rights of Rodney King. This time, the trial was held in Los Angeles District Court, and a racially mixed jury found two of the officers guilty. As the verdicts were announced, the city deployed 3,200 police officers—about ten times the normal number. Additionally, the county sheriff's office dispatched 1,400 officers, and the National Guard deployed over 600 guardsmen at local armories.[29] Ultimately, the verdicts resulted in no significant public disorder. Lou Cannon, the author of the definitive recounting of the King trials and riots, wrote that it was as if all of the people of Los Angeles had breathed a sigh of relief.[30] Several months later, Rodney King himself sued the city for police brutality and reached a civil settlement that awarded him more than one million dollars.

For a number of reasons it is difficult to consider the Rodney King trials as examples of tabloid justice. The incident, ensuing lawsuits, eventual replacement of Daryl Gates with an African American chief of police, and the riots of March 1992 certainly raised issues of race relations and police brutality. The beating, acquittals by the Simi Valley jury, and differing ways in which the riots were perceived have sometimes supported the notion that the United States remains a deeply racist nation.[31] However, we contend that the media coverage of these events helped to fuel this drama. The repeated airing of the King videotape, well beyond any reasonable attempt to inform citizens about the story, was clearly intended to sensationalize and bring viewers into the story. Noted media scholar Doris Graber has even concluded that "overly extensive" coverage of the King beating "contributed to the frustrations that exploded in the Los Angeles riots."[32] As *Los Angeles Times* columnist Howard Rosenberg pointed out in the aftermath of the rioting, numerous local stations showed footage of the beating immediately after the verdict, which had the effect of inflaming the mounting anger over the jury's decision. Further, the morning after the verdict, with rioting still under way, NBC's *Today Show* aired footage of the beating four times in a forty-five-minute period.[33] The media emphasis on sensational images clearly embraced the principle of entertainment over measured reporting.

■ The Menendez Brothers: Abuse and Revenge

On August 20, 1989, entertainment executive Jose Menendez and his wife, Kitty, were found slain in their Beverly Hills mansion.[34] The first reports of the crime in the *Los Angeles Times* described a mob-style execution that was likely connected to one of Jose Menendez's many business dealings. Throughout the investigation, the Beverly Hills police department refused to divulge any details to the press. Nevertheless, the media reports for several months after the killings continued to speculate about the possibility of vengeful business partners in the entertainment industry. Those following the story, which in the first months of the investigation received little press attention, were shocked when the couple's two sons, Lyle and Erik, were charged with the slayings. A short time after their arrest, the brothers admitted killing their parents. They confessed to shooting their father numerous times in the head as he lay sleeping on a couch in the family den. They also confessed to wounding their mother in the initial shooting, at which time Lyle had gone to the trunk of his car, reloaded his shotgun, and returned to the house, where he fatally shot her.

Preceding the trial there were numerous delays, as attorneys for both sides wrangled over evidentiary issues and an extensive series of motions, some of which raised concerns about the prejudicial nature of the now extensive media frenzy that had developed around the case. The coverage and footage from the trial were broadcast nationally, as Court TV was permitted to carry the proceedings live. When the trial finally did get under way, more than three years after the arrests, prosecutors contended that the brothers had killed their parents in order to acquire the family's fortune, estimated at more than $14 million. The brothers' defense attorneys countered that the young men had essentially struck back at Jose and Kitty Menendez for a lifetime of physical, sexual, and emotional abuse.

From the outset, the trial centered not around the brothers' guilt, which had been admitted, but rather on the defense's argument that Erik and Lyle should not be held fully responsible for their deeds. The brothers' trials were held at the same time, and both juries initially deadlocked, leading to the declaration of mistrials for both defendants. In a second set of trials, in which Court TV was banned from showing live coverage, both brothers were convicted of first-degree murder and sentenced to life in prison, where they both continue to reside.

The final conviction and sentencing of the Menendez brothers did not occur until April, 18, 1996, more than six and a half years after the crime. This was the longest of any of the tabloid justice sagas that we investigated for this book. The attention that the crime and ensuing trials received can undoubtedly be attributed to the Beverly Hills location, the U.S. community perhaps most associated with glamour and wealth. Dominick Dunne, the well-known *Vanity Fair* correspondent who attended the opening days of the first trial, summed up the case this way:

"Two pampered and handsome young men, an execution-style killing and the brothers' lavish spending habits in the weeks after the killings."[35] As he waited for opening arguments, Dunne further commented, "I think we're going to be shocked by what we're about to hear. . . . I love covering trials."[36] In addition to Dunne, more than sixty TV and radio reporters were there for opening day to cover one of the most anticipated trials in Los Angeles history. Hector Tobar, a *Los Angeles Times* reporter, compared the scene of the courtroom on opening day to a made-for-television drama. The attention paid to the Menendez case can be considered, up until that point, to have been the clearest presentation of "crime for entertainment."[37] The case simply contained no overriding or broader public issues, and yet, several years later, most Americans are able to recall numerous details from this story.

O.J. Simpson: Media Circus of the Century

The basic facts surrounding O.J. Simpson's criminal trial are familiar to most Americans. Over a period of nearly three years, the media inundated the public with detailed and repetitive coverage of almost every aspect of this story. As evidence of the country's broad level of attention, it has been reported that fully 80 percent of the public either watched or listened to the live announcement of the verdict.[38] This case, which has repeatedly been referred to as the "trial of the century," a moniker that had previously been applied to many other cases,[39] centered on a brutal, although not uncommon crime.

On the night of June 12, 1994, Nicole Brown Simpson, the ex-wife of football legend O.J. Simpson, and Ronald Goldman, a waiter and aspiring actor, were found murdered in the wealthy southern California community of Brentwood. The murders took place outside Nicole Brown Simpson's condominium, where her two children slept upstairs. She died from a knife slash to her throat; Goldman died from sixty-four separate stab wounds.[40] The story broke modestly, with a small front-page article in the *Los Angeles Times* reporting the death of "football great O.J. Simpson's former wife and a 26-year-old man."[41] From these early reports, though, the story catapulted to heights of media coverage that surely could not have been predicted, and which have only recently been exceeded by the coverage of the Clinton-Lewinsky scandal and impeachment trial.

Four days after the murders, the Los Angeles police department ordered O.J. Simpson to turn himself in, informing him that he would be arrested and charged with both murders; Simpson agreed to turn himself in by eleven o'clock on Friday, June 17, but the deadline for Simpson to surrender passed with his whereabouts unknown. Simpson apparently fled. In a public announcement, Simpson's lead attorney at the time, Robert Shapiro, urged Simpson to turn himself over to the police. Robert Kardashian, a friend of Simpson's, read a letter written by Simpson, which sounded to many people like a suicide note.[42]

The following hours produced a media spectacle. O.J. Simpson, accompanied by his longtime friend Al Cowlings, was spotted traveling on a Los Angeles freeway. Simpson and Cowlings led police on what the *Los Angeles Times* called "the most spectacular pursuit in Los Angeles police history."[43] All of the major television networks provided live coverage of the chase; NBC even interrupted coverage of the National Basketball Association finals. Ultimately, Simpson drove back to his home and surrendered to police. Although the drama of the Bronco chase had come to an end, the legal odyssey, which would end 474 days later with a jury's decision to find O.J. Simpson not guilty of the slayings, was only just beginning.

Simpson assembled what the media labeled a legal "dream team," which included Johnnie Cochran, a prominent Los Angeles lawyer; F. Lee Bailey, who had made his name, in part, by winning the release of Sam Sheppard in the 1960s;[44] and Alan Dershowitz, a Harvard law professor who won the release of Claus von Bulow in a celebrated case of the 1980s.[45] The Los Angeles District Attorneys' office assigned long-time prosecutors Marcia Clark and Bill Hodgman to lead an unusually large group of prosecutors. Christopher Darden later joined the team, in effect replacing Hodgman in the courtroom.

Both inside and outside the courtroom, the Simpson trial made for great theater. In terms of trial strategy, the prosecution built its case on DNA and blood evidence, which the district attorney's office believed proved conclusively Simpson's guilt. The defense team sought to show that the prosecution's case was built on sloppy, unreliable police work. Moreover, the defense argued that certain officers involved in the case were overzealous and racially motivated in their pursuit of Simpson as the lone suspect. The actual trial, which lasted almost nine months, was a collage of skirmishing lawyers, expert witnesses, lengthy and often dull descriptions of scientific evidence, aggressive cross-examinations, daily defense team press conferences, and judicial posturing. In describing this spectacle, veteran trial reporter Theo Wilson asserted that the media presentation in the Simpson case was all "flash and trash," with the important legal and evidentiary questions often taking a backseat to the tabloid-style coverage of the case outside of the courtroom.[46] Wilson notes, for example, that both Marcia Clark and Johnnie Cochran were the subjects of extensive and often humiliating tabloid news stories about their personal lives.[47]

The Simpson saga did not end with the not-guilty verdict in the criminal trial. The parents of Ronald Goldman spearheaded a wrongful death civil suit against Simpson. Although the actual legal proceeding was quite different, with different rules of evidence, no camera in the courtroom, the mandatory testimony of O.J. Simpson, and so forth, the civil proceeding perpetuated further rumination and discussion about the Simpson criminal case. Much of the media apparatus focusing on the criminal trial continued to cover and analyze the civil case. In March 1997, the jury in the civil suit found Simpson "responsible" for the deaths of Nicole Brown Simpson and Ronald Goldman, and he was ordered to pay more than $33 million in damages. This brought the legal saga to its conclusion, although many citizens found themselves wondering about a legal system that would find someone responsible for the murder of two people, yet not be required to serve any jail time.

What factors made the Simpson cases so extraordinary? Why did it become a national obsession? A convergence of many factors, both large and small, catapulted this trial into the public spotlight. Foremost, the crime involved a popular and wealthy celebrity whom many Americans considered a hero. Much commentary suggested that Simpson's ability to fight his criminal prosecution was clearly an example of a very rich man simply "buying an acquittal."[48] Further, the crime involved a black defendant and white victims, a circumstance that ignited many deep-seated passions about race and the law. In addition to this racial angle, the Simpson case provided a venue for raising public awareness of important gender dynamics in society. O.J. and Nicole Brown Simpson's violent marital relationship, marked by almost ten years of documented violence by the defendant, raised questions about how the legal system deals with husbands who abuse their wives.[49]

Thus, the trial of O.J. Simpson tapped into many of the most divisive social fault lines in U.S. culture. Coupled with some of the more mundane and logistical components of the case, such as the presence of cameras in the courtroom, the length of the trial, and the expanding role and presence of cable TV, these notable class, racial, and gender overtones produced a recipe for a national drama of unprecedented proportions.

Louise Woodward: Murderous
Nanny or Accidental Death?

The media machinery that developed over the course of the Simpson trials undoubtedly spurred the coverage of the Woodward murder trial.[50] This coverage began to intensify after the verdict in the Simpson civil trial. Louise Woodward, a teenaged British nanny, was accused of first-degree murder for allegedly shaking to death eight-month-old Matthew Eappen, the infant she baby-sat. Prosecutors said that Woodward became so impatient with Matthew's crying that she shook him violently to quiet him. Woodward then allegedly slammed the infant against a hard surface to silence him. State medical examiners said Matthew hit the floor with the "force equivalent to a fall from a second-story window." Matthew suffered a fractured skull and later died from his injury. Woodward's defense team claimed that some prior incident, or a genetic defect, contributed to the baby's skull fracture. The defense also claimed that the Eappens' two-year-old son, Brendan, who was the only other person at home at the time, could have caused the fatal injury.

Woodward was imprisoned without bond after the incident, which caused considerable controversy. Her supporters, in both Massachusetts and Great Britain, argued that she should not be kept in a state women's prison with hardened criminals. They also claimed that Woodward did not understand the U.S. justice system and should have been released on bail. Prosecutors countered that Woodward would likely leave Massachusetts if released from custody.

Toward the end of the long, divisive, technically complex, media-saturated trial, the prosecution filed a motion asking Judge Hiller Zobel to allow the jury to consider charges of voluntary and involuntary manslaughter, in addition to the first-degree murder charge they had originally requested. The prosecutors proposed that the jury have the option of convicting Woodward on one of these lesser charges. Defense attorneys sharply objected, wanting the jury only to have the more narrow option of convicting Woodward on either first- or second-degree murder or acquitting her altogether. Judge Zobel sided with the defense, allowing the jury only the narrower set of options. Upon immediate review by the Supreme Judicial Court of Massachusetts, the ruling was upheld.

In what came as a surprise to many observers, and certainly to the judge and the defense attorneys, the jury returned a conviction of second-degree murder, which carried with it a mandatory prison sentence of fifteen years. During the sentencing phase of the trial, the defense requested that Judge Zobel set aside the conviction and dismiss the case entirely, set aside the verdict and hold a new trial, or reduce the conviction to manslaughter. In a stunning development, Judge Zobel agreed with the defense, dismissed the jury's verdict, and reduced the conviction to involuntary manslaughter. He sentenced Woodward to 279 days in jail, which was "time already served," and released her from custody immediately. The ruling was not only unusual but was also delivered in an unorthodox fashion—the judge posted the decision and his full opinion on the Internet and presented considerable legal and historical support for his right, even his duty, to overturn what he believed to be a fundamentally unjust conclusion to the trial. He stressed that the decision should not be construed as a criticism of the jury, because he had not even given them the option of convicting on the involuntary manslaughter charge. However, Zobel explained that "a judge is a public servant who must follow his conscience."[51]

The judge's actions, which seemed to undermine the premises of the jury system, stunned prosecutors and law enforcement officials, as well as many outside legal observers. Nevertheless, the Massachusetts high court upheld Zobel's decision. Woodward returned home to England, and the Eappen family filed a wrongful death civil suit against her. Woodward continued to maintain her absolute innocence but defaulted, claiming that she could not afford the costs of a prolonged civil trial.

There have been numerous trials with defendants being charged with the murder of an infant who was in their care, but none of these trials has reached the national audience. What are the factors that explain the rise of this case to national prominence? *Boston Globe* reporter Mark Jurkowitz, who covered the Woodward trial, has identified a formula for high-profile trials that appears to fit the facts of the Woodward case quite well. The case must be seized upon early by active local news media. This occurred through extensive coverage provided by the *Boston Globe* and *Boston Herald*. In addition, the presence of cameras in the courtroom allowed the local Boston affiliates to show the case live and give it extensive coverage on the local newscasts. And finally, a national audience becomes attracted to the case through the exposure on Court TV. Once these factors fell into place, the trial garnered extensive national attention and became the most watched trial since the Simpson events.[52]

■ Clinton, Jones, and Lewinsky: Tabloid Justice
Reaches the Presidency

It is important to understand that the Clinton-Lewinsky episode represents a fitting and predictable coda to the tabloid justice decade.[53] It not only contained all the elements that aroused the intense, personalized media scrutiny of the 1990s, but it also epitomized the conflation of serious politics, important legal matters, public posturing by numerous participants, and the primacy of entertainment in the late-twentieth-century United States.

The origins of the Clinton-Lewinsky saga can be traced to 1994, when a three-judge federal court of appeals panel named Kenneth Starr, a former solicitor general and federal appellate judge, as an independent counsel charged with investigating an earlier Arkansas real estate deal involving the Clintons. This came to be known as the Whitewater investigation. On May 6, 1994, in a seemingly unrelated event, Paula Corbin Jones filed a federal lawsuit claiming that then-Arkansas governor Bill Clinton sexually harassed her in a Little Rock hotel room in 1991. The Clinton administration denied the incident and claimed that, while in office, the president should enjoy immunity from civil suits, at least those that did not arise from actions while he was president. However, in May 1997, the U.S. Supreme Court ruled that Jones's lawsuit could proceed; presidents were due no broad immunity from such proceedings.

In December 1997, Paula Jones's lawyers named Monica Lewinsky, an otherwise anonymous former White House intern, as a potential witness in their lawsuit. On December 19, Lewinsky was subpoenaed to appear at a deposition for the Jones suit and to turn over any gifts she may have received from Clinton. Soon after, Lewinsky signed an affidavit claiming she had had no sexual relationship with the president. In the meantime, another former White House employee, Linda Tripp, approached Kenneth Starr and his team of investigators with evidence that contradicted the sworn affidavit of Lewinsky. Starr then requested and was granted permission from a federal judicial panel to widen his investigation to include the Lewinsky matter. In January 1998, Clinton testified in the Jones civil suit that he never engaged in any sexual activity with Monica Lewinsky. Linda Tripp's now infamous tape recordings of graphic accounts of Lewinsky's liaisons with President Clinton in the White House, however, called the president's truthfulness into question. Tripp had turned the tapes over to Kenneth Starr's deputies, and thus began the investigation that ultimately led to the Senate impeachment trial.

At the very outset of the scandal, many in the media portrayed the developments in the most sensational of terms. The day that the scandal broke, Tim Russert, host of the respected Sunday morning program *Meet the Press*, commented on the air that "one of [Clinton's] best friends told me today, 'If this is true he has to get out of town.' Whether it will come to that, I don't know, and I don't think it's fair to play the speculation game. But I do not underestimate anything happening at this point. The next 48 to 72 hours are crucial."[54] A few days later, long-time ABC News White House correspondent Sam Donaldson asserted on the program *This Week*, "If [Clinton is] not telling the truth, I think his presidency can be numbered in days. This isn't going to drag out. . . . If he's not telling the truth, the evidence shows [he] will resign, perhaps this week."[55] With very few facts at their disposal, respected journalists jumped to astounding conclusions about the gravity of the situation. By discussing the case in such terms, one could argue that the media were creating a set of expectations about the investigation that almost mandated the intensity of coverage that it received.

As the scandal story gained dominance throughout the nation's media outlets, the Clinton administration sprang into damage-control mode. The president gave a television appearance in which he emphatically denied ever having had "sex with that woman, Ms. Lewinsky." Several of Clinton's lawyers and aides speculated that Lewinsky was a stalker or a deeply disturbed compulsive liar. Hillary Clinton went on NBC's *Today Show* and attributed the scandal to a vast right-wing conspiracy that was bent on destroying her husband. Only seven months later, on August 17, 1998, when it was confirmed that Lewinsky had saved a blue dress, stained with the president's semen, did Clinton tell a grand jury and the American people that he had engaged in "an inappropriate relationship" with Monica Lewinsky.

The president's somewhat defiant statement about the relationship did not deter Independent Counsel Starr. Lewinsky, who now enjoyed immunity from prosecution for her own apparent perjury in the affidavit, gave extensive testimony detailing the affair. In September, Starr and his team delivered to the House of Representatives thirty-six boxes of material, including a scathing report that Starr believed contained compelling evidence that Clinton had committed potentially impeachable offenses. The House of Representatives voted overwhelmingly to begin an impeachment investigation. The Judiciary Committee, one of the most partisan and polarized in Congress, voted narrowly to post the Starr Report on the Internet and to make public Clinton's videotaped grand jury testimony. The public gained exposure to a wealth of lurid, graphic, and embarrassing details of Clinton and Lewinsky's numerous sexual encounters. Nevertheless, public opinion polls indicated that nearly two-thirds of all Americans opposed impeachment.

In December 1998, after one of the most bitter, personalized, and partisan debates in memory, the House of Representatives narrowly approved two articles of impeachment. Within a month, the Senate voted, under the watchful eye of Chief Justice William Rehnquist, to acquit Clinton on both counts. The president gave a brief public statement calling for a period of healing and renewal. Strong rebukes from both sides of the Senate aisle clearly diluted his "victory." A year of unprecedented scandal and investigation ended, and Bill Clinton narrowly avoided becoming the first president in history to be removed from office.

The manner in which the media covered the Clinton scandal and impeachment proceeding has perhaps caused more media introspection than any news event in recent history. *New York Times* columnist Russell Baker referred to the Clinton-Lewinsky story as the great "media meltdown of 1998" and accused members of his own profession of "actions that were variously foolish, shameful, dangerous to democracy, and destructive for the reputation of the news industry."[56] News anchor Jim Lehrer, reflecting on the coverage of the Clinton-Lewinsky scandal, concluded that the journalism on display was "akin to professional wrestling—something to watch rather than believe."[57]

Many journalists and those who write about the media asked a number of questions in the aftermath of the impeachment trial. Was the story overcovered? Were too many salacious and extraneous details reported? Was there a rush to judgment? Were journalistic practices of verifying anonymous sources discarded? These and many other questions will be pondered and debated for years as historians think back to the media performance during this scandal. For our purposes, it is crucial to understand the pervasive nature of the coverage that accompanied almost every aspect in this story. We will turn to this coverage more fully in Chapters 2 and 3.

The JonBenet Ramsey Investigation: Death of a Child Beauty Queen

More than three years after the death of six-year-old JonBenet Ramsey, a grand jury investigation of the child's murder closed without having charged a suspect.[58] Patricia Ramsey, JonBenet's mother, telephoned police early on December 26, 1996, to report that her daughter was missing from their Boulder, Colorado, house; she found a ransom note demanding $118,000 for JonBenet's safe return. Patricia Ramsey reportedly found the handwritten ransom note on a back stairway. The writer claimed to represent a "foreign faction." The police arrived at the Ramsey house shortly before six in the morning, and a police detective arrived at the home by eight, as all parties expected imminent contact from the kidnappers. Police also searched the home but found no sign of the missing child. Eight hours later, after police searched the house, JonBenet's father, John, found his daughter's body in a small, secluded basement closet the police inexplicably failed to search. Wrapped in a blanket, with her wrists tied above her head, her mouth covered with tape, and a nylon cord wrapped around her neck, JonBenet had been beaten, bound, and strangled. An autopsy showed that she suffered a severe blow to the head and died by strangulation from the nylon gar-rote. Thus, what had hours earlier been a kidnapping case became an intensive murder investigation that has yet to reveal either a killer or even a motive.

A month later, Boulder district attorney Alex Hunter said the parents were "the obvious focus of the investigation." The Ramseys vehemently denied involvement in their daughter's murder. A year later, Hunter said the Ramseys, who continued to maintain their innocence, remained "under an umbrella of suspicion." Theories about JonBenet Ramsey's death abound: The kidnap note was real, and an intruder murdered the child; one or both parents killed their daughter and wrote the ransom note themselves; the parents are covering for a relative or friend who killed the girl; JonBenet and her parents were involved in a child pornography ring operating on the edge of the child beauty pageant subculture. Investigators have asked five family members for fingerprints, palm prints, and DNA samples.

But the police and the district attorney in Boulder have come under fire in the search for JonBenet's killer, too. In September 1998, for example, detective Lou Smith resigned from the district attorney's

office, convinced of the Ramseys' innocence and Hunter's determination to prosecute them. Also in late 1998, Detective Steve Thomas, a
Boulder Police investigator, left the force, accusing Hunter of protect-
ing the Ramseys. The district attorney has also drawn intense criticism
for failing to indict the parents in the face of supposedly overwhelming
circumstantial evidence.

Meanwhile, John Ramsey started a new computer business in
Atlanta, and the couple's son Burke enrolled in a private school. The
governor of Colorado has suggested he may appoint an independent
prosecutor to expedite a resolution to the case and minimize political
infighting among the public officials involved. As of early 2000, the
grand jury in the case had been dismissed, although the murder remains
under investigation.

The reason that the Ramsey case became national news is not entirely clear. Some have suggested that the eerie and somewhat startling pictures of JonBenet Ramsey wearing adult outfits and makeup while performing in beauty pageants provided intriguing images that captured
public attention. In much the same style as with the Rodney King video,
many media outlets have repeatedly shown the photos of JonBenet
Ramsey in her pageant outfits even when there were no news developments in the story. Another possible reason for the ascension of this story
was the newspaper rivalry in Denver between the *Denver Rocky Mountain
News* and the *Denver Post*, which was one of the last major metropolitan
areas with two competing newspapers. As these papers battle for readers,
they may have helped to propel the case forward as they both jostled to
break the next big development in the case.[59] Regardless, several media
commentators have already posited that if there is ever a trial in this case,
it will unquestionably become the next "trial of the century."

CONCLUSION

This chapter introduced several major tabloid justice news stories from
the 1990s and presented summaries of the cases to which we will return
throughout the remainder of this book. Although these investigations
and trials share a number of important characteristics, there are also
significant differences among them. Two of the cases, the Rodney
King–related trials and the investigation of President Clinton, presented legitimate and important issues of national concern. Questions of
police brutality and possible criminal conduct by the president warrant

significant media exposure. However, despite the obvious merit of such issues, much of the press coverage of these cases was sensationalistic and superficial. Furthermore, we would argue that the rest of the preceding cases did *not* present issues of national significance that would warrant such extensive media attention. They were simply trials involving individual tragedies and traumas.

In reflecting back on the cases that we have just presented, we are able to draw several conclusions. First, because of the lack of national importance of many of these trials, it becomes clear that the media have used these cases as a means of entertainment rather than education. The commodification of television trials identified by Ray Surette is clearly evident in the 1990s. Second, the process of selling trials as entertainment makes it difficult for citizens to distinguish issues of real importance. For instance, the King and Clinton cases raised important legal, social, and political issues. However, when a presidential scandal receives virtually the same style of media treatment as the Simpson murder case, the media do not offer any way for the public to gain perspective. The lines between assessing what is important and what is merely interesting become blurred.

In Chapter 2, we turn to an exploration of changes in the news business that have contributed to this blurring of the lines between news and entertainment. We also discuss how this process has led to the tabloid justice coverage that now dominates stories about criminal investigations and trials.

NOTES

1. Steve Chapman, "Could 2000 Be the Real Year of the Woman?" *Chicago Tribune*, January 7, 1999, p. A19.

2. Jonathan Alter, "Reversal of Fortune: The O.J. Legacy," *Newsweek*, February 17, 1997, p. 24.

3. Neil Gabler, *Life: The Movie* (New York: Alfred Knopf, 1998), p. 82.

4. See Richard Davis and Diana Owen, *New Media and American Politics* (New York: Oxford University Press, 1998), p. 11.

5. Philip Schlessinger and Howard Tumber, *Reporting Crime: The Media Politics of Criminal Justice* (Oxford: Clarendon Press, 1994), pp. 13, 51–52.

6. See, for instance, Doris Graber, *Crime News and the Public* (Westport, Conn.: Praeger, 1980), p. xvii; and Gregg Barak, "Media, Society, and Criminology," in Gregg Barak, ed., *Media, Process, and the Social Construction of Crime: Studies in Newsmaking Criminology* (New York: Garland, 1994), pp. 3–45.

7. See Richard Davis, *The Press and American Politics*, 2d ed. (Upper Saddle River, N.J.: Prentice-Hall, 1996), pp. 129–130; Herbert Gans, *Deciding What's News: A Study of CBS Evening News, NBC Nightly News, Newsweek, and Time* (New York: Vintage Books, 1979), pp. 11–12; and Gilbert Geis and Leigh B. Bienen, *Crimes of the Century* (Boston: Northeastern University Press, 1998), pp. 3–11.

8. For more on this argument, see Cecil Greek, "Crime and the Media Course Syllabus and Lectures," online without pagination at www.fsu. edu/~crimdo/grade&m.html#lectures; and David L. Althheide, "TV News and the Social Construction of Justice," in Ray Surette, ed., *Justice and the Media* (Springfield, Ill.: Charles C. Thomas, 1984), pp. 292–304.

9. Ray Surette, *Media, Crime, and Criminal Justice: Images and Realities*, 2d ed. (Belmont, Calif.: Wadsworth Publishing, 1998), p. 72. Also see William Haltom, *Reporting on the Courts: How the Mass Media Covers Judicial Actions* (Chicago: Nelson-Hall, 1998), pp. 186–189.

10. See Edward W. Knappman, ed., *American Trials of the 20th Century* (Detroit, Mich.: Visible Ink Press, 1995).

11. Surette, *Media, Crime, and Criminal Justice*, p. 73.

12. Haltom, *Reporting on the Courts*, p. 186; and Paul Thaler, *The Watchful Eye: American Justice in the Age of the Television Trial* (Westport, Conn.: Praeger, 1994), pp. xx–xxi.

13. See Doris Graber, *Mass Media and American Politics*, 5th ed. (Washington, D.C.: Congressional Quarterly Press, 1997), pp. 104–108, for a discussion of how violence can be exaggerated in crime reporting.

14. In support of this argument see Barry Brummett, "Mediating the Laws: Popular Trials and the Mass Media," in Robert Hariman, ed., *Popular Trials: Rhetoric, Mass Media, and the Law* (Tuscaloosa: University of Alabama Press, 1990), pp. 179–193.

15. For an example of this type of coverage, see Kendall Hamilton, "Marcia Clark Goes Straight," *Newsweek*, April 24, 1995, p. 72.

16. For an example of such coverage, see Bill Briggs, "Talk Swirls About Merits of Child Beauty Pageants," *Denver Post*, January 12, 1997, p. A4.

17. Reported on the ABC National News radio broadcast of January 24, 1999.

18. Further, the growing competition among news sources and the selling of news stories much like other commercial products has been commented on in both journalistic and scholarly settings. For instance, see Jonathan Alter, "In the Time of the Tabs," *Newsweek*, June 2, 1997, p. 32. For an earlier discussion of the effects of competition on print media, see Robert Entman, *Democracy Without Citizens* (New York: Oxford University Press, 1990), chapters 5 and 6.

19. Jeffrey Toobin, *The Run of His Life: The People v. O.J. Simpson* (New York: Touchstone, 1997), p. 125.

20. Where not otherwise cited, the facts of the William Kennedy Smith case are drawn from *Boston Globe* coverage of the case between April and December of 1991. The case was covered extensively in the Boston media because of the Kennedy family's connections to Massachusetts. We also con-

sulted the Court TV website, http://www.courttv.com/casefiles/; Timothy Clifford, "Curtain Goes Up on Palm Beach Trial," *Newsday*, December 1, 1991, p. 5; Larry Tye, "Lights, Action As Smith Trial Opens Today," *Boston Globe*, December 2, 1991, p. 1; Steve Wick, "Rape Experts Look to Future Trials," *Newsday*, December 12, 1991, p. 7; and Marvin Kitman, "The Trial: Dat's All, Folks," *Newsday*, December 16, 1991, p. 45.

21. Clifford, "Curtain Goes Up on Palm Beach Trial," p. 1.

22. Tye, "Lights, Action As Smith Trial Opens Today," p. 1.

23. Ibid.

24. Wick, "Rape Experts Look to Future Trials," p. 7.

25. Ibid.

26. The facts of the Rodney King–related trials, where not otherwise cited, are based on accounts presented in the *Los Angeles Times* between March 1991 and April 1993.

27. Richard A. Serrano and Tracy Wilkinson, "All Four in King Beating Acquitted," *Los Angeles Times*, April 30, 1992, p. A1.

28. Alfred H. Knight, *The Life of the Law: The People and the Cases That Have Shaped Our Society, from King Alfred to Rodney King* (New York: Oxford University Press, 1996), p. 244.

29. Lou Cannon, *Official Negligence: How Rodney King and the Riots Changed Los Angeles and the LAPD* (New York: Times Books, 1997), p. 485.

30. Cannon, *Official Negligence*, p. 486.

31. Lori Leibovich, "Rethinking Rodney King," *Salon Magazine*, March 1998, online without pagination at http://www.salon.com/.

32. Graber, *Mass Media and American Politics*, p. 152.

33. Howard Rosenberg, "TV's Double-Edged Role in Crisis," *Los Angeles Times*, May 1, 1992, p. F1.

34. The basic facts of the trials for Lyle and Erik Menendez, where not otherwise cited, are based on the detailed summaries that can be found in Court TV's case files section at http://www.courttv.com/casefiles/.

35. Hector Tobar, "Disorder in the Court As Trial Starts," *Los Angeles Times*, July 21, 1993, p. B1.

36. Ibid.

37. Ibid.

38. *The Gallup Poll Monthly*, October 1995, p. 35.

39. Two recent books have devoted attention to the phrase "trial of the century." See Knight, *The Life of the Law*, epilogue; and Ronald Goldfarb, *TV or Not TV: Television, Justice, and the Courts* (New York: New York University Press, 1998), chapter 1.

40. This description comes from prosecutor Christopher Darden's post-trial memoir (co-written with Jess Walter), *In Contempt* (New York: ReganBooks, 1996), p. 118.

41. Eric Malnick and David Farrell, "O.J. Simpson's Ex-Wife Found Stabbed to Death," *Los Angeles Times*, June 14, 1994, p. A1.

42. For an analysis of the letter, see Sheryl Stolberg, "Picture of a Lost Person," *Los Angeles Times,* June 19, 1994, p. A14.

43. Jim Newton, "'I'm Sorry for Putting You Guys Out': Simpson Collapsed in Officers' Arms; Details of Bizarre Day Are Revealed," *Los Angeles Times,* June 19, 1994, p. A1.

44. For useful information on the Sam Sheppard case, see F. Lee Bailey with Harvey Aronson, *The Defense Never Rests* (New York: Stein and Day Publishers, 1971).

45. For a description of the Claus von Bulow case, see Alan Dershowitz, *Reversal of Fortune* (New York: Random House, 1986); and William Wright, *The Von Bulow Affair* (New York: Delacorte Press, 1983).

46. Theo Wilson, *Headline Justice* (New York: Thunder's Mouth Press, 1997), chapter 1.

47. Ibid.

48. Polling data reveals this to be the widespread perception of the public. See *The Gallup Poll Monthly*, October 1995, p. 34.

49. The level of domestic violence in the Simpson marriage is in some dispute. In Simpson's civil trial, he denied ever striking Nicole Brown Simpson. However, prosecutor Chris Darden's book *In Contempt* carefully chronicles the many documented episodes of domestic violence at the Simpson household.

50. Information about the Louise Woodward trial, where not otherwise cited, is based on the *Boston Globe*'s coverage between February and November 1997. The case was covered extensively in the Boston media. We also consulted Court TV's case files at http://www.courttv.com/casefiles/.

51. A complete transcript of Judge Zobel's ruling can be found online at http://www.courttv.com/casefiles/.

52. Mark Jurkowitz, "A Nation of Jurors Has Arisen: The Woodward Ruling," *Boston Globe*, November 12, 1997, p. A1.

53. This account is adapted generally from coverage in the *New York Times*, especially the following articles: "Key Events in the Clinton Investigation," February 13, 1999, pp. A8–A11; David Stout, "From a Modest Start to a Threat to the Presidency," November 15, 1998, p. 34; Stephen Labaton and Jeff Gerth, "Clinton Emphatically Denies an Affair With Ex-Intern," January 27, 1998, p. A1; James Bennet, "Clinton Admits Lewinsky Liaison to Grand Jury; Tells Nation 'It Was Wrong,' but Private," August 18, 1998, p. A1; R. W. Apple, Jr., "House, in a Partisan 258–176 Vote, Approves a Broad, Open-Ended Impeachment Inquiry," October 9, 1998, p. A1; and Alison Mitchell, "Clinton Acquitted Decisively: No Majority for Either Charge," February 13, 1999, p. A1.

54. Richard Harwood, "Searching for Facts in a Sea of Speculation," *Nieman Report* 53 (summer 1999): 61.

55. Ibid.

56. Jim Lehrer, "Blurring the Lines Hurts Journalism," *Nieman Report* 53 (summer 1999): 65.

57. Ibid.

58. The facts involved in the Ramsey murder investigation, where not otherwise cited, are based on coverage of the story in the *Denver Post* and the *Denver Rocky Mountain News*. Both of these papers have devoted extensive

coverage to the investigation. Also consulted in this summary was "JonBenet Ramsey Case Still Unsolved After Two Years," *CNN Interactive*, December 26, 1998, online without pagination. For additional material, see the CNN website at http://cnn.com, which maintains an extensive archive of JonBenet-related materials.

59. For a discussion of media coverage in the Ramsey investigation, see Lynn Bartels, "Professor Lambastes JonBenet Coverage," *Denver Rocky Mountain News*, July 5, 1998, p. 4A; and Howard Rosenberg, "A Clear Case of Media Mayhem," *Los Angeles Times*, September 28, 1998, p. F1.

2

The Mainstream Media Go Tabloid

If we were doing O.J. every night, I think our ratings would be soaring. It's tempting. But we'd be giving up our moral high ground.

—Ted Koppel, host of *Nightline*[1]

It is not much of a secret anymore . . . that the agenda formerly known as tabloid has picked up and moved—to the front page of the *New York Times*. After years of being disdained by the mainstream media, traditional supermarket-tabloid subjects have become everybody's subjects, whether it's JonBenet, Monica, O.J., Princess Di— or for that matter, diet and health tips.

—Richard Turner, writer for *Newsweek*[2]

Criminal trials and investigations make for fascinating news stories. They are filled with suspense, human tragedy, violence, and, occasionally, shocking sexual behavior. They can surpass the drama of Hollywood's best-scripted police or courtroom thrillers. In some ways, because they are filled with real people and events, and their outcomes are unpredictable, criminal cases have even more entertainment value than television programs or motion pictures. The trials of O.J. Simpson, the Menendez brothers, and Louise Woodward have all made for engrossing and intriguing television.[3] In a 1994 poll, 60 percent of the U.S. public said that following the Menendez trial was as interesting as or more interesting than watching crime dramas on TV. More than 50 percent said the same thing about the Bobbitt trial.[4]

This is not to say that Americans' fascination with crime is anything new. High-profile criminal cases have always captured the attention of the public and the mass media.[5] From the bizarre murder trial of Leopold and Loeb in 1924 to the trial concerning the kidnapping and murder of the Lindbergh baby in 1935 to the two murder trials of Sam Sheppard in 1954 and 1966, Americans have closely followed sensational criminal court dramas.[6] During the twentieth century, these and several other cases were even been dubbed the "trial of the century."[7] Trial reporter Theo Wilson notes that the drama and human tragedy involved in these cases gave them a theatrical quality equal to a performance of *Hamlet* or *Macbeth*.[8]

This book is not a history of famous criminal trials; hence, we do not delve extensively into the many high-profile criminal cases of the twentieth century. This is because we believe that, though intensive media coverage of the occasional trial of the century is clearly nothing new in U.S. history, and these cases occurred with greater frequency in the 1990s, the almost total cultural immersion involved in such events as those involving Rodney King, O.J. Simpson, JonBenet Ramsey, and Monica Lewinsky represents a new phenomenon. Even before a case goes to trial, journalists now often quickly spin out supermarket-quality books telling true crime stories in explicit and graphic detail.[9] Tabloid outlets such as the *National Enquirer*, the *Star*, and the *Globe* swarm to these stories, and television programs like *Hard Copy, A Current Affair*, and *Inside Edition* rush to provide coverage.[10] The tabloids have treated us to stories about the love life of O.J. Simpson prosecutor Marcia Clark, described the rumored "sex shows" that Monica Lewinsky performed for President Clinton, and have speculated about JonBenet Ramsey's incestuous experiences with her older brother. In some sense, by providing salacious coverage of personal topics, the tabloid press now does what scandal sheets have always done. The distinguishing feature of the present media culture is the alarming regularity with which *mainstream* media sources now focus on these same personalized crime stories.

Material formerly relegated to the tabloid press now pervades the mainstream press as well. News stories formerly covered only by the tabloid press have found their way into journalism's most respected sources of "hard news" in the United States: CBS, NBC, and ABC, along with the nation's most esteemed newsmagazines and newspapers. *Time, Newsweek, U.S. News and World Report,* the *New York Times,* the *Washington Post,* and the *Los Angeles Times* have become regular purveyors of tabloid-type stories. Moreover, the mainstream press now exploits crime stories that have little or no bearing on anyone other than the immediate participants in the case. The media regularly use criminal investigations and trials as entertainment fodder for attracting viewers. As television journalist Geraldo Rivera, who has worked in both the hard news and tabloid media, suggests, "The difference between a program like *Dateline NBC,* for example, and one of the tabloid shows— say, *Hard Copy* or *Inside Edition*—is in degree, not substance."[11]

In his 1998 book, *Life: The Movie,* Neal Gabler argues that the mass media now present real life as entertainment.[12] The lines separating actual tragedy, important public events, and dramatic entertainment have become blurred, as have the differences between personalized tabloid titillation and substantive legal or political information. Our analysis of the high-profile cases of the past ten years reveals clear evidence of this phenomenon. During 1997, for instance, the investigation into the death of JonBenet Ramsey received significantly more attention from television news than did issues such as poverty, health-care reform, welfare reform, and mass suffering in Africa.[13] After President Clinton's affair with Monica Lewinsky became public in January 1998, pundits and journalists spent literally thousands of hours of television airtime discussing the case. An examination of such programs as MSNBC's *Internight* or *The Big Show* reveals that for the first eight months after the Lewinsky scandal was uncovered, virtually every evening's broadcast focused on that story.[14] Keith Olberman, host of *The Big Show,* commented with dismay that he had done more than "240 consecutive shows on Monica Lewinsky."[15] Discourse on the Clinton-Lewinsky scandal proceeded without respite throughout 1998, even though on most days no new information about the case surfaced. Even the 1997 sexual assault trial of sportscaster Marv Albert, a case totally lacking in societal importance, made its way to the front page of the *New York Times,* perhaps the most esteemed media institution in the nation.[16] Coverage of these and other similar cases indicates an important shift: The mainstream media have abandoned many of their self-imposed standards for avoiding tawdry and sensational topics.[17]

In this chapter, we argue that the mainstream media—the ostensibly trusted distributors of hard news—now focus an inordinate amount of attention on criminal trial stories that previously might have been fodder only for tabloid media outlets. We consider, from a legal, political, and educational standpoint, whether the entertainment value of such stories has overshadowed their newsworthiness. In other words, have the media chosen to focus so heavily on tabloid justice cases because of their appeal as entertainment, as opposed to their objective importance as hard news? Also, we begin to delineate how this shift in media attention has given the mass public the closest and most detailed portrait of the legal system it has ever seen. Further, we note that media representations of the legal system viewed in the context of these highly anomalous cases may distort the public's view of that system, an idea we develop throughout our remaining chapters.

To examine this transformation, we have divided this chapter into three sections. The first section specifically describes the mainstream press and the standard journalistic practices of mainstream media organizations. Section two briefly discusses changes in the dynamics of the news and information business during the decades preceding the 1990s. Finally, we examine more closely recent newspaper, magazine, television news program, and television newsmagazine coverage of tabloid legal proceedings.

IDENTIFYING THE MAINSTREAM MEDIA

Americans have come to associate the mainstream media, or hard news outlets, with the reporting of serious issues. One media scholar has defined hard news sources as those to which people turn for late-breaking reporting on the most important stories of the day.[18] Because national news sources play a critical role in establishing the news priorities of local news organizations throughout the country, they are the outlets with which we are primarily concerned.[19] These news outlets have increasingly focused their attention on criminal trials and investigations, and regardless of the appropriateness of such attention, this has heightened the public's exposure to the workings of the justice system. When Americans watch the coverage of tabloid justice cases, especially live images emanating from the courtroom, they see firsthand the behavior of lawyers, judges, and defendants. The presentation of evidence and courtroom testimony are now common media topics, and a significant portion of the public may potentially have gained a working familiarity with the basic aspects of the judicial process. Recent polls also show that the public has gained an increased awareness of the judicial process through such coverage; therefore, the media have fulfilled their agenda-setting function in this regard.[20] Accordingly, former trial court judge Burton Katz, now a radio talk show host, has commented that the people who call his show have more familiarity with the criminal justice system than ever before.[21]

In addition to setting the agenda for the nation's legal and political discourse, there exists an agenda-setting function *within* the media. When *ABC News* or the *New York Times* covers a story, that story gains instant legitimacy for media outlets across the nation.[22] The coverage thus cues local news broadcasts and local newspapers to a story's importance and appropriateness for media attention.

As we consider how the media have increased their coverage of criminal trials and investigations, and the manner in which they have given such stories a more tabloid-like slant, it is important to distinguish tabloid cases from what we deem important legal proceedings—those which possess broad legal, social, or public policy implications. Clearly, some criminal cases have a national significance. Nearly all of the rulings of the U.S. Supreme Court could be characterized this way. Further, many trials effectively demonstrate the functioning of the legal system and raise political or legal questions that transcend the experiences and interests of the individual participants in them. For instance, the murder trial of Sirhan Sirhan for the assassination of U.S. senator and presidential candidate Robert Kennedy in 1968, and the trial of John Hinckley for the assassination attempt on President Ronald Reagan in 1981 were of great public importance. All U.S. citizens share a legitimate interest in the protection of political leaders and in the stability of the regime. Similarly, the trial of Timothy McVeigh, who was convicted for the bombing of a federal government building in Oklahoma City, falls into this category, though some critics of the media's obsession with trials as entertainment have included McVeigh in their analyses.[23] And the public has a legitimate interest in proceedings that involve emerging civil liberties issues, such as the trials of Jack Kevorkian, the Michigan doctor who has waged a one-person crusade for the legalization of assisted suicide. However, some have argued that the television newsmagazine *60 Minutes* went too far when it aired footage of Kevorkian administering a lethal injection to a patient.[24]

Whereas the aforementioned cases seem to warrant sustained national media attention, others seem to fall almost entirely into the realm of crime entertainment. The cases involving William Kennedy Smith, Lorena Bobbitt, Susan Smith, Louise Woodward, JonBenet Ramsey, Marv Albert, and O.J. Simpson had few broad societal implications.[25] The trials involving Rodney King and President Clinton, however, raised questions of national importance, but the sensationalistic style of coverage devoted to them makes it difficult to distinguish them from the more clearly tabloid cases. Below, we examine two prominent hard news sources, as well as the journalistic ethics standards that supposedly govern the behavior of reporters for these organizations. Cable news-talk channels, such as CNN and MSNBC, which we also consider to be hard news outlets, are included in a later discussion of new media in Chapter 3.

▨ Daily Newspapers and Weekly Newsmagazines

According to most observers, the foundation of all serious journalism remains the top-rated daily urban newspapers.[26] These papers include the *New York Times,* the *Washington Post,* the *Wall Street Journal,* and the *Los Angeles Times.* Newspaper coverage is crucial because the dailies set the tone for the subjects that appear on network and cable news programs later in a given day. Although newspapers lack the ability to present late-breaking stories, they possess a level of credibility missing from much of modern journalism. Newspapers have the capacity to cover criminal trials and investigations in a manner that is impossible to duplicate in the typical thirty-minute television newscast.[27]

Weekly newsmagazines round out the top tier of the print medium. *Newsweek, Time,* and *U.S. News and World Report* are generally considered the core of the hard news weeklies.[28] Although the publication cycle of weekly magazines does not allow them to compete with other news outlets in terms of reporting on breaking news, they have the opportunity to offer more in-depth stories and include more extensive analysis and contextual detail.[29] Ironically, this ability to provide relatively deeper coverage has recently contributed to the tendency of moving the newsmagazines in the direction of the tabloid exposé.

▨ Network Television News Organizations

The three major television networks—ABC, NBC, and CBS—devote considerable resources to news coverage.[30] Each of these organizations presents nightly national news broadcasts with a highly credible image based on its significant role in the history of modern media. These nightly broadcasts have a tradition of legendary journalism behind them, with such figures as Edward R. Murrow, Walter Cronkite, Chet Huntley, and David Brinkley having occupied the anchor's chair. This presentation of the nation's most important stories of the day, however, takes place within the confines of a thirty-minute time restraint, and at least a quarter of that time is used for commercial breaks, a formula that has changed little over the past thirty-five years. The typical broadcast begins with what is deemed to be the most important story of the day, followed by two or three stories also considered to be of national significance. Thus, these newscasts are rarely able to spend more than two to three minutes on any one story.[31] We should note that ABC has an additional nightly news broadcast, *Nightline*, which runs after the prime time entertainment schedule. Anchored by Ted Koppel, *Nightline* usually focuses on a single topic for most of the half hour, providing only brief updates on a few other important stories of the day.

In addition to the nightly news broadcasts, the "big three" networks have several other venues in which to present hard news. The morning shows—NBC's *Today*, ABC's *Good Morning America*, and CBS's *The Early Show*—offer a combination of news, features, interviews, friendly chatter, and consumer advice. Importantly, these programs also devote considerable attention to serious stories. Also, the Sunday morning talk shows—CBS's *Face the Nation*, NBC's *Meet the Press*, and ABC's *This Week*—have long been considered forums for prominent journalists to ask questions of national figures and politicians. The Sunday morning programs have often been criticized as dull viewing fare, as they tend to heavily emphasize "inside the beltway" Washington politics. Finally, television news magazines, such as ABC's *20/20*, NBC's *Dateline*, and CBS's *48 Hours* and *60 Minutes*, are now very popular outlets for the networks to provide more in-depth coverage than the nightly newscasts allow. This has long been true of *60 Minutes*, which first aired in 1968, but the number of these programs has increased tremendously in the 1990s. The fact that these shows, which air between 7:00 P.M. and 11:00 P.M., compete for viewers with sitcoms, dramas, and movie channels has encouraged them to move in the direction of news entertainment. Prime time viewers now often have a choice between entertaining news and just plain entertainment.[32] In sum, the television newsmagazines have played an integral role in fueling the news media's transition toward a stronger entertainment focus.[33]

THE ETHICS OF HARD NEWS ORGANIZATIONS

Taken together, the print and television news organizations, as well as some cable news outlets, are the sources of mainstream news that the public relies on for reporting important public events. A tradition and perceived legacy of journalistic integrity distinguishes these organizations from other news outlets. Reporters working for these organizations have historically been bound by a code of ethics, such as that promulgated by the national Society of Professional Journalists (SPJ).[34] This code presents a wide-ranging list of standards of conduct meant to assure both ethical and competent journalism. The SPJ's full code includes more than thirty topics, such as those pertaining to privacy, "sourcing" guidelines, and the maintenance of objectivity. Below is a list of seven standards of behavior particularly relevant to our focus on criminal trial coverage:

1. Only an overriding public need can justify intrusion into anyone's privacy.
2. Show good taste. Avoid pandering to lurid curiosity.
3. Make certain that headlines, news teases and promotional material, photos, video, audio, graphics, sound bites and quotations do not misrepresent. They should not oversimplify or highlight incidents out of context.
4. Be sensitive when seeking or using interviews or photographs of those affected by tragedy or grief.
5. Recognize that gathering and reporting information may cause harm or discomfort. Pursuit of the news is not a license for arrogance.
6. Be judicious about naming criminal suspects before the formal filing of charges.
7. Balance a criminal suspect's fair trial rights with the public's right to be informed.[35]

In the past fifty years, the mainstream press has, for the most part, *arguably* upheld these standards. In the coverage we analyze in this book, however, it appears that many of these principles and standards of behavior have been discarded on a regular basis.

CHANGES IN THE NEWS BUSINESS SINCE THE 1970S

Although the mainstream news providers described above still exist in their historic institutional form, there have been some fundamental changes in the news business since the 1970s, and particularly during the 1990s. Perhaps most significant is that newspaper readership has declined dramatically since the 1960s. As newspaper readership dropped, the prominence of television news grew substantially during the 1970s and 1980s. Today, 80 percent of Americans identify television as their number one source of news.[36] The big three network news organizations' audience share, however, fell in the 1990s. Accompanying this decline has been the expansion of the cable television industry. Currently, five cable channels are devoted almost entirely to news. Further, the Internet now plays a substantial role in the presentation and dissemination of news and information.[37] Table 2.1 displays several of these trends.

Because of these important changes in how people access news, mainstream news organizations have experienced a consistently shrinking audience. To maintain ratings and attract viewers, they have implemented both structural and substantive changes. All of the news organizations, both print and television, for example, have gone online with sophisticated, interactive websites. NBC has aggressively moved into the cable television arena with two new channels, CNBC and MSNBC. And beyond these structural changes, the traditional hard news outlets have changed their practices, too, now focusing more heavily on sensational, tabloid-style, human interest and consumer-oriented stories.

Table 2.1   Changes in News and Information Dissemination Since 1970

Year	% of People Who Read a Newspaper Daily[a]	% of Households Viewing Network News Broadcasts on Any Given Evening[b]	Number of Households Linked to Internet[c]	Number of Cable Television Channels Devoted to News[d]
1970	75	75	n/a	0
1980	61	72	n/a	1
1990	n/a	59	n/a	3
1991	51	57	n/a	3
1992	n/a	55	992,000	3
1993	46	57	1,776,000	3
1994	49	57	3,212,000	3
1995	n/a	51	6,642,000	3
1996	42	50	12,881,000	5
1997	n/a	49	19,540,000	5
1998	43	49	36,739,000	5

Note: "n/a" means data not available for that year.
[a] Data are from the General Social Survey, Roper Center, University of Connecticut.
[b] Based on information provided by Nielsen Media Research.
[c] Based on Network Wizards study of Internet sites; see http://www.nw.com.
[d] Compiled by the authors through analysis of program guides.

▨ THE TABLOID CONVERSION OF THE MAINSTREAM PRESS

To some degree, the mainstream media have left behind the journalistic principles that have guided them since the 1950s. Whether they are a print or television forum, news organizations have redefined what constitutes appropriate coverage. They now spend considerable time covering tabloid-type stories, not all of which involve crime and trials (for instance, extensive attention is paid to the activities of celebrities). So, why do these trials and investigations receive such attention? The answer may lie in the fact that these events, unlike most other types of news stories, present an opportunity for the press to provide prolonged, detailed, and relatively inexpensive coverage. On the one hand, stories about hurricanes, earthquakes, floods, fires, and other natural disasters (historically favorites of the media), for instance, can be sustained only for a few days. There might be a series of short reports on predisaster anxiety and preparations, several pictures and descriptions of the actual event itself, and a culmination with postdisaster victim reaction and cleanup efforts. Stories about trials and investigations, on the other hand, can be sustained for weeks, months, or even years. In fact, the length of criminal proceedings actually allows for suspense and interest to grow over time. Further, the relatively slow-moving nature of the criminal justice system allows these cases to become national melodramas embedded in the social fabric of U.S. culture.

Clearly, the length of trials and investigations is part of what makes them such ideal stories for news organizations. They can dispatch correspondents to a trial and leave them there for the entire duration of the proceedings. Table 2.2 shows the length of the formal legal portion of the tabloid justice cases we consider in this book. It lists the time from the initial crime or charge through the legal proceedings, though the national conversation about these cases often continues long after the formal legal proceedings conclude. This has certainly been true in the cases of William Kennedy Smith, Rodney King, and O.J. Simpson.

Perhaps surprisingly, the public often expresses little direct interest in these trials. Rather, people regularly indicate that they consider these cases boring sagas and believe that the media spend too much time covering them. In a series of Times Mirror polls, 90 percent of respondents believed that the media gave too much attention to the Simpson case, 71 percent felt the same about the William Kennedy Smith trial, and 51

Table 2.2   Number of Months Each Case Continued in the Legal System

Case	Duration of Legal Proceedings (months)
Menendez brothers murder trial (crime occurred August 21, 1989; final sentence handed down July 2, 1996)	70
Rodney King beating trial (videotaped beating of King first aired March 3, 1991; second trial of officers concluded April 17, 1993)	25
William Kennedy Smith rape trial (crime reported April 3, 1991; trial concluded December 11, 1991)	8
O.J. Simpson murder trials (crime occurred June 12, 1994; civil trial concluded February 10, 1997)	33
JonBenet Ramsey murder investigation (crime occurred December 26, 1996; investigation continues; months counted through 1999)	36
Louise Woodward trial (murder charges filed February 9, 1997; judge overturned verdict November 9, 1997)	9
Bill Clinton/Paula Jones/Monica Lewinsky investigation (first mass media reports of Paula Jones's sexual harassment suit occurred in February 1994; impeachment inquiry involving Monica Lewinsky ended in February 1999)	60

Note: Cases are listed chronologically from the time of initial news reports. Number of months is rounded up.

percent voiced this opinion about the trial of Lorena Bobbitt.[38] In contrast, news organizations point to increased ratings as justification for programming choices, and polling evidence also suggests that the public does pay considerable attention to these stories (see Table 4.1).[39]

It is difficult to be certain if the coverage of these trials *is* merely the media's response to public demand, for this demand is, in effect, denied by the citizenry in polls. Alternatively, there may exist a set of internal media imperatives driving the coverage of these cases, such as the need to promote ratings or maintain a competitive edge over other media outlets. In any event, the vastly increased level of viewer exposure to the inner workings of the legal system in recent years cannot be divorced from the attention paid to tabloid justice cases. We will assess some of the ramifications of public exposure to the legal system in Chapters 4 and 5.

▇ NEWSPAPERS AND MAGAZINES: FROM HARD NEWS TO SCANDAL SHEETS

Although television has become a much more prominent medium, print journalism remains important in understanding the growth of tabloid-style legal coverage. People rely more heavily on television news, and they believe, perhaps surprisingly, that TV news is more credible than print news.[40] This distinction is somewhat meaningless, though, as print journalists actually conduct much of the investigative work reported on television and in radio broadcasts.[41] Within the journalism profession, itself, however, reporting in major daily newspapers carries a very high level of credibility.

Table 2.3 provides an illustration of the sheer volume of tabloid justice stories presented in major newspapers and newsmagazines. We include as major newspapers the forty-five top daily papers in the United States and the twenty most prominent international daily papers as identified by Lexis-Nexis, an archival and Internet search engine. Our analysis of newsmagazines relies on *Time, Newsweek,* and *U.S. News and World Report.*[42] Table 2.3 reveals that the hard news print media have devoted considerable attention to tabloid justice sto-

Table 2.3   Volume of Coverage and Front-Page Articles on Tabloid Justice Stories in Major Newspapers and Newsmagazines, 1989–1998

Story	Major Newspapers		News Magazines	
	Total Articles	Front Page	Total Articles	Cover Stories
Menendez brothers murder trial (1989–1996)	1,131	36	37	0
William Kennedy Smith rape trial (1991)	1,958	71	46	0
Rodney King beating trial (1991–1993)	6,847	447	104	6
Lorena Bobbitt mutilation trial (1993–1994)	1,562	49	12	0
Paula Jones sexual harassment suit (1994–1998)	5,351	361	165	6
O.J. Simpson murder trials (1994–1997)	22,610	1,471	173	10
JonBenet Ramsey murder investigation (1996–1998)	2,090	79	47	1
Louise Woodward trial (1997)	1,823	62	16	1
Clinton-Lewinsky investigation (1998)	25,975	1,959	497	25

Note: Number of articles for each story is based on a Lexis-Nexis search. The Lexis-Nexis definition of "major newspapers" includes the sixty-five domestic and international newspapers with the highest circulations. Newsmagazines considered were *Newsweek, Time,* and *U.S. News and World Report.* For search instructions, see Appendix A.

ries. In fact, many of these stories have received front-page or cover story status, which places them in a category of considerable importance.

The increased volume of coverage of tabloid stories is not the only way the hard news print media have shifted their focus. Front-page newspaper headlines from around the country are now often written in a decidedly tabloid style as well. Importantly, the headlines assume that their readers already possess a substantial familiarity with each case; these stories are part of our national consciousness. A brief glance at several headlines about the Louise Woodward case and the JonBenet Ramsey murder investigation illustrate these trends: [43]

> "In a Startling Turnabout, Judge Sets Au Pair Free," *New York Times*
> "British Au Pair Is Found Guilty of Killing Baby," *Los Angeles Times*
> "British Nanny Sobs After Guilty Verdict: 'Why Did They Do This to Me?'" *Orlando Sentinel*
> "Foreign Faction Threatened to Kill JonBenet in Ransom Note," *Buffalo News*
> "Killing of Tiny Beauty Queen Becomes a Riveting Mystery," *Atlanta Journal and Constitution*
> "Ramsey's Trip to Spain Strictly Business, Friend Says," *Denver Rocky Mountain News*
> "No Semen Found at Ramsey Slay Scene," *Denver Post*

These headlines discuss these cases as if every American knows who the British nanny and the Ramseys are. Tabloid-style article headlines covering the Ramsey investigation, the Marv Albert trial, the Menendez brothers trial, and the scandal involving President Clinton and Monica Lewinsky can also be found in each of the three major newsmagazines: [44]

> "The Strange World of JonBenet," *Newsweek*
> "JonBenet: Taking the Hunt into His Own Hands," *Time*
> "A Body in the Basement [JonBenet]," *Newsweek*
> "Marv Goes to the Showers," *Newsweek*
> "He's Out of the Game [Marv]," *U.S. News and World Report*
> "Murder 90210: Crime Styles of the Young, Rich and Impatient [Menendez]," *Newsweek*

"Papa Bill, Mama Linda, Baby Monica: The Dysfunctional
   Family at the Heart of the Scandal," *Time*
"He [President Clinton] Was Thinking with Another Head,"
   Newsweek

These headlines are similar in tone to those presented in the three
top-selling supermarket tabloids: the *National Enquirer*, the *Star*, and
the *Globe*. For instance, headlines taken from articles appearing in the
National Enquirer include "Monica: What Shrinks Think"; "JonBenet
Arrest Drama"; and "Menendez Brother Weds Wealthy Widow Behind
Bars."[45] It becomes clear that distinguishing subject matter and style of
presentation between the tabloids and the serious newsmagazines can
be difficult.

The falling sales of the tabloids themselves since the 1980s provides further evidence of the major daily newspapers and newsmagazines' shift toward tabloid justice topics. Twenty years ago, the
tabloid papers were alone in covering what today has become the news
agenda for all news organizations. Table 2.4 illustrates the shrinking
market for the tabloids. Although news magazines have also struggled,
they have largely managed to maintain their readership over the years.
The *National Enquirer*, traditionally the leader of the tabloids, and its
closest competitor, the *Star*, have experienced a virtual sales free fall

**Table 2.4   Average Weekly Sales of Newsmagazines and Tabloids Since 1970
(in millions)**

Year	Newsweek	Time	National Enquirer	Star
1970	2.6	4.3	2.0	n/a
1980	3.0	4.6	5.0	3.4
1990	3.2	4.1	4.0	3.5
1991	3.4	4.2	3.7	3.2
1992	3.2	4.2	3.4	2.9
1993	3.2	4.2	3.4	3.0
1994	3.2	4.1	3.1	2.7
1995	3.2	4.1	2.6	2.4
1996	3.2	4.1	2.5	2.3
1997	3.2	4.2	2.3	1.9
1998	3.2	4.2	2.2	1.9

Source: Audit Bureau of Circulation, 1998 (through June 30).
Note: "n/a" means data not available for that year.

since the early 1980s; their total readership has dropped by almost 60 percent. As *Newsweek* writer Richard Turner asks, "With dollops of sleaze on your doorstep and your TV everyday, who needs the tabs?"[46]

Unquestionably, the print media have moved away from the principles of journalism espoused, though not always adhered to, by the old beat writers of the 1950s, 1960s, and 1970s.[47] The detailed coverage of the Simpson trial, the Ramsey case, and the Louise Woodward trial demonstrated a clear violation of many of the standards articulated in the journalistic code of ethics listed previously. Coverage of many of these cases involved significant invasions of privacy, rarely accompanied by any overriding public need. In many instances, reporters also pandered to the public's lurid curiosity. Several of the headlines listed above, most notably the reference to semen stains, do not involve details or issues that the public had an objective need to know.

THE TRANSFORMATION OF TELEVISION NEWS

The considerable evidence of a tabloid shift in the print media pales in comparison to the "tabloidization" of television news. This is hardly surprising, given TV's disproportionate impact on U.S. culture generally.[48] Political scientists and media scholars have long pointed to events such as the first Nixon-Kennedy debate in 1960 and the coverage of the Vietnam War in the 1960s and 1970s as evidence of the power of visual images to influence the public's response to political and social issues. Some have speculated that TV images of a striking and youthful John F. Kennedy propelled him to victory over Richard Nixon in the 1960 presidential election, and that the shocking war pictures coming out of Vietnam and broadcast on the evening news turned public opinion against the war and played a major role in ending the conflict.[49]

The current period of tabloid justice includes similarly striking images. Most Americans have seen the videotaped beating of Rodney King, the footage of six-year-old JonBenet Ramsey performing in beauty pageants, the police pursuit of O.J. Simpson's white Ford Bronco on a Los Angeles freeway, and the image of President Clinton hugging a smiling, beret-wearing Monica Lewinsky. In fact, without the presence of such memorable video images, these cases may not have risen to such elevated levels of media frenzy. Doris Graber contends that the 1992 trial of serial killer and cannibal Jeffrey Dahmer did not receive extensive media attention because no striking visual images were associated with the crime.[50] Images are crucial to the success of a story.

A careful analysis of television news coverage shows that there has been a dramatic shift in the style of coverage in the past thirty years. To examine this change, we sought to quantify the volume of trial coverage that the networks have presented in their newscasts. Table 2.5 identifies the number of trial-related news stories presented by the three nightly network newscasts since 1968, the first year such broadcasts were archived. Utilizing the Television News Archives at Vanderbilt University, we used the key word *trial* to identify the number of segments that featured trial coverage on ABC, CBS, and NBC national news broadcasts.[51] Thus, our analysis in Table 2.5 includes literally any type of trial, from simple murder cases to those involving Vietnam War crimes. This general measure of trial-related segments is important, because trial coverage of any type potentially exposes the public to information about the judicial process.

Since the late 1960s, there have been three distinct periods of intensive trial coverage. The first period, between 1968 through 1974, was one of the most tumultuous times in recent U.S. history. This six-year span included trials concerning the assassinations of three major American political figures. In 1968, Clay Shaw was charged with conspiracy to assassinate John F. Kennedy.[52] That same year, Sirhan Sirhan was tried for the murder of Robert Kennedy,[53] and James Earl Ray was successfully prosecuted for the assassination of Martin Luther King, Jr.[54] This extraordinary period also included the criminal investigations and trials of the Weathermen Underground, the Black Panther Party, the Symbionese Liberation Army, and the Chicago Seven.[55] The infamous Pentagon Papers case arose during this time as well. All of these cases clearly meet the previously identified baseline standard of broad social and political importance, as their significance transcended the individual participants.

In the second period, from 1975 through 1989, no clear pattern of trial coverage emerges. A number of important stories, including the ABSCAM and Iran-Contra affairs, received considerable coverage, but they did not dominate the news as heavily as did trials and investigations in the earlier period. Yet during the second period, we see the media turn to more individual and personal types of crime cases. These include the trials of Claus von Bulow, John Wayne Gacy, and Wayne

**Table 2.5   Coverage of Trials and Major Criminal Investigations on Network
News Broadcasts, 1968–1998**

Year	Number of News Segments Focusing on a Trial	Top Cases
First period		
1968	57	Sirhan Sirhan, Huey Newton
1969	470	Sirhan Sirhan, Chicago 7, James Earl Ray
1970	438	Chicago 7, Black Panthers, My Lai massacre
1971	437	Charles Manson, Vietnam war crimes
1972	280	Daniel Ellsberg, Angela Davis, Harrisburg 7
1973	257	Pentagon Papers, Watergate break-in
1974	725	Kent State shooting, Watergate
Second period		
1975	331	Joan Little, Patty Hearst, John Connelly
1976	352	Patty Hearst
1977	238	No marquee trials
1978	281	No marquee trials
1979	285	No marquee trials
1980	290	ABSCAM, Burt Lance, Ford Corporation
1981	226	ABSCAM
1982	371	John Hinckley, Claus von Bulow, Wayne Williams
1983	138	John DeLorean
1984	195	John DeLorean
1985	269	Papal assassination, Claus von Bulow
1986	214	No marquee trials
1987	257	Bernard Goetz
1988	213	No marquee trials
1989	363	Iran/Contra, Lyn Nofzinger, Jim Bakker
Third period		
1990	277	Iran-Contra, Marion Barry
1991	168	Manuel Noriega, William Kennedy Smith
1992	277	Jeffrey Dahmer, Mike Tyson, Amy Fisher
1993	343	Menendez brothers
1994	679	O.J. Simpson
1995	882	O.J. Simpson
1996	318	No marquee trials
1997	676	O.J. Simpson, Timothy McVeigh, JonBenet Ramsey
1998	632	Paula Jones, Monica Lewinsky

Source: Television News Archives, Vanderbilt University.

Note: Entries indicate total number of news segments on the *CBS Evening News, NBC
Nightly News,* and *ABC World News Tonight* that reference a criminal trial. "Top cases" are
listings of the most covered or most famous cases of that year. For search instructions, see
Appendix A.

Williams, all of which were stories of individuals who stood accused of murder. The latter two cases did involve serial killers whose crimes were extraordinary, however.

In the third period examined, from 1990 through 1998, the total volume of trial coverage increased dramatically. This period started off slowly in terms of the number of trial segments covered by the media, but such stories soon proliferated. In fact, four of the five years in which trials received the greatest media attention occurred between 1994 and 1998. The only exception is 1974, the height of the Watergate scandal and President Richard Nixon's resignation from office, when many in the Nixon administration stood trial for their involvement in that affair. And yet, with the exception of Panamanian dictator Manuel Noriega's case, none of the marquee trials of the early part of the 1990s involved political leaders or serious political questions. Aside from the Clinton-Lewinsky affair, trial coverage in the 1990s has been almost entirely concerned with crimes between individuals (husbands killing their wives, wives attacking husbands, men attacking women, parents killing children). Without question, these cases involve severe individual tragedy and pain, but individually they have little broader significance or societal implications.

Although the number of trial-related stories has fluctuated over the years, Table 2.5 shows that total coverage increased dramatically in the 1990s. More specifically, the data presented in Table 2.5 make clear that a sea change in the media's coverage of tabloid justice cases occurred with the 1994 criminal trial of O.J. Simpson. The mean number of trial stories per year for the period between 1968 and 1974 was 381. This number drops off considerably for the second period, with the mean number of trial-related news stories falling to 269. Turning to the third period—the era of tabloid justice—there was an average of 497 stories. Since 1994, the average number of trial or criminal-investigation segments on the national nightly news broadcasts each year was 637. This dramatic increase appears to have arisen, not coincidentally, in the wake of the Simpson case.

It is also important to consider the different forms of media that characterize each time period. Traditional, mainstream news sources—newspapers, newsmagazines, network television, and wire services—dominated the first period (1968–1974). The second period (1975–1989) witnessed the increased speed of communication and delivery of news via cable TV, computers, satellites, and fax machines. It was in the 1990s, however, that the speed with which information could be transmitted increased exponentially. Thus, the increase in media coverage of criminal trials and investigations is closely correlated with technological developments. The emergence of cable television and the Internet, for example, have greatly expanded the number of forums where discussion and coverage can continue long after the traditional media have abandoned a given trial.

COMPARING TRIAL COVERAGE: CHARLES MANSON, CLAUS VON BULOW, AND O.J. SIMPSON

One way to illustrate the changes in media coverage over the three previously delineated time periods is to compare the media's treatment of three murder trials that had comparable levels of newsworthiness. From our first time period, we selected the trial of Charles Manson. The leader of a cult called "The Family," Manson stood accused of orchestrating the brutal and grotesque murders of actress Sharon Tate, wife of film director Roman Polanski, and six other Los Angeles residents. The bizarre motive for the killing spree, according to Manson, was to bring about an inevitable war between blacks and whites in the United States. He believed that blacks would ultimately win this war and turn to him for guidance on how to govern a new society. Three decades later, Manson still languishes in a California prison.[56]

We illustrate the second media period with the trial of Claus von Bulow, a member of the wealthy elite of Rhode Island. Around Christmas of 1980, von Bulow's wife, Sunny, slipped into a coma, in which she remains today. The prosecutor in the case charged her husband with attempted murder and accused him of injecting his wife with near fatal dosages of insulin. The prosecutor argued that with a $14 million inheritance and a beautiful young mistress at his side, von Bulow had a powerful motive for murdering his wife.[57] The trial we selected to represent our third time period is the 1995 double-murder trial of O.J. Simpson. (See Chapter 1 for a description of the facts of this case.)

Although the comparisons among these cases are certainly imperfect, they share several similar characteristics. All three involve some degree of celebrity, as well as substantial wealth by some trial participants. Furthermore, all three trials involved murder or attempted murder charges. Table 2.6 shows the number of story segments on the three major network news broadcasts that featured each of the crime stories.

Table 2.6   Number of Network Television News Segments Covering Cases Involving Charles Manson, Claus von Bulow, and O.J. Simpson

Case	CBS Evening News	NBC Nightly News	ABC World News	Total
Charles Manson				
1969 (crime occurred August 9)	9	8	8	25
1970 (trial began June 15)	32	34	23	89
1971 (verdict March 29)	8	12	9	29
Total				143
Claus von Bulow				
1980 (crime occurred December 21)	0	0	1	1
1982 (trial began January 11)	14	26	23	63
1983–1984 (case on appeal)	3	2	3	8
1985 (second trial ended April 25)	13	11	9	3
Total				105
O.J. Simpson				
1994 (crime occurred June 12)	132	116	105	353
1995 (trial began January 24 and ended October 3)	241	242	195	678
1996 (civil trial began October 22)	34	36	34	104
1997 (civil trial verdict February 10)	32	28	30	90
Total				1,225

Source: Television News Archives, Vanderbilt University.

Most striking about the data presented in Table 2.6 is the staggering number of national news segments devoted to the Simpson trial. This case received roughly eight times the coverage of the Manson trial and more than ten times the coverage given to the von Bulow trial. In 1994, before the trial had even begun, the Simpson case led the news twenty-two times on NBC, twenty-three times on CBS, and twelve times on ABC.[58] Placing a story at the top of a national newscast has historically been done to signify that it is the most important one of the day. In contrast, the Manson and von Bulow stories never led the national news broadcasts.

The comparisons of these three cases help demonstrate the media transformation we have suggested. The Simpson trial did not receive so much more attention simply because it was more newsworthy; it garnered more attention because it transpired in the era of tabloid justice. In fact, the Manson case was, arguably, far more intriguing than the Simpson case. The saga of a murderous doomsday cult orchestrating a race war with the goal of achieving political power seems far more intrinsically interesting than the relatively common story of an abusive husband allegedly murdering his ex-wife. Granted, the racial dynamics of the Simpson case added an important element, as did Simpson's fame and celebrity.[59] As we discuss in Chapter 5, however, "racialized" coverage of the case may have fueled the racial overtones of the Simpson proceedings.

In terms of the legal issues at stake, the von Bulow and Manson cases were perhaps more interesting than the Simpson trial, which was often dominated by lawyerly wrangling. Manson, for example, was not even present for the killings with which he was charged. In the von Bulow case, renowned criminal defense attorney and Harvard Law School professor Alan Dershowitz convinced the Rhode Island Supreme Court to overturn the attempted murder conviction and order a new trial. In the second trial, von Bulow was acquitted.

TODAY'S TABLOID NEWS COVERAGE

We now turn more specifically to the prominance of tabloid coverage within national news broadcasts. The three network nightly news broadcasts now regularly report on criminal trials and investigations that they believe will pique the nation's interest. To illustrate the promi-nent role of tabloid cases in mainstream media fare, Table 2.7 illustrates the programming schedules for the nightly news on important days dur-ing the Menendez, Simpson, and Woodward cases. We present the broadcast schedule for one edition of the evening news for each net-work. Table 2.7 demonstrates how the networks emphasize tabloid tri-als and de-emphasize more politically and socially meaningful topics. For each of these specific broadcasts, the tabloid justice story received more coverage than any other topic. In ABC's broadcast, coverage of the Menendez trial matched only the duration of the news feature "Person of the Week," which is a profile of a "worthy citizen." In this same broadcast, however, additional coverage was devoted to the tabloid-like story concerning figure skaters Tonya Harding and Nancy Kerrigan. CBS's trial coverage of Louise Woodward, and NBC's cov-erage of O.J. Simpson, exceeded by three times any other story covered that day.

In his 1979 study of the CBS and NBC newsrooms, Herbert Gans identified some very specific norms, procedures, and imperatives that drove network news organizations' choices. Gans found that most lead

**Table 2.7   Programming Schedules for Three Nightly Network News
Broadcasts When Tabloid Justice Stories Were Covered**

ABC World News Tonight January 28, 1994		*NBC Nightly News* July 7, 1994		*CBS Evening News* October 31, 1997	
Story	Time	Story	Time	Story	Time
Clinton crime bill	2:10	*Simpson murder case*	9:10	*Au pair murder trial*	8:50
Menendez murder trial	4:30	Colorado wild fires	2:00	Campaign fundraising	:30
Kerrigan/Harding		Floods in the South	1:50	U.S.-China relations	:10
investigation	2:00	Clinton policy on Haiti	2:20	Stock market report	1:20
Deadbeat dad case	2:10	Russian coup trial	:20	Beef plant shutdown	:30
Earthquake relief abuse	:20	New York police		Pepper spray attack on	
Cleveland flood	:10	corruption	2:10	environmentalists	2:00
Race and drug laws	2:20	Abortion protests in		El Niño/weather	:20
Stock market report	:20	Arkansas	:20	Saccharin and cancer	:30
Death of silent film star	:20	Medical cost of smoking	:20	Halloween in France	:10
Bosnia civil war deaths	:20	Stock market report	:20	Travel in New Orleans	2:30
Economy and politics		Dinosaur research	1:30		
in Russia	1:30				
Person of the week	4:30				

General Totals	ABC	NBC	CBS
Introduction/previews/commercials	9:20	9:30	11:00
Total news time	20:40	20:30	19:00
Tabloid crime coverage	6:30	9:10	8:50

Tabloid Crime Story As a Percent of Total News		
31	45	46

Source: Television News Archive, Vanderbilt University.
Note: Numbers represent minutes and seconds. Tabloid stories appear in italics.

news stories received two to three minutes of attention. He noted, however, that "when events that journalists deem to be world-shaking take
place . . . the normal daily format may be set aside, with 8 to 10 minutes or more given to one story."[60] This norm, which has been followed
by the national news broadcasts since they went to the half-hour format
in the late 1950s, was clearly discarded in the 1990s.

What else could explain the levels of media attention given to the
trial of Louise Woodward illustrated in Table 2.7? Woodward, an
unknown nineteen-year-old woman, came to the United States from
Great Britain to work as an au pair. The toddler she was accused of

shaking to death was not a well-known figure in the United States, and neither were his parents. The trial raised few issues of broad public concern.[61] Yet the story of Louise Woodward received substantially more airtime than did stories with potentially important domestic and foreign policy implications, such as the visit of Chinese premier Jiang Jemin to the United States, the congressional debate on campaign finance reform, and a violent attack on environmentalists who were attempting to save a redwood forest in California.

To provide a broader look at the media coverage that now pervades our social and political world, we provide a more extensive look at coverage in 1997. Table 2.8 shows the aggregate number of network news segments devoted to twenty-six news stories or topics in 1997. Segments are generally anywhere from ten seconds to three or four minutes. We divided the stories into four categories: tabloid justice dramas, domestic and human-interest topics, U.S. foreign policy, and domestic public policy issues. We also broke down the analysis by the number of segments on each particular television network.

The most covered story of 1997 was the trial of Oklahoma bombing suspect Timothy McVeigh. Although this cannot be considered a tabloid justice story in the manner of the Simpson or Woodward cases, it did provide the public with an explicit view of the legal system. Other topics that received considerable attention included U.S. relations with China, the death of Princess Diana, and the civil war in Bosnia. The Princess Diana coverage certainly bordered on sensationalism, particularly when the media began to follow the police investigation into the causes of the fatal car crash. Tabloid justice cases constitute the next tier of most covered stories. Alarmingly, most of the tabloid stories received more media attention than did public policy topics. Many recent critics of journalism in the United States would find this reality troubling but not surprising.[62]

Based on our analysis of nightly network news broadcasts, we can draw two conclusions. First, the networks have increasingly come to spend more time covering human-interest trials that would formerly have been the domain of the tabloid press. The William Kennedy Smith case in 1991 triggered this coverage, but it began in earnest with O.J. Simpson's criminal trial in 1995. Second, this analysis lays the groundwork for our contention that at no time in history have the media so frequently and thoroughly inundated the public with portrayals of the workings of the U.S. judicial system.

Table 2.8   Number of Nightly National News Segments Devoted to Twenty-six Stories in 1997

Story	CBS Evening News	NBC Nightly News	ABC World News	Total
Tabloid justice				
O.J. Simpson civil trial	32	28	30	90
JonBenet Ramsey investigation	37	22	27	86
Gianni Versace murder investigation	22	19	15	56
Paula Jones sexual harassment suit	22	15	11	48
Louise Woodward trial	20	13	14	47
Ennis Cosby murder trial	22	11	13	46
Marv Albert sexual assault trial	2	6	4	12
Domestic and human interest				
Timothy McVeigh trial	97	82	70	249
Princess Diana's death	44	43	37	124
UPS strike	23	18	22	63
Septuplets	10	11	11	33
Heaven's Gate	13	7	9	29
Hamburger recall	10	7	6	23
Foreign policy				
China relations	78	53	93	224
Bosnia	28	37	37	102
Yeltsin and Russian politics	19	18	24	61
UN inspectors in Iraq	14	11	14	39
Public policy				
Medicare	17	24	17	58
Abortion	22	11	18	51
Affirmative action	17	13	13	43
Welfare policy	14	13	13	40
Health care	12	10	13	35
Social security	8	6	10	24
HMO reform	8	7	5	20
Campaign finance reform	3	8	8	19
Federal budget	9	5	0	14

Source: Television News Archives, Vanderbilt University.
Note: For search instructions, see Appendix A.

TELEVISION NEWSMAGAZINES: HARD NEWS OR ENTERTAINMENT?

Accompanying the network news broadcasts' embrace of tabloid justice stories has been the tremendous growth in the number of television newsmagazines that air during prime time. These shows have become

Table 2.9 **Growth in the Number of Prime Time Newsmagazines on the Major Networks**

		Number of Editions of Each Program Shown Every Week	
Network	Program	1993	1999
NBC	*Dateline*	1	5
ABC	*20/20*	1	3
CBS	*60 Minutes*	1	2
CBS	*48 Hours*	1	1
Total		4	11

Source: Prime time television listing for the 1998/1999 season provided by www.ultimatetv.com.

an important component in creating the media frenzy surrounding criminal investigations and trials. Table 2.9 illustrates the proliferation of such programs since 1993. Although some media scholars consider these programs to occupy the distant periphery of serious news, we believe that they should be considered alongside the flagship news broadcasts.[63] The basis for this contention is that the same journalists now appear on both types of programs. For instance, Dan Rather, the longtime anchor of the *CBS Evening News*, also hosts the newsmagazine *48 Hours*. Tom Brokaw, anchor of the *NBC Nightly News*, is a frequent contributor to *Dateline*. Similarly, for the program *20/20*, ABC uses its topflight reporters, including noted interviewer Barbara Walters, White House correspondent Sam Donaldson, and prominent journalist Diane Sawyer.

The television newsmagazines play a crucial role in the era of tabloid justice. First, they air on the major networks during prime time, and they enjoy the largest regular audience of any type of news programming. Second, the format allows for much more detailed analysis of criminal trials and investigations. An hour in length, the newsmagazines are usually divided into two or three fifteen-minute segments, with the rest of the hour devoted to commercials and shorter stories and updates. Often, these programs devote the entire hour to a single criminal case. CBS's *48 Hours* is based on this format, whereas NBC's *Dateline* has done this on numerous occasions. These newsmagazines' segments are often structured as mystery stories, with twists and turns in a plot that remains unresolved until the very end of the program. Below are some examples of titles from the segments included in episodes from the 1990s:[64]

"Free to Kill: The Boy Next Door" (murderer Kenneth McDuff set free in Texas to murder again), *48 Hours*, April 28, 1993

"Fatal Encounter: Death in the Night" (Adrian Crump shoots teenager who has broken his window with a slingshot), *48 Hours*, August 4, 1993

"Why Did Eric Kill?" (investigation, trial, and verdict in the case of a thirteen-year-old boy brutally murdering a four-year-old), *48 Hours*, August 31, 1995

"Fortunate Son?" (why John du Pont killed Dave Schultz), *Dateline NBC*, January 30, 1996

"Murder for Hire" (trial of David Lusskin, accused of trying to hire a man to kill his pregnant girlfriend), *Dateline NBC*, February 9, 1996

"Haunting Vision" (after twenty-seven years of secrecy, a young woman accuses her father of her mother's murder), *Dateline NBC*, March 15, 1996

"While She Was Sleeping" (murder trial of small-town banker and mayor), *Dateline NBC*, May 20, 1997

As their titles indicate, these programs present true crime stories as dramatic entertainment. Rarely is there an attempt to place them into the context of the real workings of the legal system, the findings of scholars, or general trends in U.S. society. The crime presentations of newsmagazines clearly epitomize that to which we referred in Chapter 1 as commodification—"the packaging and marketing of crime information for popular consumption."[65]

Beyond the anecdotal nature of the story titles presented above, Table 2.10 documents the commanding presence of crime stories on several television newsmagazines. The entries in Table 2.10 represent the percentage of broadcasts in a given year that included a crime story. For this analysis, we defined a crime story as anything involving a crime of an individual against another individual. In our coding of the programs, we did not include more general news stories on crime, such as investigative reports on capital punishment or racism in the criminal justice system. Table 2.10 reveals that television newsmagazines frequently cover tabloid criminal cases. *Dateline* and *48 Hours* increased their crime coverage during the 1990s, and in 1997

Table 2.10   **Percentage of Television Newsmagazine Broadcasts That Contained a Tabloid-Style Crime Story, 1991–1998**

Year	60 Minutes (CBS)	48 Hours (CBS)	Dateline (NBC)	20/20 (ABC)
1991	22	n/a	16	21
1992	14	n/a	15	12
1993	10	20	18	22
1994	14	24	31	21
1995	12	24	45	23
1996	19	23	35	21
1997	16	48	29	23
1998	20	47	36	19

Note: "n/a" means data not available for that year.

and 1998, more than 40 percent of all *Dateline* and *48 Hours* programs included interpersonal crime stories. "True crime" stories were less prominent on *60 Minutes* and *20/20*, and neither of these programs increased its crime coverage over the course of the decade. Nonetheless, roughly 20 percent of their broadcasts included a tabloid justice segment as well.

The television newsmagazines, in conjunction with the national news broadcasts, have worked together to promote the media frenzy that surrounds tabloid cases. An interested viewer can watch the latest trial developments on the nightly news, tune in for more in-depth reporting to one of the prime time newsmagazines, and then wake to the morning network broadcasts to receive an update on each case. This level of media saturation was particularly prevalent in the Simpson and Clinton legal proceedings. News presented so obsessively and constantly almost begins to suppress other news. The public becomes very knowledgeable about irregular legal proceedings, and particularly the personalities involved, but learns little about broader issues in the legal system.

A NOTE ON TELEVISION RATINGS

The pursuit of viewers has often been cited as the primary reason behind the mainstream media's increasingly more sensational styles and formats. In some instances, particularly on cable television, it is indisputable that tabloid stories have helped to boost ratings substantially.[66] Evidence from the mainstream media, however, is not as clear.

Some media outlets appear to have benefited from covering these events, whereas others have not.[67] For instance, the evening network newscasts may actually have suffered from their constant coverage of the Simpson case. In the 1994–1995 television season, when the networks covered the Simpson case in epic proportions (see Table 2.6), the ratings share for the nightly news programs dropped to the lowest levels in years (see Table 2.1). The CBS *Evening News* and the NBC *Nightly News* recorded their lowest shares of viewers since before 1970. ABC *World News Tonight* scored its lowest rating since 1978.[68] Although the decline in viewers for the nightly newscasts certainly relates to broader trends, at the very least we can conclude that the networks' decisions to cover these cases did not inhibit their descent.

However, the ratings of other mainstream news programs, such as ABC's *Nightline* and the television newsmagazines, appear to have thrived in the era of tabloid justice. Almost seventy *Nightline* programs focused on the Simpson criminal case.[69] Significantly, the average rating for these programs was 11 percent higher than programs focusing on other subjects.[70] Various accounts of managing news editors and news producers reveal that they were often torn between continuing to cover the Simpson case and moving on to a topic they deemed more important. The lure of ratings made this a very difficult decision. In any event, the importance of ratings as a factor in determining a broadcast's focus becomes even more striking in our consideration of the cable television outlets.

CONCLUSION

When *Newsweek* writer Jonathan Alter wrote an article at the end of 1994 asserting that nothing could match the string of tabloid stories that paraded across our television screens that year, he probably did not expect to write a similar article in 1997.[71] In 1994, we saw extended coverage of Lorena Bobbitt, Tonya Harding, Paula Jones, O.J. Simpson, and Susan Smith. In 1997, Kelly Flynn (a female fighter pilot forced to resign from the air force over charges of sexual misconduct), Marv Albert, Kathy Lee Gifford (the popular talk show host whose famous husband was caught on camera in a sexually compromising position), JonBenet Ramsey, Louise Woodward, and O.J. Simpson (again) made the headlines. In describing the news environment in 1997, Alter lamented "No wars? No news? No problem. The news media can just entertain us into a stupor."

Further, Alter claims that as a result of the media's blurring of scandal and hard news, much of the public can no longer differentiate between important public events and entertainment.[72]

Two basic conclusions emerge from the data presented in this chapter. First, it is important to recognize the role of the mainstream media as the foundation of the news media generally. As the flagship media outlets in the United States turn aggressively toward the coverage of criminal justice dramas, they in effect give a green light to the rest of the mass media at all levels to follow suit. The competition in the news business compels ever-greater degrees of sensationalism. The news media sources we discuss in the following chapter have seized upon the mainstream media's validation of these cases, thereby immersing U.S. society and culture in tabloid-style crime coverage.

Second, we reiterate the point that, beginning with the William Kennedy Smith trial in 1991, Americans have been exposed to an unprecedented amount of detailed information about the legal system.[73] And though we argue that this exposure has on balance been a mixed blessing, it has nevertheless been substantial. The Smith trial, for instance, illustrated to the public firsthand the treatment of a woman bringing a charge of rape. The Simpson trial treated the public to lengthy explanations of evidence and legal rules. The Paula Jones sexual harassment case exposed the public to lengthy and technical discussions of the legal definitions of perjury and obstruction of justice. Thus, these cases and the coverage of them provided opportunities for the public to learn about the judicial process. Unfortunately, this opportunity for civic education and an increase in public confidence has been squandered by the style in which the media have chosen to present this information.

As the media environment rapidly evolves, the hard news outlets discussed in this chapter constitute only one source of what David Shenk has called the "data smog" that pollutes everyone's personal orbit.[74] The tabloidization of the media becomes substantially more apparent when we consider the new media that have cranked up both the amount and volume of tabloid justice coverage. We turn to the role of these new media outlets in our next chapter.

NOTES

1. Howard Kurtz, *Hot Air* (New York: Basic Books, 1995), p. 138. In the end, *Nightline* aired more than seventy shows on Simpson's legal battles.

2. Richard Turner, "A Tabloid Shocker," *Newsweek,* October 12, 1998, p. 70.

3. For an early analysis of the prevalence of "crime entertainment" on television, see Joseph Dominick, "Crime and Law Enforcement in Mass Media," in Charles Winick, ed., *Deviance and Mass Media* (Thousand Oaks, Calif.: Sage, 1978), pp. 105–128. More recently see Barbara Wilson et al., *National Television Violence Study,* vol. 1 (Thousand Oaks, Calif.: Sage, 1997).

4. Andrew Kohut, "TV Trials Captivate Public," *Times Mirror Center for the People and the Press,* February 4, 1994, p. 12.

5. For a collection of earlier high-profile cases, see Lloyd Chiasson, Jr., ed., *The Press on Trial* (Westport, Conn.: Praeger, 1997).

6. For a brief description of these and other famous cases of the twentieth century, see Edward Knappman, ed., *American Trials of the 20th Century* (Detroit, Mich.: Visible Ink Press, 1995). Also see Ronald Goldfarb, *TV or Not TV: Television, Justice, and the Courts* (New York: New York University Press, 1998), pp. 4–5.

7. Identifying the one true trial of the century has become an amusing debate topic for a number of scholars and journalists. See Goldfarb, *TV or Not TV,* chapter 1; and "What Was the 'Trial of the Century'?" *Newsweek,* August 24, 1998, p. 9.

8. Theo Wilson, *Headline Justice* (New York: Thunder's Mouth Press, 1997), p. 4.

9. For example, St. Martin's Press publishes a true crime series that often presents the story behind a given crime long before the case ever goes to trial.

10. See Linda Acorn, "Crime in Prime Time: New Shows Capture Audiences," *Corrections Today,* February 1989, pp. 44–46, 54.

11. Peter Johnson and Gary Levin, "Rivera Holds His Tongue on the Eve of 'Upfront,'" *USA Today,* August 24, 1998, p. 3D.

12. Neal Gabler, *Life: The Movie* (New York: Knopf, 1998), pp. 3–10.

13. This assessment is based on materials provided by the Television News Archives at Vanderbilt University, available online at http://tvnews.vanderbilt.edu/index.html. Also see Table 2.8.

14. Program summaries for *The Big Show* were provided by Burrelles Transcript Service, available online at www.burrelles.com.

15. Keith Olberman interview on *Imus in the Morning* radio program, December 4, 1998.

16. Michael Janofsky, "Marv Albert Pleads Guilty and Is Dismissed by NBC," *New York Times,* September 26, 1997, p. A1.

17. For further evidence of this transformation, see Richard Davis and Diana Owen, *New Media and American Politics* (New York: Oxford University Press, 1998), pp. 94–107. Although these authors do not address media coverage of the legal system and judicial process per se, they effectively present an account of how the new media culture interacts with the broader political system.

18. Richard Davis, *The Press and American Politics,* 2d ed. (Upper Saddle River, N.J.: Prentice-Hall, 1996), pp. 108–109.

19. For a discussion about how national wire services play a significant role in establishing news for *all* types of news organizations, see David L. Paletz, *The Media in American Politics* (New York: Longman, 1999), pp. 62–63; and David Morgan, *The Capitol Press Corps: Newsmen and the Governing of New York State* (Westport, Conn.: Greenwood, 1978), p. 134.

20. For a discussion of how the media set the agenda for policy debates in the criminal justice system, see Ray Surette, *Media, Crime, and Criminal Justice: Images and Realities*, 2d ed. (Belmont, Calif.: Wadsworth Publishing, 1998), pp. 201–203.

21. Burton S. Katz, *Justice Overruled: Unmasking the Criminal Justice System* (New York: Warner Books, 1998), pp. 2, 260.

22. Davis, *The Press and American Politics*, chapter 8.

23. Gabler, *Life,* pp. 181–184.

24. For a recounting of the *60 Minutes* decision to run the videotape, see Ira Byock, "Snuff Film," *Washington Post*, December 6, 1998, p. C7.

25. Many would argue that these cases, particularly the criminal trial of O.J. Simpson, did raise important national issues. We would argue that the Simpson case only came to symbolize larger issues, such as race or gender relations, *as a result* of the enormous levels of media coverage involved in the case.

26. Doris Graber, *Crime News and the Public* (Westport, Conn.: Praeger, 1980), p. 44.

27. For a description of how newspaper writers have covered trials in the past, see Wilson, *Headline Justice*, pp. 3–11.

28. Stephen Ansolabehere, Roy Behr, and Shanto Iyengar, *The Media Game* (New York: Macmillan, 1993), p. 40.

29. Herbert Gans, *Deciding What's News: A Study of CBS Evening News, NBC Nightly News, Newsweek, and Time* (New York: Vintage Books, 1979), p. 4.

30. Certainly CNN could be considered in this category, as it is a widely and highly regarded television news network. We have chosen to address CNN in Chapter 3 in our discussion of cable news outlets.

31. Gans, *Deciding What's News*, pp. 3–5.

32. The difference between crime news and crime shows can become blurred, as Surette points out in *Media, Crime, and Criminal Justice*. See also Paletz, *The Media in American Politics*, p. 299.

33. Teresa Ortega, "Dateline Dominates," www.utlimatetv.com/.

34. The Society of Professional Journalists posts its code of ethics on the Internet at http://www.spj.org/ethics/index.htm.

35. Ibid.

36. "General Social Sciences Survey, 1993," Roper Center, University of Connecticut.

37. See Joe Abernathy, "Casting the Internet: A New Tool for Electronic News Gathering," *Columbia Journalism Review*, January/February 1993, p. 56.

38. "Simpson Story Loses Audience: Democratic Congressional Prospects Worsen," *Times Mirror Center of the People and Press*, October 13, 1994, p. 4.

39. For a discussion of audience interest levels and the marketing of the Simpson case, see George Lipsitz, "The Greatest Story Ever Sold: Marketing and the O.J. Simpson Trial" in Toni Morrison and Claudia Brosky Lacour, eds., *Birth of a Nation'hood: Gaze, Script, and Spectacle in the O.J. Simpson Case* (New York: Pantheon Books, 1997), pp. 3–29.

40. Ansolabehere, Behr, and Iyengar, *The Media Game*, pp. 42–45; and Mathew Robert Kerbel, *Remote and Controlled* (Boulder, Colo.: Westview Press, 1995), p. 12.

41. See Bill Kovach and Tom Rosenstiel, *Warp Speed: America in the Age of Mixed Media* (New York: The Century Foundation, 1999).

42. It is common to rely on these three newsmagazines. See Martin P. Wattenberg, *The Decline of American Political Parties: 1952–1988* (Cambridge, Mass.: Harvard University Press, 1990), pp. 92–98.

43. Carey Goldberg, "In a Startling Turnabout, Judge Sets Au Pair Free," *New York Times*, November 11, 1997, p. A1; David Lauter and Rebecca Mowbray, "British Au Pair Is Found Guilty of Killing Baby," *Los Angeles Times*, October 31, 1997, p. A1; "British Nanny Sobs After Guilty Verdict, 'Why Did They Do This to Me?'" *Orlando Sentinel*, October 31, 1997, p. A1; "Foreign Faction Threatened to Kill JonBenet in Ransom Note," *Buffalo News*, September 3, 1997, p A1; Jay Croft, "Killing of Tiny Beauty Queen Becomes a Riveting Mystery," *Atlanta Journal and Constitution*, January 12, 1997, p. A1; Lisa Levitt Ryckman, "Ramsey's Trip to Spain Strictly Business, Friend Says," *Denver Rocky Mountain News*, February 6, 1998, p. 1A; and Marilyn Robinson, "No Semen Found at Ramsey Slay Scene," *Denver Post*, March 15, 1997, p. A-1.

44. Jerry Adler, "The Strange World of JonBenet," *Newsweek*, January 20, 1997, p. 43; Richard Woodbury, "JonBenet; Taking the Hunt into His Own Hands," *Time*, August 4, 1997, p. 12; Marc Peyser, "A Body in the Basement," *Newsweek*, January 13, 1997, p. 38; Matthew Cooper, "Marv Goes to the Showers," *Newsweek*, October 6, 1997, p. 40; Dorian Freedman, "He's Out of the Game," *U.S. News and World Report*, October 6, 1997, p. 8; Jerry Alder, "Murder 90210: Crime Styles of the Young, Rich and Impatient," *Newsweek*, August 2, 1993, p. 60; Walter Kirn, "Papa Bill, Mama Linda, Baby Monica: The Dysfunctional Family at the Heart of the Scandal," *Time*, October 5, 1998, p. 36; and "He Was Thinking with Another Head," *Newsweek*, February 2, 1998, p. 17.

45. These headlines can be found in the archives of the *National Enquirer* website: http://www.nationalenquirer.com.

46. Turner, "A Tabloid Shocker," p. 70.

47. Wilson, *Headline Justice*, pp. 3–11.

48. The argument that we are now a "snapshot culture" has been put forward by a number of scholars in different fields. For instance, see Neil Postman, *Amusing Ourselves to Death: Public Discourse in the Age of Show Business* (New York: Viking Penguin, 1986); Michael Parenti, *Inventing Reality* (New York: St. Martin's, 1986); and Arthur Asa Berger, *Manufacturing Desire* (New Brunswick, N.J.: Transaction Publishers, 1996).

49. For an analysis of the role of image in presidential debates, see David J. Lanoue and Peter Schrott, *The History, Impact, and Prospects of American*

Presidential Debates (Westport, Conn.: Greenwood Press, 1991). For the role of media in Vietnam, see Daniel C. Hallin, *The "Uncensored War" : The Media and Vietnam* (New York: Oxford University Press, 1986).

50. Doris Graber, *Mass Media and American Politics*, 5th ed. (Washington, D.C.: Congressional Quarterly Press, 1997), p. 152.

51. We included, in the totals for 1997 and 1998, segments mentioning JonBenet Ramsey and Monica Lewinsky that did not include the term "trial."

52. For a discussion of the criminal investigation and trial proceedings, see Jim Garrison, *On the Trail of Assassins* (New York: Sheridan Press, 1988).

53. See John Christian and William Turner, *The Assassination of Robert Kennedy* (New York: Random House, 1978).

54. For a discussion of all three of these assassinations see Stephen Goode, *Assassination! Kennedy, King, Kennedy* (New York: Watts, 1979).

55. For a description of many of these and other notable cases, see Knappman, *American Trials of the 20th Century.*

56. For a full account of the Manson crimes and trial as written by the lead prosecutor in the case, see Vincent Bugliosi with Curt Gentry, *Helter Skelter: The True Story of the Manson Murders* (New York: W. W. Norton, 1974). Also see Tex Watson, *Will You Die for Me?* (Old Tappan, N.J.: Fleming Revell, 1978).

57. For a full account of the case, see Alan M. Dershowitz, *Reversal of Fortune* (New York: Random House, 1986); and William Wright, *The Von Bulow Affair* (New York: Delacorte Press, 1983).

58. These tabulations are based on an analysis of the Television News Archives, Vanderbilt University.

59. It has been noted that O.J. Simpson is the most famous person ever to be tried for murder in the United States and that this automatically dictated that there would be a tremendous amount of interest in the crime.

60. Gans, *Deciding What's News*, p. 3.

61. It was asserted that the trial had become a story of national interest because the death of a small child at the hands of a child-care worker evoked the fears of many who trust their children to babysitters or daycare facilities. But although this may explain some of the interest, this case would not appear to raise these issues any more clearly than hundreds of other similar cases each year.

62. Many who study the mass media, particularly in the arena of politics, have concluded that there is very little issue coverage. See, for instance, Guido H. Stempel III and John Windhauser, *The Media and the 1984 and 1988 Elections* (Westport, Conn.: Greenwood Press, 1991).

63. See Paletz, *The Media in American Politics*, p. 357, for a brief but concise explanation of why newsmagazines are difficult to classify.

64. Program descriptions for *Dateline NBC* and CBS's *48 Hours* are based on the program schedules maintained by Burrelles Transcript Service.

65. Surette, *Media, Crime, and Criminal Justice*, p. 71.

66. Cynthia Littleton, "Verdict Propels Tabloid Ratings," *Broadcasting and Cable*, October 1, 1995, p. 7.

67. Joe Mandrese and Thomas Tyler, "Simpson Shakes New TV Season," *Advertising Age*, October 16, 1995, p. 8.

68. Information received directly from Nielsen Media Research, 1998.

69. Based on ABC News Program Listing guide, provided by ABC NEWS, Livonia, Michigan.

70. Based on *Nightline*'s ratings for the period of June 12, 1994, through October 10, 1995, provided by Nielsen Media Research.

71. Jonathan Alter, "America Goes Tabloid," *Newsweek*, December 26, 1994, p. 34.

72. Ibid.

73. Howard Kurtz, "TV in Court: Healthy or 'Debasing' Eye on Justice?" *Washington Post*, December 12, 1991, p. A1.

74. For a wide-ranging discussion of the role of "information" in the daily lives of citizens, see David Shenk, *Data Smog: Surviving the Information Glut* (San Francisco: Harper, 1998).

3

Tabloid Justice and the Evolution of New Media

I have dedicated over two years of my life to covering the Simpson case and I will see it through to the end.

   —Geraldo Rivera, host of CNBC's *Rivera Live*[1]

We cover this story [Monica] 28 hours out of every 24. . . . There are days now when my line of work makes me ashamed, makes me depressed, makes me cry.

   —Keith Olberman, host of *The Big Show*[2]

When news oozes 24 hours a day it's not really news anymore. The TV becomes ambient noise. The newspaper becomes wallpaper. Finding the patterns of importance becomes hard. It's easier—and more profitable—just to make the consumer gape.

   —Jonathan Alter, writer for *Newsweek*[3]

We have entered an age in which news and information are available at a moment's notice. Gone are the days of eagerly awaiting delivery of the morning newspaper to learn what was going on in the world. Now, the *New York Times* and the *Washington Post* are rarely the first to break a big story, and even if they are, the story is likely to be reported the night before on a cable television news outlet such as CNN or MSNBC, or on the Internet. For example, in the summer of 1998, the

New York Times received the first word that President Clinton planned to change his previous story and admit to a sexual relationship with Monica Lewinsky. Long before the article appeared in the morning paper, cable television widely broadcast the revelation. Brian Williams, the host of MSNBC's nightly broadcast called *The News*, reads and discusses interesting newspaper headlines slated to appear the following day. In addition, all of the major newspapers now have online websites, where they reprint and update the news before the papers go to press and occasionally throughout the day of publication. In essence, we live in an environment where we no longer wait for the news—today's news is immediate, and it permeates our lives.

In the midst of this fast-paced news environment, the stream of tabloid justice coverage has become omnipresent. Stories and news about O.J., Monica, and JonBenet flow, it seems, from everywhere. Nightly newscasts contain information about these cases. Morning newspapers carry headlines about the trials. Magazine covers depict the players. And as we stand in supermarket checkout lines, tabloid headlines provide further rumors and details. Nowhere is the discussion of these cases more prominent and more enduring, however, than in the new and emerging forms of mass media.

The primary forms of new media on which we focus in this chapter are cable television and the Internet, but we also briefly assess the importance of talk radio. Each of these sources has provided extensive and ongoing coverage of the tabloid cases. In 1994 and 1995, for instance, several cable talk television programs, most notably *Rivera Live* and *Charles Grodin*, discussed the Simpson case almost every evening. In fact, roughly 400 *Rivera Live* programs covered the Simpson case.[4] Even the October 3, 1995, conclusion of the Simpson criminal trial did not end the news media's coverage. Rather, it marked the beginning of yet another new phase—the *civil* trial. In 1996 and 1997, the cable talk programs also devoted intense coverage to the Paula Jones case and the JonBenet Ramsey murder investigation. In 1998, cable talk shows turned their full attention to the presidential scandal involving Monica Lewinsky. A relentless drumbeat of talk television "analysis" surrounds these tabloid justice trials and investigations.

Alongside cable news programs, the Internet has also emerged as the newest and in many ways most complex form of new media. The Internet combines almost all forms of media—print journalism, visual news reporting, interactive news websites, and citizen reporting and commentary. Simply typing the key words "JonBenet," "Paula Jones," or "Monica Lewinsky" yields a vast array of news stories, games, video and audio clips, and editorials on these subjects. In the modern media age, talk, news, and information are always easily available and readily accessible.

In this chapter, we argue that the emergence of new media has substantially inundated and presented the public with information about tabloid trials and investigations. The almost-constant news and commentary about these cases keep them in the forefront of our national consciousness. Long after more traditional media outlets move on to other stories, the new media outlets continue to prod, discuss, dissect, and examine tabloid stories from every possible angle. As a result, Americans now receive previously unmatched amounts of information about the criminal justice system. In this era of expanded coverage, the public has the opportunity to view firsthand the judicial process and its actors, such as judges, lawyers, law enforcement officers, criminologists, and expert witnesses. In many instances, the viewer also may consider the same evidence that jurors see. Anecdotal evidence suggests that Americans, in particular those of younger generations, now learn much of what they know about the legal system through exposure to tabloid justice cases.

To explore the prevalence and impact of new media in the era of tabloid justice, we have divided this chapter into two sections. First, we offer a specific description of new media and identify the central features of the new media environment. Second, we analyze the manner in which the twenty-four-hour news television channels, pundits, the Internet, and talk radio programs help to fuel the frenzy that surrounds tabloid cases.

DEFINING THE "NEW MEDIA"

The creation of new technologies has always precipitated broad changes in the delivery and focus of the news. Media scholars Richard Davis and Diana Owen assert, however, that defining the "new media" and its impact in the 1990s is a particularly difficult task, as the role the media play in people's lives is now so multifaceted.[5] They argue that a complicated mix of "rapidly changing technology, increased public discussion, and a limitless potential to educate" distinguishes the new media from the more traditional hard news outlets.[6] Even the Pew

Research Center for the People and the Press, which offers a purely technological definition of new media (simply, cable television and the Internet), emphasizes that the U.S. media culture changed dramatically during the 1990s.[7]

Prior to discussing the structural factors that have converged to create the new media environment and its corresponding characteristics, it is important to refer to several noteworthy events in the early 1990s that provided an impetus for ushering in the new media era. Some analysts identify CNN's coverage of the Persian Gulf War in 1991 as the event that lent credibility to around-the-clock news.[8] Coverage of the conflict in the Gulf provided viewers with continuous footage of "smart bombs," fighter plane and missile deployments, and military press briefings. The coverage that accompanied the conflict allowed Americans, for the first time, to follow the finer nuances of the war closely and visually. Although there has been some serious criticism of CNN's war coverage, the increase in viewer ratings indicated to news organizations that twenty-four-hour news channels could be successful.[9] In sum, although CNN's nonstop news format had already existed for more than a decade, the Gulf War validated the credibility and usefulness of this approach.

The 1991 trial of William Kennedy Smith and the 1991 Senate confirmation hearings of Supreme Court nominee Clarence Thomas were two other events central to ushering in the new media, albeit in different ways.[10] As previously discussed, the Kennedy Smith episode served as the first marquee trial to receive gavel-to-gavel coverage on Court TV. The dramatic confirmation hearings of Thomas, who faced charges of sexual harassment by former government employee Anita Hill, riveted the country for three days. Many cable and noncable networks chose to air the hearings in their entirety. More than 80 percent of the U.S. public claimed to have watched at least some of the live hearings.[11] These events, which included lurid and explicit language about pornography, rape, and sex, may have helped to normalize the presentation of specific details about sexual and criminal allegations in mainstream news broadcasts.

As the 1990s unfolded, a number of structural and social factors converged to create a new media environment. Not only had technology changed, but the boundaries of acceptable subject matter appeared to be changing as well. It is important to note that most of the new media outlets on which we focus share many of the fundamental characteristics of the traditional media discussed in Chapter 2. Because many cable television news outlets and Internet sites are formally affiliated with mainstream news organizations, they acquire the same veneer of legitimacy with which the major networks and more respected print outlets are regarded. But despite the new media's similarity to the traditional outlets, at least three characteristics—*new technology*, *commercialism*, and *populism*—distinguish the new media environment.[12]

First, throughout the 1990s there has been rapid growth in new technology and especially in the new uses of old technology. In recent years, the importance of cable television as a news medium has grown dramatically. And although cable is not a new outlet, per se, its widespread use as a setting for all-news channels is unprecedented. Beyond the growth of cable, the biggest change in the technological environment involves the emergence of the Internet. Never before has an information source provided thousands of pages of information about virtually any topic from an endless array of sources. The Internet is now used by journalists and writers to research stories, and by news organizations to present information and interact with consumers.[13] Online-only magazines such as *Salon*, *Slate*, and the *Drudge Report* broke major news stories about Paula Jones and Monica Lewinsky.

More important, a significant portion of the public now looks to the Internet as a primary source of news, information, and entertainment. The number of Americans who can access information online has increased exponentially. A 1998 survey by the Pew Research Center found that 41 percent of Americans have Internet access, and more than 50 percent of those regularly access news on the Net.[14] Although it is still too early in the evolution of this technology to comprehend its ultimate impact on the dissemination of news and information, the Internet has clearly become an important vehicle for political, legal, and social discourse.[15]

A second important aspect of the new media environment is commercialism. Historically, numerous commentators have raised concerns about the objectivity and fairness of the news media.[16] Many have suggested that the news cannot be delivered objectively when news organizations must compete for viewers and profit.[17] Other observers have voiced concerns about the trend toward corporate consolidation of media outlets.[18] The imperative to attract viewers, readers, or computer users may undermine the many idealized media roles discussed in our introductory chapter. Further, competition spurred by the new media environment may corrupt decisions about newsworthiness by allowing commercial considerations to trump the intrinsic importance of a story.

In providing coverage of tabloid justice cases, the new media outlets emphasize the characteristics of serialization and personification, which we discussed in Chapter 1. The news media benefit from lengthy trials, which allow anticipation and drama to build to an often unpredictable verdict. The serialization of these proceedings is particularly important for cable television because of the high number of programs that are devoted to legal proceedings. The constant tracking and regular updating of cases appears to garner a larger audience. To help create interest, the new media also strongly emphasizes personification. Apparently, criminal trials and investigations are more engaging to consumers when they have intimate knowledge of the individuals involved, even at the expense of a particularly clear understanding of the legal and structural components of these dramas.

A final characteristic of the new media environment is populism. In the 1990s, news and information outlets encouraged—and in some cases, overtly relied upon—mass citizen input and participation. As Richard Davis and Diana Owen explain, "The new media enhance the public's ability to become actors, rather than merely spectators."[19] Talk radio, which gained popularity in the late 1970s, was the first venue to incorporate citizen participation (via listener calls) into the basic format of most programs. The top talk radio hosts of the late 1990s based their shows almost exclusively on the opinions and comments of citizen callers. Additionally, Tom Leykis, a national talk radio host who frequently discusses tabloid justice cases, often uses listener e-mail to establish the subject of each program.

Beyond radio, many cable television news programs, such as CNN's *Larry King Live*, the Fox News Channel's *Hannity and Combes*, and MSNBC's *News Chat*, take live phone calls from viewers as well. But even though talk radio and talk television encourage the active participation of their audiences, the Internet offers an even more accessible—and less demanding—means for citizen participation in the realm of news and commentary.[20] Most news organizations now have interactive websites, many of which ask people to reply to questions or post their opinions on timely topics, often including tabloid justice cases. Electronic "chat rooms" have also created an opportunity for people to carry on cyber-conversations with complete strangers. In today's news environment, citizens need not merely absorb information or settle for passive entertainment. They can easily become a part of the news themselves.

THE RISE OF CABLE NEWS CHANNELS

Cable television's twenty-four-hour presentation of news plays a prominent role in creating the media frenzy surrounding high-profile criminal trials. Viewers surfing through various cable channels repeatedly hear the names O.J. Simpson, JonBenet Ramsey, Louise Woodward, and Monica Lewinsky. CNN (Cable News Network) has been the pioneer in this around-the-clock news coverage. It first went on the air in 1980 and added a second twenty-four-hour news channel, Headline News, in 1982. CNN's ratings languished for much of the 1980s, though, and the network did not gain full recognition as a news leader until its 1991 coverage of the Persian Gulf War.[21] CNN now presents a diverse schedule of programming, which includes narrowly tailored shows dealing with sports, entertainment, fashion, business, travel, and politics. Headline News offers a continuous succession of thirty-minute national broadcasts.

Although CNN and Headline News were the only cable news channels to emerge during the first several years of the 1980s, a number of other news-related cable channels, such as CSPAN, the Discovery Channel, Lifetime, the History Channel, and ESPN, all began to develop during the mid-1980s. This major expansion helped to promote cable television as an outlet for news and other kinds of increasingly specialized programming. By the end of the 1980s and throughout the 1990s, several additional news channels developed. CNBC, for example, concentrates heavily on business news, although during prime time its format changes to talk television, with programming that emphasizes legal and political commentary. MSNBC and the Fox News Channel, the two newest entrants in the twenty-four-hour news business, embrace formats that are most likely to encourage constant discussion about tabloid cases. Their programming schedules are almost entirely devoted to general news and commentary. For the purposes of our discussion, we also include Court TV, which presents twenty-four-hour coverage of various legal proceedings (heavily skewed toward murder trials). This channel also provides news and analysis about trials and legal issues throughout the country. In 1997

Table 3.1   Start-up Dates of Twenty-four-Hour News Channels

Channel	Start-up Date
CNN	June 1, 1980
CNN's Headline News	January 1, 1982
CNBC	April 17, 1989
Court TV	July 1, 1991
MSNBC	July 15, 1996
Fox News	October 17, 1996

Source: Network offices.

Court TV began broadcasting reruns of dramatic fictional crime series as well, further blurring the line between the real judicial process and criminal justice infotainment. Regardless of programmatic nuances, each of these channels has devoted extensive attention to the tabloid cases of the 1990s. A listing of these news channels and their start-up dates are presented in Table 3.1.

THE STYLE AND SUBSTANCE OF CABLE NEWS PROGRAMS

To provide a better sense of the formats of these twenty-four-hour news stations, we have broken down the types of programs they offer in Table 3.2. We have not included either Headline News, which is all "straight" broadcast news, or Court TV, which offers programming

Table 3.2   Time Devoted to Three Types of News Programs on Twenty-four-Hour Cable News Channels (hours)

Type of Program	CNBC	CNN	MSNBC	Fox News
Guests/pundits[a]	4.0	3.5	12.0	5.0
Straight news[b]	3.0	11.5	9.0	16.0
Focused program[c]	17.0	8.0	3.0	3.0
Total	24.0	24.0	24.0	24.0

Source: Based on weekday program schedules of November 30, 1998.

[a] Programs that center on analysis by a roundtable of commentators.

[b] Programs that utilize a traditional news broadcast format.

[c] Shows that focus on a particular news area, such as sports, entertainment, politics, or business.

exclusively on the legal system. Programs fall into three categories: guests/pundits, straight news, and focused programs.

The guests/pundits format is usually organized around a topic or topics of the day and offers a panel of "expert" commentators typically composed of lawyers and political activists, although politicians and actual trial participants often appear on these broadcasts, too. The panels engage in lively and, at times, quite rancorous discussions of the topic du jour. The straight news category includes programs with anchors and short news stories, a format similar to that of traditional newscasts and TV newsmagazines. The third category, focused programs, comprises shows that cover a specific news area, such as sports, travel, fashion, or entertainment. We should note that most focused programs do not lend themselves to much discussion of legal issues. Shows such as the *Cavuto Business Report* on Fox, as well as most of the business-oriented programming on CNBC, are not conducive to a sustained discussion of tabloid trials. Some of the focused programs identified in Table 3.2, however, are programs dedicated primarily to politics, legal issues, and discussions of the legal process. For instance, CNN's *Burden of Proof* offers daily discussions of legal issues involved in ostensibly newsworthy cases. During 1998, MSNBC offered *White House in Crisis*, a program that covered the Monica Lewinsky and Paula Jones stories exclusively.

If a story is deemed to merit special coverage, though, the twenty-four-hour news stations adapt their programming accordingly. In fact, the cable news outlets are much more likely to devote significant time to these criminal trials and investigations than the major networks (ABC, CBS, and NBC), which are more likely to stay with their normal programming schedules. Even narrowly focused cable news programs readily alter their schedules to present interesting criminal investigations and trials. For instance, during the months of O.J. Simpson's criminal trial, CNN provided extensive live coverage that preempted much of its normal schedule. In another example, in August 1998, the Fox News Channel, CNN, and MSNBC each broadcast the entire four hours of President Clinton's previously recorded grand jury testimony. Table 3.3 shows MSNBC's programming scheme for November 1998, which allows for a shift to continuous coverage of a major trial or story of the day without altering the basic prearranged schedule.

Table 3.3 shows that the daily MSNBC schedule consists of about 50 percent straight news programming with a traditional anchorperson and about 50 percent flexible format shows involving a host, changing

Table 3.3   Programming Schedule of MSNBC, November 1998

Time Slot	Program Title	Program Type	Show Description
6 A.M.–9 A.M.	*Imus in the Morning*	Guests/pundits	Political and news talk, with daily guests who are politicians, media members, and authors— often crude and irreverent.
9 A.M.–10 A.M.	*Watch It*	Guests/pundits	Hosted by Laura Ingram, conservative activist. Show covers current events and has politicians and media members as guests.
10 A.M.–12 P.M.	*Morning Line*	Straight news	Traditional news broadcast, with desk anchors and correspondents in the field.
12 P.M.–1 P.M.	*Judge and Jury*	Focused programs	Show hosted by Judge Burton Katz; it discusses major legal issues of the day.
1 P.M.–3 P.M.	*NBC News Today in America*	Straight news	Traditional news broadcast, with anchors and correspondents in the field.
3 P.M.–4 P.M.	*NBC News @ Issue*	Straight news	Traditional news broadcast, with desk anchors and correspondents in the field.
4 P.M.–5 P.M.	*Newsfront*	Straight news	Traditional news broadcast, with desk anchors and correspondents in the field.
5 P.M.–7 P.M.	*News Chat*	Guests/pundits	Various hosts. Format includes a panel of commentators and calls from the public.
7 P.M.–8 P.M.	*Internight*	Guests/pundits	Hosted by John Gibson. Format includes a panel of commentators.
8 P.M.–9 P.M.	*The Big Show*	Guests/Pundits	Hosted by Keith Olberman. Format includes a panel of commentators.
9 P.M.–10 P.M.	*The News with Brian Williams*	Straight news	Traditional news format, with occasional individual "expert" commentators.
10 P.M.–11 P.M.	*Time & Again*	Guests/pundits	Panel of experts examining today's impact of historical events.
11 P.M.–12 A.M.	*White House in Crisis*	Focused programming	Program focused on Clinton-Lewinsky.
12 A.M.–1 A.M.	*The News with Brian Williams*	Straight news	Replay
1 A.M.–2 A.M.	*Time & Again*	Guests/pundits	Replay
2 A.M.–3 A.M.	*White House in Crisis*	Focused programming	Replay
3 A.M.–4 A.M.	*Internight*	Guests/pundits	Replay
4 A.M.–5 A.M.	*Time & Again*	Guests/pundits	Replay
5 A.M. – 6 A.M.	*White House in Crisis*	Focused programming	Replay

Source: MSNBC network offices.

panels of commentators, and viewer telephone calls. These shows have no set subject matter and can thus be reconfigured on a moment's notice to focus on a given day's most compelling story.

In fact, NBC News division president Andrew Lack, who also presides over programming of MSNBC, has said that the purpose of MSNBC is to focus on the "one or two" big news events that occur each day.[22] The logic behind this is to create an outlet where anyone can flip on the television and get the latest on the "big story." The consequence is that concentrating on the one great story of the day creates a troubling connection between commodification and agenda-setting. When a respected news outlet, like CNN or NBC (via MSNBC), covers one main issue all day, it signals to the public that the story is very important. This propels ratings because the public, taking its cue from the media, often tunes to stories that garner intensive coverage. Also, by covering a story almost exclusively, the cable media outlets set a very narrow agenda. When MSNBC chose to cover only the Clinton investigation, for example, the network precluded the viewing public from learning about any other foreign or domestic issues. Coverage of tabloid cases, in essence, may come at the expense of other important news.

To demonstrate further the manner in which the cable talk programs often focus on tabloid justice cases, consider the programming of several shows during the Louise Woodward trial. On November 10, 1997, Judge Hiller Zobel reduced Woodward's sentence from second-degree murder to involuntary manslaughter. This event dominated coverage on four of CNBC's prime time programs. *Equal Time* and *Rivera Live* focused exclusively on the Woodward story, while *Charles Grodin* and *Hardball* featured lengthy segments on the case. On MSNBC, the Woodward trial was the only story covered on *Internight*, and it served as the lead story on *The Big Show*. All of these programs share a "talk-television" format, whereby the host presides over a panel of "experts" who discuss the central topic of the evening. Guests often interrupt one another, and discussions regularly degenerate into shouting matches, with the host pleading for civility and order. Sensationalism and conflict drive the programs.

In terms of sensationalism, these programs tend to characterize the investigation or trial under examination as an "astounding," "incredible," or "earth-shaking" event, with wide-ranging significance. For instance, on the day of the verdict in the O.J. Simpson criminal trial, this is how Geraldo Rivera, host of *Rivera Live*, began his program:

"Not Guilty" is our inevitable title. It's—it's the end of an incredible saga, an incredible story, an incredible chapter of American history. The defining story of our times, certainly the defining story for the end of the twentieth century here in the United States of America.[23]

Rivera characterizes the O.J. Simpson drama as, apparently, more important than the Vietnam War, the civil rights movement, Watergate, or any presidential election. The hyperbole of this assessment again demonstrates the level of sensationalism that prevails in the era of tabloid justice.

In another example, on MSNBC's *The Big Show*, Jack Ford, NBC's legal affairs correspondent, summed up the judge's reversal of the jury's verdict in the Louise Woodward trial:

I have tried cases for about sixteen years, I've been covering cases for about thirteen years, and between them, I can't remember as dramatic a change in as serious a case as this.[24]

The broadcast never made clear why Ford considered this to be such an important case. After all, in 1996 almost 2,000 children were murdered in the United States, and many of these cases went to trial. Because of the public interest associated with the Woodward case, however, the outcome could be discussed in such dramatic terms.[25]

In a final example, on January 21, 1998, the day the Monica Lewinsky affair became public, Rivera opened his program by saying:

Is this now, ladies and gentlemen, "Zippergate"? Hi, everybody. I'm Geraldo Rivera. And for the first time, there are scandalous allegations of such immense proportions that they could conceivably unravel the Clinton presidency.[26]

Certainly, a case involving the president of the United States is by definition an important story. However, it is worth noting that Rivera's pronouncements came on the first day that this story became public, at a point when very few facts about the case had been revealed.

Beyond the urgent tone of these programs, the quality of debate and discussion tends to emphasize conflict. In *Amusing Ourselves to Death*, Neil Postman comments that television is a very poor medium for thoughtful discussion or conversation. Postman notes that the imperatives of television offer little opportunity to *think*, because showing someone thinking does not make for interesting television. The consequence is that whenever discussion and analysis occur on television, the arguments or ideas presented are usually simplistic and poorly articulated.[27] Postman would undoubtedly be dismayed by the quality of comment and discussion that is rampant on cable television talk shows. For instance, on *The Big Show*, California deputy district attorney James Curtis offered this assessment of Judge Hiller Zobel's ruling in the Woodward trial:

> I think he is an idiot. I mean, this is—this is ridiculous. Not only is this entirely inappropriate given the state of the evidence that this jury considered in this case—this woman killed an eight-month-old child—his analysis is flawed. He is an old man who's taken into consideration a cherub-faced young white defendant and has sent a message throughout the country.[28]

This style of overly personal attack is a staple of talk television programs. The example below, drawn from MSNBC's *Internight,* illustrates what constitutes "discussion" on news talk programs. With guests interrupting one another and speaking in increasingly belligerent tones, host John Gibson, a panel of attorneys, and a judge discuss the final verdict in the Woodward trial:

> Jeralyn Merritt (criminal defense attorney): And I think judges have complete discretion in sentencing. And he considered what he considered to be the relevant factors. And in his opinion today, he stated that he thought she was frightened. . . . But he didn't think that she intended to kill this baby . . . and I think that he was correct in saying "Let's just get all this behind us." He wasn't trying to minimize . . . [cut off]
>
> Cynthia Alksne (former prosecutor): John, I can't believe that . . . [cut off]
>
> Merritt: . . . what happened to the Eappen baby, but . . . [cut off]
>
> Mike Hanley (criminal defense attorney and former prosecutor): But, John . . . [cut off]
>
> Merritt: . . . and that really wasn't his job.
>
> John Gibson: Cynthia.
>
> Merritt: His job was to take—to sentence her as—as an individual.
>
> Gibson: Cynthia, I heard you interrupting.
>
> Alksne: I mean, ge—get—get us all—get it all behind us? The Eappens can't get it all behind them; their baby is dead. This—it is

outrageous to me that this baby's life is worth so little money. And I'll tell you what this is; this is an argument . . . [cut off]

Gibson: So little time.

Alksne: . . . for mandatory sentencing guidelines, because in . . . [cut off]

Gibson: But there are mandatory sentencing guidelines.

Alksne: No, that—they're not mandatory in this case. They were volun—there's some sort of guidelines that have not been adopted in Massachusetts, and that would be three and five years.

Dan Abrams (news correspondent): And—and . . . [cut off]

Gibson: Dan Abrams.

Alksne: But this child's. . . [cut off]

Abrams: And, John—John—John . . . [cut off]

Alksne: . . . life was worth nothing. This is justice denied.[29]

And so it goes night after night on the talk television circuit. Lawyers talk over one another, attempting to be heard by making ever-bolder assertions. Geraldo Rivera often tells his panel of guests, "Fight amongst yourselves," and breaks up the argument only after complete chaos has erupted.[30]

Such discussions clearly provide entertainment and diversion first, and serious legal and political discourse second. More serious is that the polarizing and truncated nature of the discussion provides little room to explore the more subtle aspects of a given position or interpretation, or the context within which a story takes place. Guests are usually forced to take diametrically opposing positions—in fact, they are often invited on the show specifically to advance a particular side. There seems to be no room for any middle ground on such programs.[31]

Before we dismiss these programs as inconsequential infotainment, however, we must recognize their high degree of credibility among political, legal, and journalistic elites. Noted criminal prosecutors, professors of law, high-level politicians, and well-known defense attorneys appear on these programs regularly. One *Larry King Live* roundtable discussion, for example, featured six U.S. senators discussing the Clinton impeachment and fielding calls from viewers. U.S. Representative John Conyers, the top Democrat on the House Judiciary Committee (conducting the House impeachment inquiry), appeared on *Rivera Live* several times during the course of the committee hearings. Viewers, therefore, may grant greater levels of seriousness and newsworthiness to tabloid cases for no reason other than the presence of well-known guests and experts discussing them on these shows.

Perhaps the most distressing tendency of the cable news-talk programs is how they blur the line between serious issues and tabloid sensationalism. This problem has already been noted in Chapter 2, which attributed this characteristic to the networks and major newspapers as well. CNBC's November 10, 1997, episode of *Hardball* serves as a prime example of the cable news programs' failure to differentiate between entertainment and nationally significant news. Host Chris Matthews began the program with a report on the ruling in the Woodward case. In the second segment, Matthews, Congressman Sherrod Brown of Ohio, and *Time* magazine journalist Margaret Carlson discussed President Clinton's push for trade legislation in Congress. This conversation led the three to consider the Democratic Party race for the presidency in the year 2000. Following a commercial break, though, Matthews moved away from hard news and identified his "winners and losers of the week," a segment that included portions of an interview with Marv Albert, the New York sportscaster who was accused of sexual assault. After another commercial, the host and four journalists returned to the Woodward ruling and the public's reaction to it.[32] Trade legislation and the race for the presidency were presented as relatively incidental in comparison to the Woodward trial.

Airing on the same night as this *Hardball* episode, the *Charles Grodin* program (on CNBC) provides another striking example of the blurred distinction between different categories of current events. Grodin, a former comedic actor, hosted a program that discussed a major foreign policy issue and two tabloid justice criminal cases. He began by assessing the possibility of U.S. military action against Iraq. Grodin then proceeded to present his views on the Woodward and Marv Albert cases. Linda Kenney (a criminal defense lawyer) and Victoria Toensing (a former federal prosecutor and a regular guest on the cable news–talk circuit) joined Grodin in an extended discussion of the significance of the Woodward and Albert cases. The host then returned to foreign policy, introducing a panel of experts to discuss the military situation in Iraq. The program allotted significantly less time to U.S. foreign policy toward Iraq than to two criminal trials having few public ramifications.[33]

Although it is common for a news program to present a variety of stories, both of the aforementioned examples illustrate the common juxtaposition of important national and international issues with extended commentary on *relatively* meaningless tabloid cases.

Typically, cable television hosts and guests make no distinction as to the relative importance of either topic. It is common for the same panel of guests to discuss many completely disparate topics and for viewer telephone calls to prompt discussions that veer far away from the original topic. These examples also highlight the high priority that is currently extended to the judicial process in the era of tabloid justice.[34]

■ Comparing Cable Talk Programs: *Internight, Hardball,* and *Rivera Live*

Programs such as MSNBC's *Internight* and CNBC's *Rivera Live* tend to discuss criminal trials and legal proceedings almost exclusively. Although this was not the original mission of either of these shows, they appear to have evolved in this fashion because focusing on legal proceedings attracted the largest number of viewers.[35] Even *Hardball*, a program originally intended to cover national politics, now regularly examines tabloid cases. The show enjoys a high degree of credibility among political elites and often invites members of the House of Representatives and the U.S. Senate, and members of the presidential cabinet and White House staff to discuss important political issues. For example, in 1999 most of the major candidates for the Republican nomination for president appeared on *Hardball*. Table 3.4, which displays the programming schedules for all three of these programs in 1997, reveals a clear emphasis on tabloid justice cases.

The subject matter of these three programs illustrates the high degree to which twenty-four-hour news stations' prime time programming focuses on tabloid justice investigations and trials. We should note that we include the Oklahoma City bombing trial in this analysis not because we consider it a tabloid case but simply because it serves as an example of the manner in which trial coverage provides the public with another view of the legal system. We also included the investigation into Princess Diana's death, as this event fueled an ongoing discussion of police tactics and possible criminal activity. Of the programs detailed in Table 3.4, *Rivera Live* clearly focused the most thoroughly on criminal trials. In fact, Geraldo Rivera declared that his was "the program of record" for the O.J. Simpson trials.[36] Since the period of the Simpson criminal trial in 1995, *Rivera Live* has turned to a wide assortment of other tabloid cases. *Internight* has followed suit, with more than three-quarters of its broadcasts in 1997 centered on criminal cases.

Table 3.4   Presence of Tabloid Cases in Cable Programs in 1997

	Rivera Live (CNBC)	Hard Ball (CNBC)	Internight (MSNBC)
Total number of programs	257	250	253
	Number of Programs That Discussed the Case		
Topics			
O.J. Simpson	84 (33)	29 (12)	38 (15)
JonBenet Ramsey	97 (38)	22 (9)	30 (12)
Oklahoma City	84 (33)	3 (1)	25 (10)
Louise Woodward	24 (9)	5 (2)	19 (8)
Marv Albert	17 (7)	7 (3)	13 (5)
Paula Jones	16 (6)	21 (8)	9 (4)
Princess Diana	27 (11)	17 (7)	36 (14)
Ennis Cosby	35 (14)	7 (3)	4 (2)
	% of Programs Focusing on Legal or Tabloid-Style Cases		
	97	44	78

Source: Program summaries provided by Burrelles Transcript Service.
Note: Entrees in parentheses represent the percentage of programs that discussed the case.

Perhaps most striking is *Hardball*'s programming schedule. Although the show does not appear to obsess about these cases to the same extent that others do, at least 40 percent of its broadcasts included coverage of legal and tabloid justice cases. Host Chris Matthews has admitted that his program focuses heavily on the "hot topics" in the news.[37] He is also quite open about the fact that "hot" is not necessarily the same as "important." Still, the fact that the show covers hot topics and important national and international affairs on the same program lends tabloid cases an air of legitimacy they may not always warrant.

In 1998, all three of these programs covered the Monica Lewinsky and Paula Jones cases in almost every broadcast. In a sense, the Clinton-Lewinsky matter not only supplanted 1998's other potential tabloid justice stories, but it also reduced extended coverage of all other political and legal issues. Clearly, the fact that the investigation involved the president of the United States conveyed a sense of legitimacy to the media's obsession with the Lewinsky matter. That perceived legitimacy was suspect, however, for news outlets initially tended to cover the case in the same salacious manner with which they handled the Simpson trial and other tabloid cases.

Cable news–talk programs continued to trot out the same experts to comment on the intimate details of the independent counsel investigation and the activities of Congress as were used for discussions of the JonBenet Ramsey murder and the Menendez trial. In a particularly illuminating example of this news/entertainment conflation, a CNN advertisement for its program *Investigating the President* superimposed an image of President Clinton over an image of O.J. Simpson. The tabloid overtones, which resulted in a journalistic focus on the interpersonal and sexual details of the case for the better part of a year, once again highlight the melding of news and entertainment, even regarding substantive cases involving important public figures.

Twenty-Four-Hour Cable Channels and the Ratings Game

The actual number of viewers who watch cable news talk channels at any given time is quite small. The ratings of individual programs, like *Rivera Live* or *Hardball,* are usually less than one-tenth those of the network news programs like *Dateline* or *20/20.* However, the number of people who tune into cable news channels each day, at least for a few minutes, is quite large. In 1998, the average citizen turned on CNN roughly 2.5 times per week, the Fox News Channel 1.9 times per week, and CNBC and MSNBC 1.5 and 1.3 times per week, respectively. These tune-in averages are higher than those of the three network news broadcasts of CBS (1.5), NBC (1.4), and ABC (1.3).[38] The emerging success of the cable news stations should further be considered in light of the fact that a number of these channels did not even exist before the mid-1990s.

In examining ratings over time for the cable stations, tabloid justice cases have clearly been quite important. When a tabloid case is at the forefront of current events, ratings increased dramatically. During the second half of 1998, when the Clinton-Lewinsky scandal peaked, MSNBC and Fox News Channel's ratings more than doubled.[39] In 1995, the year of the O.J. Simpson criminal trial, CNN clearly reaped dividends from its extensive trial coverage, as it enjoyed ratings that were roughly 80 percent higher than in the years preceding and succeeding the case. Table 3.5 shows the yearly average ratings for several cable news channels. Clearly, as the volume and intensity of a tabloid

Table 3.5   Ratings of Twenty-four-Hour News Channels, 1995–1998

Year	Court TV	CNBC	CNN	MSNBC	Fox News
1995	122	111	573	n/a	n/a
1996	17	117	331	n/a	n/a
1997	28	158	339	n/a	17
1998	33	244	360	101	45

Source: Data provided by Nielsen Media Research.
Note: "n/a" means data not available for that year. Entries indicate average number of households (in thousands) viewing each station at any given time.

justice story increase, ratings increase as well. In Table 3.5 ratings for Court TV and CNN were noticeably higher in 1995, the year of the O.J. Simpson trial, than in the succeeding years. All of the networks (except MSNBC, for which no ratings numbers were available for 1997) also experienced a jump in ratings for 1998, the year of the intense coverage of the Clinton-Lewinsky investigation.

To explore further the importance of scandal and tabloid coverage to the ratings of cable news stations, we examine the overnight ratings of two tabloid stories: the criminal trial of O.J. Simpson and the presidential scandal involving Bill Clinton and Monica Lewinsky. Table 3.6 displays both the yearly ratings average for CNN, CNBC, MSNBC, and the Fox News Channel and the ratings for the days that major events occurred in each of these stories. The data in Table 3.6 suggest that scandal is important business for the cable television stations. Throughout the lengthy O.J. Simpson drama, major events such as the infamous "Bronco chase," the trial's opening arguments, and the day of the verdict's announcement led to a doubling or tripling of the ratings for CNN. This effect was not as clear for CNBC, whose level of attention to the case evolved more slowly during the year

Turning to the coverage of the Clinton-Lewinsky investigation, we see that the story started out relatively slowly. A small upturn in the ratings occurred on the day the media reported that President Clinton may have been sexually involved with a White House intern. As the scandal began to unfold, however, ratings for the four cable news programs soared. On the day that President Clinton's grand jury testimony was televised, Fox News' ratings were five times their 1998 daily average, while CNN's were four times higher. Further, Table 3.6 illustrates that by the time of the impeachment vote in the House of Representatives, cable ratings had fallen and were only a little above the yearly average. The

Table 3.6   Ratings of Twenty-four-Hour News Channels During Time of Scandal

Scandal	CNN	CNBC	MSNBC	Fox News
O.J. Simpson criminal trial				
Average for 1995	573	111	n/a	n/a
Day of the Bronco chase (in 1994)	1,841	45	n/a	n/a
Day of opening arguments	1,248	128	n/a	n/a
Day verdict was announced	1,705	350	n/a	n/a
Clinton-Lewinsky scandal				
Average for 1998	360	244	101	45
Day Lewinsky story broke	500	297	130	50
Day of president's grand jury testimony and apology	1,297	415	314	193
Day grand jury testimony was aired	1,657	328	471	259
Day full House voted to open impeachment inquiry	385	329	163	65

Source: Nielsen Media Research.
Note: Entries indicate the number of households (in thousands) tuned on that particular day. MSNBC and Fox News were not in operation for the Simpson criminal trial.

public had grown weary of this story, and the outcome of the trial never seemed in doubt, as an overwhelming majority of Americans never believed that President Clinton would be removed from office. In essence, the drama and ensuing ability to sell the story had run its course.

If we turn our attention more specifically to *Rivera Live*, the ratings leader in tabloid justice coverage, we can see more clearly the manner in which the defining moments of scandals affect ratings. The ratings for *Rivera Live* increased dramatically in 1995, the year of the Simpson criminal trial. Subsequently, though, viewer levels fell in the succeeding two years, which lacked such a single dominating tabloid case. *Rivera Live*'s ratings then rose again in 1998, a calendar year in which the program focused almost exclusively on the Clinton-Lewinsky matter. Figure 3.1 shows the weekly ratings for *Rivera Live* in 1998. The highest ratings weeks correspond directly with critical moments in the investigation, impeachment, and Senate trial. Substantial boosts in ratings occurred the day the story broke in January, the dates in August and September when President Clinton acknowledged his relationship with Lewinsky and testified before the grand jury, the day the news channels aired his grand jury testimony, and the day the House voted to impeach the president.

Figure 3.1   Television Ratings for *Rivera Live* in 1998

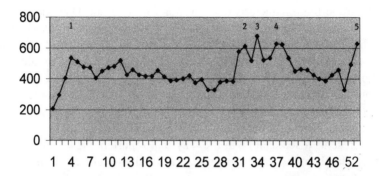

Notes: The vertical axis represents number of viewing households (in thousands). The horizontal axis represents the weeks in 1998. The number "1" represents the week the Lewinsky story broke; "2" represents the week Clinton gave his grand jury testimony and public admission of an "inappropriate relationship"; "3" represents the week the Starr Report was released to the public; "4" represents the week President Clinton's grand jury testimony was aired on television; "5" represents the week the full House of Representatives voted two articles of impeachment against the president.

Tables 3.5 and 3.6 and Figure 3.1 demonstrate the importance of a good serialized scandal or trial in attracting viewers. As in any TV drama or soap opera, more compelling moments attract more interested viewers. It is quite plausible to conclude that commercial considerations drive the substantive emphasis of such programs. What else could explain a news program devoting so much time to certain stories? Indeed, if we subscribe to the notion that the media simply cover stories of interest to the public, these programs would probably be foolish not to emphasize such stories. Although this tactic may make business sense, it also clearly reveals that the commodification of tabloid events has trumped any idealized vision of the role that the news media should play in a democracy.

THE RISE OF PUNDITRY

The culture of talk, argument, and irreverence constitutes a critical component of the new media era. The new media environment, or what

Jonathan Alter has called the "American wilderness of noise," is dominated by heated—and at times, rather undignified—discussion by pundits of all types.[40] This differs greatly from both the traditional, sober reporting characteristic of Walter Cronkite and Dan Rather, as well as that of the established Sunday morning political talk shows, such as *Face the Nation*, *This Week*, and *Meet the Press*. In the recent past, journalists who covered legal and political news events did not enjoy a forum in which to argue with other journalists and lawyers about the proper interpretation of legal events. The discussion on the news-talk programs often focuses on nothing more than how the media covered an event, as opposed to the substance of the story. This dynamic represents a sea change in the way that reporters view themselves, and certainly in the way that they interact with the subjects of their stories. On a regular basis, reporters from all types of publications and programs argue with members of Congress and previously obscure trial attorneys about how to interpret the day's legal and political developments.

Regardless of the subject, the cable news channels regularly feature panels of political and legal experts jousting with members of the news media about various topics. Just as any issue can apparently be presented in this manner, guests are presented as authorities on any topic that happens to arise during a program. The same guests discuss everything from Marv Albert, the Oklahoma City bombing, and the death of Princess Diana to the midterm congressional elections, the history of presidential impeachment, and Monica Lewinsky's future professional prospects. In an episode of *Hardball* discussed previously, the same panel of experts discussed trade legislation, the 2000 presidential campaign, and the verdict in the Louise Woodward trial. And, although it is reasonable for reporters to cover a number of disparate topics, it is quite another situation when reporters are presented as experts on virtually all public issues that arise.

A number of pundits who have entered the talk show circuit, or have even become hosts of their own news-talk shows, rose to prominence during the O.J. Simpson criminal trial. Table 3.7 presents the names of several pundits whose involvement in the coverage of the O.J. Simpson case either launched or rejuvenated their media careers. Many of the actual trial participants now either host programs or frequently comment on other legal proceedings. In an important sense, these pundits, as well as many others, have become public educators about the legal and political system. In sum, this group constitutes a sort of

Table 3.7   Media Careers Launched by the O.J. Simpson Trial

Name	Role in Simpson Trial	New Media Role
Trial participants		
Marcia Clark	Lead prosecutor	Legal affairs journalist for MSNBC
Johnnie Cochran	Lead defense attorney	Hosts program *Cochran & Co.* on Court TV
Barry Scheck	Defense attorney	Frequent commentator on talk television
Alan Dershowitz	Defense attorney	Frequent commentator on talk television
F. Lee Bailey	Defense attorney	Frequent commentator on talk television
Henry Lee	Forensic pathologist, expert defense witness	Frequent commentator on talk television
Jo Ellan Dimitrius	Defense jury consultant	Frequent guest on talk television
Cato Kaelin	Witness	Radio show host (canceled)
Fred Goldman	Father of murder victim	Radio show host (canceled)
Media commentators		
John Gibson	Correspondent for CNBC	Hosts *Internight* on MSNBC
Greta Van Sustern	Correspondent for CNN	Co-hosts *Burden of Proof* on CNN
Roger Cossack	Correspondent for CNN	Co-hosts *Burden of Proof* on CNN
Burton Katz	Frequent commentator	Hosts *Judge and Jury* on MSNBC
Revolving pundits		
Joe DiGenoa	Former independent counsel	
Victoria Toensing	Former federal prosecutor	
Julianne Malveaux	Criminal defense attorney	
Paul Rothstein	Law professor	

revolving roundtable of talking heads. These figures reappear on numerous news-talk shows, apparently willing to discuss any topic.[41]

The rise of punditry as an aspect of general reporting marks a significant shift that has occurred in the era of tabloid justice. This phenomenon has received considerable analysis based on journalistic reporting throughout the Clinton-Lewinsky scandal. In their recent book *Warp Speed*, veteran journalists Bill Kovach and Tom Rosenstiel contend that in the initial days of the scandal, over 40 percent of the industry output on the Clinton-Lewinsky affair "was not factual reporting at all but was instead journalists offering their own analysis, opinion, speculation, or judgments—essentially, commentary and punditry."[42] After citing a litany of examples in which journalists offered opinionated and completely speculative comments on both network news and cable news outlets, Kovach and Rosenstiel conclude that the scandal showed the "degree to which the supposed information revolution is not actually about gathering information, but instead about commenting on information that others have gathered."[43] The emerging dual role of journalists as news reporters and commentators is a change that carries with it important consequences for the role of journalists and merits further exploration both within that profession and by those who study the mass media.

THE INTERNET AND TABLOID JUSTICE

Although scholarly analysis of the broader impact of the Internet is just beginning to emerge, a number of studies have assessed the importance of the Internet in terms of the political process.[44] This medium now plays an important role in covering criminal trials and creating and maintaining the culture of tabloid justice. Foremost, hundreds of news and information websites deal with crime and criminal trials. The Internet has even been used to fight crime, as information posted on the Web has led directly to the arrests of several fugitives and criminal suspects.[45] Further, in several high-profile cases, legal institutions have themselves used the Internet as a means of disseminating important information. When Judge Hiller Zobel overruled the jury in the Woodward trial, he first issued his ruling online. The U.S. House of Representatives posted the infamous Starr Report on the Internet, ostensibly to make Bill Clinton's impeachment an open and accessible process. The Net is now clearly regarded as a legitimate and respectable medium for the dissemination of news.

Of course, the Internet, as cyber-gossip and online magazine editor Matt Drudge has asserted, also allows any citizen the opportunity to be a reporter or publisher of news and information.[46] It is relatively easy to create an online report covering Monica Lewinsky, JonBenet Ramsey, or some other tragic "tabloidized" figure. The Internet also gives anyone the ability to publish information on any topic and make that information available to a potentially worldwide audience. Top news organizations, government agencies, think tanks, and interest groups have developed home pages. Many well-known authors and scholars also have personal home pages, and many of these sources of information possess the same legitimacy as broadcast networks and top newspapers and newsmagazines.

At the other end of the continuum, there exist many sites sponsored by highly partisan, extremely opinionated, openly conspiratorial, vaguely criminal citizens and organizations. What is more, online chat rooms allow users to carry on real-time conversations about almost any subject imaginable. This interactive component of the World Wide Web has fostered an essential technological populism; anyone can be a part of the discourse.

Since the Internet's explosion in popularity and accessibility in the mid-1990s, it has played a significant role in fueling the news media's focus on tabloid justice cases and fostering a public interest in them. Many Internet home pages provide information about criminal trials. Court TV's home page, for example, lists all of the "major trials" going on in the country at any given time. The Court TV site also contains an elaborate database of stories dealing with "famous trials" and a glossary of legal terms, courtroom simulations, links to government documents, and, of course, advertising.[47] This website, which exists for those very attentive to the legal issues in high-profile cases, has been praised by both the *Los Angeles Times* and the *New York Times* as an example of good journalism on the Internet.[48]

The Internet also contains a bewildering array of far less reputable information. The average user must wade through a jumbled list of relatively traditional hard news and highly subjective and factually suspect information. For instance, a search using the key words "Lance Ito" (the trial judge in the Simpson criminal case) yields a link for the Court TV home page, followed by a link for the Lance Ito, Eat My Burrito! site.[49] The keywords "John and Lorena Bobbitt" confront the user with a suggestion to try the Ballad of the Bobbitt Hillbillies page.[50] "Monica Lewinsky" leads to a website that reprints the Report of the Office of the Independent Counsel but also a page that markets the "Gen-U-Wine, Multi-Purpose, Monica Lewinsky-approved, kneeling mouse pad."[51] In short, there is little organization, context, or quality control in terms of information obtained online.

To illustrate the wealth of information about tabloid justice cases on the Web, we conducted searches using key words associated with our selected cases. Table 3.8 reveals the number of webpages for each of the cases that we have been considering. Unfortunately, because we ran our searches in November 1998, much of the Web information pertaining to the earlier cases in the decade had been removed. We omitted searches for the Rodney King and William Kennedy Smith trials because both of these occurred before the Internet became a widespread source of information. Instead, we conducted searches on the Marv Albert and Lorena Bobbitt trials. We also conducted separate searches for Monica Lewinsky and Paula Jones. Because each Internet

Table 3.8   Number of Webpages Mentioning Tabloid Justice Stories on Yahoo! and Netscape

Tabloid Story	Number of Webpages Found by Yahoo!	Number of Webpages Found by Netscape
Marv Albert	65,825	202,582
Menendez brothers	117,358	228,644
Lorena and John Bobbitt	5,835	8,758
O.J. Simpson	8,120	498,932
Louise Woodward	36,472	132,950
JonBenet Ramsey	27,531	32,116
Monica Lewinsky	94,267	126,410
Paula Jones	458,322	495,669

Note: Web browser searches conducted in November 1998. For search instructions, see Appendix A.

search engine classifies a webpage differently, it is important to examine the results from several search sites. Table 3.8 reveals the search results for two of the most well-known search engines—Yahoo! and Netscape.

The disparate numbers in Table 3.8 reveal again that the two search engines have different methods for identifying sources. Nevertheless, in each case, typing a few key words produces literally thousands of sources pertaining to these cases. To put the numbers in Table 3.8 into perspective, we also ran searches on other topics. A Netscape search for "poverty" produced 105,790 "hits"; "Bosnia" resulted in 53,133 sites found; and "racism" produced 40,340 webpages. The results from Yahoo! were similar, with "poverty" resulting in 22,257 hits, "Bosnia" yielding 62,790 webpages, and "racism" generating 40,340 links. These searches on major issues of public policy produced fewer citations than those associated with Marv Albert, the Menendez brothers, O.J. Simpson, Louise Woodward, Monica Lewinsky, or Paula Jones, thereby indicating that tabloid justice is a booming enterprise on the Internet.

A NOTE ON TALK RADIO

Talk radio has further propelled tabloid justice cases to high levels of prominence. And even though talk television and the Internet have stolen much of talk radio's thunder, radio remains an important element in the new media environment. Talk radio is still the fastest growing radio format, with the number of talk radio stations in the United States having doubled between 1992 and 1998.[52] Although talk radio cannot be considered a new media outlet, its popularity and growth in the 1990s makes it a noteworthy phenomenon. The pinnacle of talk radio's influence has often been associated with the national midterm elections of 1994. At that time, syndicated radio host Rush Limbaugh fostered a strong antigovernment and anti-Clinton sentiment among his listeners. Many analysts viewed this as a crucial factor in the Republican takeover of both houses of Congress that year.[53]

A number of commentators have identified talk radio as a critical component in the development of contemporary political attitudes in the United States.[54] In her book *The Angry American*, Susan Tolchin very effectively illustrates the influential role that talk radio has played in setting the political agenda.[55] For instance, scholars have demonstrated that talk radio has played an important role in motivating its listeners to contact their representatives and other public officials.[56] On issues ranging from gun control, abortion, and trade policy to the impeachment of President Clinton, talk radio fosters a sense of efficacy and activism among its listeners. Tolchin also persuasively argues, however, that talk radio fueled the general feeling of antigovernment anger and alienation during the 1990s.

In terms of high-profile criminal proceedings, talk radio provides a forum conducive to constant discussion. Most radio markets offer a wide range of personalities who discuss the political and tabloid stories of the day. Nationally known talk show hosts, such as Rush Limbaugh, Tom Leykis, Don Imus, Howard Stern, G. Gordon Liddy, and Laura Schlesinger all offer, to varying degrees, commentary on cultural, political, and tabloid events. Many lesser-known local and regional personalities carry on these conversations, too. The topics of discussion can range from the more serious, such as "the O.J. Simpson case and race relations in the United States," or a constitutional debate on whether "Monica-gate constitutes an impeachable offense," to the more crude and bawdy, such as "Is the President a pervert?" or "Why would anyone sexually harass Paula Jones?"

Radio hosts have spent thousands of hours discussing O.J. Simpson, William Kennedy Smith, JonBenet Ramsey, Paula Jones, and Monica Lewinsky. Nationally syndicated radio talk show host Mike Gallagher has commented that even five years later, "nothing gets the phones going like the mention of O.J. Simpson."[57] The Simpson case can still be a strong commodity in attracting listeners.

CONCLUSION

Based on our analysis in this chapter we draw three conclusions. First, new media outlets grew substantially during the 1990s. The twenty-four-hour cable news channels, the Internet, and talk radio became integral aspects of the mass media universe in the final years of the twentieth century.

Second, we have suggested that the new media have become important outlets for covering tabloid criminal trials. Nightly, cable television news-talk programs, many of which are affiliated with respected network news organizations, serve as the leading source of information and analysis about tabloid justice cases. These shows sustain the sense of importance and urgency behind tabloid cases and present even the casual viewer with around-the-clock information about these events. Lloyd Chiasson, who has written extensively about trial publicity in the United States, has commented that even though crime is big news, it quickly fades from public consciousness. The prolonged nature of many criminal trials, however, fosters a sustaining sense of interest among citizens.[58] The recent explosion of new media has dramatically enhanced the tendency for tabloid justice criminal cases to linger in the public mind.

Finally, these new forms of media have given the U.S. public an unprecedented exposure to the inner workings of the legal system. In the William Kennedy Smith case, viewers not only directly watched the work of judges, prosecutors, and defense attorneys, but they also saw the difficulties confronted by alleged rape victims in pursuing justice in the courts. In the Bobbitt and Menendez trials, the public gained heavy exposure to issues such as domestic violence, child abuse, and the insanity defense. The Louise Woodward case furnished Americans with an opportunity to examine judicial behavior and discretion, as Hiller Zobel took the extraordinary measure of overturning the jury's verdict. In the Simpson criminal trial, viewers learned about everything from preliminary hearings to pretrial motions to attorney procedural maneuvering to expert witnesses to jury consultants to judicial discretion. In the presidential scandal involving Paula Jones and Monica Lewinsky, viewers were treated to extensive analysis of grand jury and impeachment proceedings, as well as extended debates about perjury and obstruction of justice.

The presence of the new media has greatly magnified the specific facts of each case and the importance of the specific topics that are raised in each instance. In short, the public has received an unprecedented level of exposure to the legal system through the presentation of these cases. The quality and accuracy of this education remains a matter of debate, however. In addition to the central concepts of the new media (new technology, commercialism, and populism), an underlying theme in this chapter has been that the conversation about the legal system that is carried out on the new media outlets may not adequately reflect the range of important public issues facing Americans in the twenty-first century. In our remaining chapters we examine the impact of this media inundation on actual public attitudes about justice in the United States.

▨ NOTES

1. *Rivera Live*, September 14, 1995, provided by Burrelles Transcript Service.

2. Cited in Majorie Williams, "Man of the Hour," *Vanity Fair*, January 1999, p. 133.

3. Jonathan Alter, "In the Time of the Tabs," *Newsweek*, June 2, 1997, p. 32.

4. This calculation is based on an analysis of each show's descriptions as provided by Burrelles Transcript Service.

5. Richard Davis and Diana Owen, *New Media and American Politics* (New York: Oxford University Press, 1998), p. 7.

6. Ibid., pp. 7–9.

7. The Pew Research Center, "Stock Market Down, New Media Up," November 9, 1997, p. 1.

8. Davis and Owen, *New Media and American Politics*, p. 53.

9. For a good discussion of many aspects of the Gulf War coverage, see Lance W. Bennett and David L. Paletz, eds., *Taken by Storm* (Chicago: University of Chicago Press, 1994).

10. Davis and Owen, *New Media and American Politics*, p. 195.

11. This figure is from a CBS News/*New York Times* poll cited in David L. Paletz, *The Media in American Politics* (New York: Longman, 1999), p. 289.

12. In describing these three components of the new media environment, we rely heavily on the definition provided in Davis and Owen, *New Media and American Politics*, chapter 1; and Barry Brummett, "Mediating the Laws: Popular Trials and the Mass Media," in Robert Hariman, ed., *Popular Trials:*

Rhetoric, Mass Media, and the Law (Tuscaloosa: University of Alabama Press, 1990), pp. 179–193.

13. Gary Selnow, *Electronic Whistle-Stops: The Impact of the Internet on American Politics* (Westport, Conn.: Praeger, 1998).

14. "Online Newcomers More Middle Brow, Less Work-Oriented: The Internet News Audience Goes Ordinary," *Pew Survey Report*, January 14, 1999.

15. See Selnow, *Electronic Whistle-Stops*; Sara Bentivegna, "Talking Politics on the Net," Joan Shorenstein Center on the Press, Politics, and Public Policy, 1998; and Richard Davis, *The Web of Politics: The Internet's Impact on the American Political System* (New York: Oxford University Press, 1998).

16. See Michael Parenti, *Inventing Reality* (New York: St. Martin's Press, 1986), pp. 27–34. Also see Arthur Asa Berger, *Manufacturing Desire* (New Brunswick, N.J.: Transaction Publishers, 1996).

17. Russell W. Neuman, *The Future of the Mass Audience* (New York: Cambridge University Press, 1991).

18. See, for instance, the first chapter, "The Endless Chain," in Ben Bagdikian, *The Media Monopoly,* 5th ed. (Boston: Beacon Press, 1997), pp. 3–26.

19. Davis and Owen, *New Media and American Politics*, p. 7.

20. See Kevin Hill, *Cyberpolitics: Citizen Activism in the Age of the Internet* (Lanham, Md.: Rowman and Littlefield, 1998).

21. Stephen Ansolabehere, Roy Behr, and Shanto Iyengar, *The Media Game* (New York: Macmillan, 1993), p. 46.

22. Williams, "Man of the Hour," pp. 132–133.

23. *Rivera Live*, October 3, 1995, provided by Burrelles Transcript Service.

24. *The Big Show*, November 10, 1997, provided by Burrelles Transcript Service.

25. Cited in Lisa Levitt Ryckman, "Legacy of JonBenet: For Friends, Cops, Neighbors, Tragedy Leaves Scars," *Denver Rocky Mountain News*, December 21, 1997, p. 5A.

26. *Rivera Live*, January 21, 1998, provided by Burrelles Transcript Service.

27. Neil Postman, *Amusing Ourselves to Death: Public Discourse in the Age of Show Business* (New York: Penguin, 1985), chapter 1.

28. *The Big Show*, November 10, 1997, provided by Burrelles Transcript Service.

29. *Internight*, November 10, 1997, provided by Burrelles Transcript Service.

30. *Rivera Live*, October 3, 1995, provided by Burrelles Transcript Service.

31. Postman, *Amusing Ourselves to Death*, chapter 1.

32. *Hardball*, November 10, 1997, provided by Burrelles Transcript Service.

33. *Charles Grodin*, November 10, 1997, provided by Burrelles Transcript Service.

34. Ibid.

35. Williams, "Man of the Hour," p. 112.

36. Rivera repeated this statement almost nightly during 1995.

37. *Hardball*, January 10, 1998, provided by Burrelles Transcript Service.

38. Frank N. Magrid Associates, cited in Michael J. Wold and Geoffrey Sands, "Fearless Predictions: The Content World, 2005," *Brill's Content*, August 1999, p. 110.

39. Williams, "Man of the Hour," p. 112.

40. Jonathan Alter, "The New Powers That Be," *Newsweek*, January 18, 1999, p. 25.

41. "Titans of 'tude," *Newsweek*, January 18, 1999, pp. 32–34.

42. Bill Kovach and Tom Rosentiel, *Warp Speed: America in the Age of Mixed Media* (New York: The Century Foundation Press, 1999), p. 17.

43. Ibid., p. 18.

44. For the most recent assessments see Selnow, *Electronic Whistle-Stops*; Tim Jordan, *Cyberpower: The Culture and Politics of Cyberspace and the Internet* (New York: Routledge, 1999); and Davis and Owen, *New Media and American Politics*, pp. 113–116.

45. Ray Surette, *Media, Crime, and Criminal Justice: Images and Realities,* 2d ed. (Belmont, Calif.: Wadsworth Publishing, 1998), pp. 232–233.

46. Drudge made these comments at the National Press Club on June 3, 1998. See Howard Kurtz, "Internet Gossip Parries the Press," *Washington Post*, June 3, 1998, p. D1.

47. See the Court TV website at http://www.courttv.com/.

48. Ronald L. Goldfarb, *TV or Not TV: Television, Justice, and the Courts* (New York: New York University Press, 1998), p. 149.

49. Yahoo! search using the key words "Lance Ito," conducted November 15, 1998.

50. Yahoo! search using the key words "John and Lorena Bobbitt," conducted November 15, 1998.

51. Yahoo! search using the key words "Monica Lewinsky," conducted November 15, 1998.

52. Michael J. Wold and Geoffrey Sands, "Fearless Predictions: The Content World in 2005," *Brill's Content*, August 1999, p. 113.

53. Robert S. Lichter and Linda S. Lichter, "Take This Campaign, Please," *Media Monitor,* September/October 1996, p. 5.

54. Peter Laufer, *Talk Radio: America's Voice or Just Hot Air?* (New York: Birch Lane Press, 1995).

55. Susan Tolchin, *The Angry American* (Boulder, Colo.: Westview Press, 1995), pp. 83–87.

56. Howard Kurtz, *Hot Air* (New York: Basic Books, 1995).

57. Mike Gallagher, speaking on his syndicated radio show, April 14, 1999.

58. Lloyd Chiasson, Jr., ed., *The Press on Trial* (Westport, Conn.: Praeger, 1997), p. x.

PART 2

The Impact of the Media Culture on Public Attitudes Toward the Criminal Justice System

4

Public Opinion, Trial Coverage, and Faith in the Criminal Justice System

I think this is a travesty of justice. I don't believe the jurors followed directions.

> —Rochester, New York, resident responding to the initial guilty verdict by the jury in the Louise Woodward trial[1]

There's a legal system—but I'm not sure there's any justice.

> —Denver, Colorado, resident responding to the Simpson verdict[2]

It's about time we get this all over and done with, but I don't like to see Clinton get off with nothing. . . . I think it's pretty clear he lied to just about everybody and broke the law. . . . He got lucky, real lucky. . . . If that were me and I'd done something like that, I'd be in jail cursing the food right about now.

> —Newbury Park, California, resident commenting the day after the impeachment trial ended[3]

As our previous chapters have shown, the public has received a steady diet of legal coverage emanating from recent criminal cases. At times, this coverage has been sensationalistic and filled with graphic details or shocking revelations. In other instances, these cases have been presented as the most important news in the nation, in that they have been given more airtime and print space than any competing stories. The public's interest in these legal proceedings has been evidenced by an increase in ratings for many news programs. Americans have been the willing recipients of news about tabloid legal proceedings, and these stories have come to pervade the national dialogue.

Nearly two-thirds of Americans claim to have had conversations about Lorena Bobbitt and the Menendez brothers.[4] These numbers are likely higher for the more heavily covered Clinton impeachment, the O.J. Simpson trial, and the JonBenet Ramsey murder investigation. But beyond general, casual conversations about the guilt, innocence, or moral culpability of the various participants, Americans have discussed these cases in far more specific and legalistic terms. Media stories have prompted widespread popular discussion of legal topics such as perjury, reasonable doubt, standards of evidence, proper police procedure, the place of judicial discretion, and the role of juries. Essentially, we have come to discuss formerly esoteric topics with a casual familiarity normally reserved for chats about our favorite sitcoms or dramatic television programs. But again, while public interest in formerly obscure legal issues and questions has presented an opportunity for civic education, the tabloid-like nature of the media's presentation has for the most part meant squandering that possibility.

Beyond a fascination with tabloid cases, the public, at least in several instances, has been dismayed by the actual result in some of these cases. Public opinion polls have shown that a clear majority of Americans disagreed with the verdicts in the O.J. Simpson criminal trial and the first trial of the officers who beat Rodney King. Smaller but still substantial numbers of Americans have been alarmed by the acquittal of William Kennedy Smith, the deadlocked jury in the first trial of Erik and Lyle Menendez, and the judicial reversal and release of Louise Woodward. A media machine that has greatly turned up the volume and criticism in its presentation of these cases has fueled public distaste with their resolution.

In this chapter, we turn our attention to the actual effects of tabloid justice media coverage on the public's attitudes about the criminal justice system. Does the current media culture really affect how citizens view the criminal justice system? More specifically, as a result of tabloid-style media coverage, do citizens have less faith that juries can do their jobs properly, that judges can adequately control their courtrooms in an objective and fair manner, or that the police will treat all Americans in a fair and lawful way? If the answer to these questions is "no," then perhaps such developments should be seen simply as a moderately interesting but ultimately unimportant pop culture phenomenon and not necessarily worthy of social scientific investigation. However, if this coverage has actually influenced how people think about the judicial process, then it is clear that scholars, policymakers, and interested citizens might want to understand it more fully.

We will address these and other concerns by examining the results of a national public opinion poll that we conducted in mid-1999.[5] Ultimately, we will argue here that the media's tabloid-style focus on these cases has undermined faith in the U.S. judicial process for a substantial number of citizens.

MEDIA COVERAGE, PUBLIC OPINION, AND THE LEGAL SYSTEM

Considering that the typical American is by far most likely to encounter "the law" at the level of local trial court proceedings, and that so much of local news is concerned with crime, it is rather surprising that very little academic research has been directed at examining citizen opinion about the criminal justice system.[6] The limited information that does exist must normally be culled from polls that have focused on broader measures of opinion. For instance, a 1994 poll conducted by the Times Mirror Center for the People and the Press sought to ascertain citizen opinion about the U.S. court system. About 43 percent of the respondents held a generally favorable view of the system, while about 53 percent harbored a generally negative view about the courts.[7] This level of generality tells us little about how citizens perceive the more specific components of the system and nothing about how they might have formed those perceptions, but it does indicate that confidence in the system is at best a mixed bag.

Since 1993, the most consistent survey tool for measuring general public attitudes toward the criminal justice system has been an annual poll conducted by the Gallup Organization. In each poll since that year, Americans have expressed lower levels of confidence here than in any other set of public institutions—no more than 20 percent of respondents have expressed strong confidence in the system. In 1994, the year in which the O.J. Simpson criminal proceeding began, the number of people expressing confidence fell to a record low of 15 percent.[8] Again, this statistic ranked the criminal justice system lower in public esteem than other frequently vilified and distrusted institutions such as the public schools, organized labor, big business, or the U.S. Congress.[9] Confidence in the legal system was already very low. So for many who viewed the system negatively before the decade of these cases, the increased exposure to the criminal justice system provided the opportunity to reinvestigate or perhaps reinforce previously existing attitudes.

Beyond the meager number of polls that address attitudes about the justice system, there is a small body of work that focuses on public views of the U.S. Supreme Court. Several such studies have claimed that mass media coverage of the Court has influenced the attitudes of citizens. Public reaction to the Court seems to be largely based on the general popularity of its decisions, rather than on any substantive knowledge about its work or its role in the broader constitutional order.[10] Simply put, politically popular decisions lead to positive public assessments of the Court, and politically unpopular decisions lead to negative assessments.[11] Although public approval levels for the Court are consistently higher than for Congress, the more that poll questions address narrower aspects of the Court's work, the more "don't know" and negative responses dominate.[12] These studies do show a correlation between coverage of the Supreme Court's decisions and public reactions to the institution. Of most relevance to our study, they indicate that public agreement with a decision in a certain case; and, more important, the *way that the issues are presented* in the media often serves as a compelling factor in how citizens assess the overall body of the Supreme Court. In general, the manner in which the High Court is presented fosters the legitimacy of that institution in the public mind. Thus, one can plausibly conclude that the type of coverage in a given case does impact public opinion.

In thinking more specifically about whether coverage of high-profile legal proceedings has influenced public opinion, a number of writers have linked the public's negative attitudes toward the legal system with the mass media's increasingly negative reporting about the U.S. judicial process.[13] In exploring the potential influences of recent crime coverage in the media, there are a number of possible consequences of this coverage. First, given that news organizations possess a limited amount of resources to expend, extensive tabloid justice coverage may reduce the attention paid to arguably more important issues of public concern. The mass public's lack of interest in, and meager knowledge of, important political and social events and issues have been well chronicled. Since the early 1960s, voter turnout is down, citizens have far less trust in the institutions of government, and public apathy about politics and government has reached an all-time high.[14] The causes of such high levels of disinterest and low levels of knowledge lie far beyond the scope of this book. Nevertheless, it is worth noting that this thirty-year decline in political efficacy in the United States closely coincides with changes in the news business during that same period, which we have chronicled in Chapters 2 and 3.[15]

It is common for news outlets to neglect important legal and political issues in the process of "chasing sleaze and celebrities."[16] Journalist Richard Krajicek and others have noted that this is particularly true of the media's coverage of crime and justice issues, as the pursuit of flashy crime dramas has led to a neglect of ostensibly more important events involving foreign policy, governmental corruption, welfare policy, campaign finance reform, the environment, and so on. Americans know and discuss the intimate details of JonBenet's final days or Monica Lewinsky's sexual proclivities, even as they are unable to find Kosovo on a map or name the chief justice of the U.S. Supreme Court. And although the public's lack of knowledge about national or current events is nothing new, the explicit coverage of tabloid events may be further eroding public awareness of important domestic or international developments. At the very least, media coverage has trivialized or marginalized important news events by giving priority to tabloid criminal cases.

A second potential consequence of the tabloid justice style of media coverage is that many Americans may routinely be misled about the legal system. This possibility stands in contrast to the traditional view that increased public awareness of the courts will result in a more informed citizenry. It is interesting to note the number of scholars and journalists who have said that the O.J. Simpson and Clinton-Lewinsky sagas have served as "grand civics lessons" for all Americans.[17] But while citizens *were* exposed to the intimate workings of the criminal justice system and the congressional impeachment process during these dramas, the processes and behavior on display were at times so unusual that the long-term educational value in conveying the reality of the legal system is questionable.

For instance, legal scholar Angelique Paul undertook a study of this tendency toward miseducation and attempted to test a number of hypotheses about how television trial coverage is miseducating the public.[18] Paul surveyed people who had watched a significant portion of the Simpson criminal trial. She found that the respondents believed that a high percentage of criminal cases are resolved through jury trials; they thought that they knew significantly more about criminal rather than civil procedure (even though civil procedures are far more common); and they believed that violent crime was far more widespread than it actually is.[19] In essence, those who had followed the Simpson trial closely had drawn highly inaccurate conclusions about the realities of the legal system. Similarly, David Harris has persuasively argued that the media's focus on murder trials leads the public to believe that all defendants receive a "generous serving of due process" protection, when in reality most cases are quickly and routinely resolved through "mumbled questions and incantations in a crowded courtroom, before a judge taking plea after plea."[20]

A final consequence, and the primary focus of this chapter, involves the possibility that tabloid-style coverage of the judicial process has resulted in increasingly negative assessments of the justice system on the part of U.S. citizens. Obviously, this concern is related to the second, that the public has been misinformed about the real operation of the system. But here we are concerned specifically with a loss of public trust, rather than with the question of what factual knowledge citizens have about the judicial process. The view of the criminal justice system that is on display during these tabloid-style cases is distinctly negative in tone. The cases selected for sustained media coverage are highly anomalous; for the most part they tend to exaggerate the inefficiencies and shortcomings of U.S. law.

For instance, the prosecution of the Menendez brothers lasted almost seven years, which is far longer than a typical murder prosecution. This conveys the sense that the system is very ineffective. Similarly, when Judge Hiller Zobel overruled the jury's verdict in the trial of Louise Woodward, the decision was dissected on the cable news talk shows as though it were a common occurrence, when in fact it is quite rare for judges to overturn jury decisions that are consistent with the judge's original instructions. Further, coverage of the Simpson trial might have given the public the impression that defense attorneys routinely give press conferences at the end of each day's trial proceedings. Not surprisingly, when Christopher Darden, one of the key prosecutors in the Simpson criminal trial, was asked what U.S. college students could learn about the criminal justice system from that case, his answer was "absolutely nothing." According to Darden, the Simpson case was so bizarre, unusual, and celebrity driven that it was impossible to understand the daily workings of the system by watching that trial on television.[21]

Inaccurate images of the judicial process were pervasive during the Simpson criminal trial. To cite just one example, it is well documented that about 80 percent of all criminal defendants in the United States are indigent, and in California 93 percent of all criminal cases are settled through the process of plea bargaining.[22] However, the Simpson case and others might lead one to conclude that defense lawyers regularly wreak havoc in courtrooms, when in reality that occurs in only a small percentage of cases.

Law professor Peter Arenella, a frequent media commentator on the Simpson case, has cautioned that the media messages emanating from the Simpson case might lead the public to demand some hasty, unnecessary, and even dangerous changes to the system. Accordingly, in the wake of the Simpson criminal trial, there were calls in California to ban cameras from courtrooms and to do away with the unanimous jury requirement in criminal trials.[23] None of these proposals has yet been passed, but all have been debated in the California Legislature.[24]

Based on the preceding analysis, both here and in Chapters 2 and 3, we have developed three hypotheses. The foundation for each is our central concern with how tabloid-style coverage affects citizen attitudes toward the legal system. The hypotheses are as follows:

1. *Public knowledge of and familiarity with the high-profile tabloid trials are extensive.* For the tabloid cases and coverage of those cases to matter, there must be public retention of some of the facts and emotions emanating from these cases.

2. *Public exposure to tabloid cases has diminished public confidence in the criminal justice system.* This hypothesis is the main focus of this chapter and is supported by some preliminary evidence that citizens have been distressed by the outcomes in several of the tabloid cases that we consider.

3. *Individual levels of news consumption will be correlated to a citizen's level of confidence in the criminal justice system.* If exposure through the media causes negative perceptions of the criminal justice system as speculated in hypothesis two, than it would logically follow that even higher levels of media exposure would result in even more negative assessments.

The remainder of this chapter is devoted to assessing these hypotheses.

■ THE PUBLIC'S KNOWLEDGE OF HIGH-PROFILE CRIMINAL TRIALS AND INVESTIGATIONS

As previously mentioned, only a handful of studies explore public attitudes about trial courts and the specific actors and components of the judicial process. Nevertheless, previous polling has shown that Americans believe they know a great deal about the seven specific cases that we focus on in this book. The Pew Research Center conducts regular polls that ask citizens about the issues in the news that they have followed most closely. Their results have relevance to our study, as they have shown that 92 percent of Americans followed the first Rodney King trial, 77 percent followed the O.J. Simpson criminal trial, 66 percent followed the William Kennedy Smith trial, and 40 percent paid attention to the Menendez trial.[25] In contrast, public awareness of, and interest in, stories such as the war in Bosnia (27 percent), social security reform (23 percent), and the Medicare debate (20 percent) lagged far behind.[26]

Our national poll focused directly on the seven tabloid justice cases that we described in Chapter 1. Conducted between April 1 and June 15, 1999, the poll revealed high levels of familiarity with these cases, even when they had occurred several years earlier. In addition to familiarity, almost 50 percent of the sample asserted that their knowledge of the legal system had increased based on what they knew about these seven tabloid cases.[27] Table 4.1 shows the public's level of familiarity with the cases that we have focused on in our analysis.

Table 4.1   Public Familiarity with Facts Surrounding Seven Tabloid Cases in the 1990s

	% Familiar[a]	% Unfamiliar[b]
Criminal trial of O.J. Simpson	97	3
Senate impeachment trial of Bill Clinton	97	4
Investigation into the death of JonBenet Ramsey	86	14
Trial of the officers who beat Rodney King	74	26
Trial of Louise Woodward	65	35
Trials of the Menendez brothers	64	36
Trial of William Kennedy Smith	51	49

Note: N = 1,003. Rows may not add to 100 due to rounding.

[a] "Familiar" is the combined responses of those saying they are "very familiar" and "somewhat familiar."

[b] "Unfamiliar" is the combined responses of those saying they are "somewhat unfamiliar" and "very unfamiliar."

Not surprisingly, the highest levels of familiarity were associated with the Simpson trial and the impeachment of President Clinton. The Simpson case, even several years after its conclusion, remains an important cultural reference point for most Americans. And Simpson himself remains a figure who is regularly covered by the press even today. Numerous stories continue to be aired and published that focus on his whereabouts, the selling and auctioning of his possessions to pay the damages awarded in the civil trial, and ongoing rumors about the status of his personal life. Further, as mentioned previously in Chapter 3, some of the central (as well as peripheral) players from the Simpson trial have gone on to enjoy successful careers in the media, and they are often called upon to discuss their involvement in the trial.

In retrospect, the media precedent established in covering the Simpson trial paved the way for the press's treatment of the Clinton-Lewinsky scandal. The Simpson criminal trial coincided with the advent of the Internet and the ascendance of cable news, and these institutions were firmly in place by the time of the Clinton impeachment drama. With the exception of violence, the Clinton episode had all of the necessary elements that have led to intensive media coverage in the 1990s: celebrity, money, power, and sex. Additionally, the president's behavior is, by definition, a legitimate news subject. Thus, the media were able to maintain that they were covering important news about the chief executive, rather than simply a sex scandal. In the end, the level of media attention given to the Clinton drama exceeded even that focused on Simpson, which was not surprising once the scandal evolved into an actual House impeachment and Senate trial.

Closely trailing the levels of public awareness associated with Simpson and Clinton, fully 86 percent of our respondents voiced familiarity with the JonBenet Ramsey case. There can be little doubt that if and when this case ever reaches a courtroom, it will be dubbed the latest trial of the century. Well over three years after JonBenet's murder, and with neither a suspect nor an indictment on the horizon, there have already been at least six books written about the case.[28] Perhaps a bit more surprisingly, several cases from the early 1990s, including those involving William Kennedy Smith (1991), the Menendez brothers (who murdered their parents in 1989), and the officers who beat Rodney King (1992), remain highly familiar to a majority of our respondents. In addition to the cases on which we polled, the Pew Research Center has detected high levels of public familiarity with the trials involving Oklahoma City bombing suspect Timothy McVeigh, fallen televangelist Jim Bakker, boxing champ Mike Tyson, and Lorena Bobbitt.[29]

We sought to place these levels of public familiarity into context by comparing them with citizen knowledge about other major political and social issues. Table 4.2 offers a brief comparison of public knowledge regarding some specific criminal trial facts with knowledge about important political figures. Table 4.2 suggests that factual knowledge about our selected criminal trials and investigations often exceeds familiarity with ostensibly more important topics and events.

When Americans can identify JonBenet Ramsey as easily as the vice president of the United States, several conclusions can be suggested. First, the notion that the public has received heavy does of tabloid justice information is made fairly clear. If we combine the levels of familiarity in Table 4.1 with the factual knowledge depicted in Table 4.2, we can conclude that the memory of these cases extends well beyond the time that the particular trial or investigation took place. This finding provides strong support for our first hypothesis. Moreover, we would reiterate that the prominent cases with which we are concerned have become a part of the fabric of U.S. popular culture.

These tables also suggest that either Americans are profoundly uninterested in news involving top government officials and political

Table 4.2   Comparison of the Public's Knowledge of Selected Tabloid and Nontabloid Topics

	% Answering Correctly
Tabloid Topics	
Amount awarded in Simpson civil trial	75
Identity of William Kennedy Smith	75
Identity of JonBenet Ramsey	70
Identity of Simpson Judge Lance Ito	64
Identity of Clinton antagonist Kathleen Willey	52
Identity of presidential adviser Vernon Jordan	41
Nontabloid Topics	
Identity of Vice President Al Gore	70
The political party that has a majority in	
the U.S. House of Representatives	49
Identity of Russian president Boris Yeltsin	47
Identity of Senate majority leader Trent Lott	15
Identity of Chief Justice William Rehnquist	12
Identity of British prime minister Tony Blair	10

Source: Data compiled by the Pew Research Center, 1991–1999.

figures, or the media have reported more news about tabloid-type criminal cases than about the activities of such political figures and events (or perhaps both). At a minimum, we know that given the public's lack of knowledge, the increasing media focus on criminal justice entertainment is directed at a receptive audience. But does public familiarity with these cases have any broader ramifications? It is to this question and our next two hypotheses that we now turn.

GENERAL PUBLIC CONFIDENCE IN THE U.S. CRIMINAL JUSTICE SYSTEM

As we begin to assess public confidence in the criminal justice system, it is important to recall that previous studies have revealed a generally declining trust in many government institutions during the past three decades.[30] That said, it is not surprising that our study revealed low levels of confidence in the criminal justice system. Our findings are consistent with previous national survey data.[31] In an effort to go beyond mere assessments of the whole system, we also asked respondents to state their level of confidence in various specific aspects of the system. Table 4.3 displays our findings and reveals low levels of confidence in the system as a whole, as well as in the police, judges, juries, defense attorneys, and prosecuting attorneys. Respondents expressed relatively more confidence in the police than in other participants in the system, but even here we found that about two-thirds of Americans *do not* express high levels of trust in law enforcement.

In our introductory chapter, we noted that there are numerous difficulties involved in attempting to measure the effects of the mass media on public attitudes.[32] Cause and effect are hard to establish, for many factors can influence one's perceptions of, in this case, the criminal justice system. Recognizing these difficulties, we used a number of methods in attempting to measure the influence of the coverage that we have been describing. First, we randomly divided our survey sample in half. We asked one group of respondents for their level of confidence in the system as a whole and in several specific criminal justice participants prior to mentioning any of the individual cases.

For the other group of respondents, we asked numerous questions about the tabloid justice cases themselves before inquiring about the person's overall level of confidence.[33] Our intent was to determine whether first cueing respondents with the names of the cases would influence their responses. Such question ordering, or priming experiment, is a common means of attempting to measure how particular events affect a person's general attitudes.[34] John Zaller, in *The Nature and Origins of Mass Opinion*, argues that public opinion measures are often the result of an individual respondent "averaging" conflicting feelings or providing an answer based on the considerations that come most quickly to mind. Zaller urges survey researchers not to view responses based on question-order effects as "methodological artifacts" but to use them to gain insight regarding what factors help to influence public opinion on a given subject.[35] He further notes that important factors shaping public attitudes can be missed in typical survey research because the respondents simply do not recall some of the elements that influence their opinions in the few moments they have with which to answer the questions posed to them.[36]

Along these lines, our research revealed that question ordering had an important impact on how respondents viewed the legal system. The second and third columns of Table 4.3 reveal a clear and statistically significant difference between the two groups of respondents in all but one of the components of the system. Those respondents who had first been reminded about the high-profile cases demonstrated *lower* levels of confidence in the criminal justice system, the police, judges, juries,

Table 4.3   Overall Confidence in the Criminal Justice System and the Impact of Tabloid Case Mentions on Confidence in the Criminal Justice System

Aspects of the Criminal Justice System	Overall Confidence Level	Confidence Level When Tabloid Cases Mentioned First	Confidence Level When Tabloid Cases Mentioned Last
		% Expressing Confidence	
Criminal justice system	20	15**	25
Police	31	24**	39
Judges	27	24*	31
Juries	29	25*	33
Defense attorneys	19	17	20
Prosecuting attorneys	20	14**	25
N	1,003	500	503

Note: Entries are the percentage of respondents who had "complete" or "quite a lot" of confidence in the listed aspects of the criminal justice system. Chi-square significance tests compare the second and third columns, ** $p < .01$ and * $p < .05$.

and prosecuting attorneys. And although these differences are not extraordinarily large, they do reveal a clear and important pattern in which recollection of the tabloid justice trials triggered more negative responses regarding the criminal justice system. The only component for which this finding did not hold was defense attorneys.

To further explore the relationship between media coverage and public attitudes toward criminal justice in the United States, we queried our sample about whether media coverage of these cases had affected their confidence in the system. We inquired as to whether respondents had come to have more, less, or the same amount of trust in the criminal justice system as a result of their exposure to these high-profile trials and investigations. Table 4.4 reveals the results of these questions.

The cases that have had the most negative effect on public attitudes are those involving O.J. Simpson and JonBenet Ramsey. Simpson's case is not surprising, as that trial was followed by an extended national discussion regarding whether the ordeal had exposed serious defects in the U.S. judicial process. A Gallup poll in 1999, more than three years after Simpson's acquittal in the criminal trial, found that 79 percent of the public continued to believe that Simpson had killed his ex-wife and Ronald Goldman.[37] Perhaps a bit more surprising is that 70 percent of our respondents claimed that the JonBenet Ramsey investigation has made them less trustful of the criminal justice system. Levels of public familiarity with the Ramsey case may be unprecedented, for at the time of this writing (early 2000), no suspect has been

Table 4.4   Influence of Tabloid Trials on Citizen Confidence in the Criminal Justice System

	% Less Confident	% More Confident	% No Change	% Don't Know
Change in confidence in the criminal justice system as a result of exposure to the following cases:				
Criminal trial of O.J. Simpson	75	3	19	3
Investigation into the death of JonBenet Ramsey	70	2	17	11
Senate impeachment trial of Bill Clinton	58	6	32	4
Trial of the officers who beat Rodney King	49	5	22	24
Trial of William Kennedy Smith	36	2	16	46
Trial of Louise Woodward	25	6	34	35
Trials of the Menendez brothers	14	25	28	33

Note: N = 1,003.

named or indicted, and no formal legal proceedings have taken place, with the exception of the impaneling of a grand jury. The investigation into the murder of the six-year-old beauty queen must surely be the most high-profile unsolved crime in the nation at the present time.

What is interesting is that, given that there has been no arrest or trial, the public's great awareness of the Ramsey case seems to be entirely based on the relentless, tabloid-style coverage presented by both the mainstream and the supermarket media outlets. For example, JonBenet's face has appeared on the cover of the *National Enquirer* more than forty times since her death on December 26, 1996, and the political talk show *Hardball* recently devoted a full thirty minutes of its one-hour show to analyzing the recent "developments" in the case.[38] This high level of public awareness is accompanied by pessimism, however. A 1998 Gallup poll found that 56 percent of Americans do not believe that JonBenet's killer will ever be brought to justice.[39]

The responses concerning the impeachment and Senate trial of President Clinton also illustrate a significant drop in public trust in the legal system. As many conservative critics warned during 1998, the impeachment ordeal seems to have weakened civic confidence. Yet it is important to realize that this negative reaction may be motivated by a number of interpretations of the series of events that led to Clinton's acquittal by the U.S. Senate in February 1999. Some respondents believe that the president unjustly avoided punishment for legitimately criminal conduct, whereas others felt that Clinton was the victim of an overzealous partisan persecutor.

Turning to the cases involving Rodney King, William Kennedy Smith, and Louise Woodward, we found that many U.S. citizens had their faith in the system tested by these events, too. In fact, the only one of our tabloid cases resulting in a net *gain* in public confidence was the murder trial of the Menendez brothers. Not coincidentally, this is also the only one of the four murder cases in which the defendants were actually found guilty and sentenced to lengthy prison terms. Americans seem to have dismissed (or forgotten) the plodding seven-year set of trials, the hung jury in the first trial, and the questionable defense tactics involved, and to have focused solely on the ultimate outcome in the case. The public appears to be results oriented, viewing the system more favorably when what they view as a just verdict has been rendered.

To further explore the link between these cases and trust in the criminal justice system we used *Pearson correlation coefficients*. We measured the relationship between an individual's general confidence in the criminal justice system and his or her assessment of how the system operated in each of the cases. That is, if a particular person held a negative view of the criminal justice system in the JonBenet Ramsey case, for instance, did that person also tend to hold a negative view of the criminal justice system as a whole? Although Pearson coefficients do not allow us to determine causation, they do allow us to determine if there is a significant relationship between the cases and trust in the overall system. The entries in Table 4.5 indicate the direction and the strength of the relationship between general trust levels and the individual cases.

The results in Table 4.5 reveal a clear pattern. Although the coefficients are small, they show that almost all of the cases are related to an individual's overall assessment of the criminal justice system. More specifically, negative reactions to each of the cases are correlated with lower levels of confidence in the criminal justice system as a whole. Every case except for the trial of the Menendez brothers revealed such a statistically significant relationship.

Based on the combined evidence presented in Tables 4.3, 4.4, and 4.5, it is clear that the media's presentation of these cases has influenced the way that some citizens view the overall criminal justice system. Each of the measures we have used—an experimental design, direct

Table 4.5   Correlation Coefficients Between General Confidence in the Criminal Justice System and the Tabloid Cases

	Correlation Coefficient
General confidence in the criminal justice system correlated with confidence in the criminal justice system in the following cases:	
Investigation into the death of JonBenet Ramsey (876)	.09**
Criminal trial of O.J. Simpson (958)	.13**
Trial of the officers who beat Rodney King (751)	.13**
Trial of William Kennedy Smith (532)	.13**
Senate impeachment trial of Bill Clinton (945)	.16**
Trial of Louise Woodward (639)	.14**
Trials of the Menendez brothers (661)	.07

Note: Sample sizes in parentheses. General confidence in the legal system was coded 1 to 5, with 1 representing the most confidence and 5 representing the least confidence. Individual cases were coded 1 to 3, with 1 representing the most confidence and 3 representing the least confidence. Entries are Pearson correlation coefficients with a two-tailed significance test, ** $p < .01$ and * $p < .05$.

questioning, and case-specific correlations to general attitudes—has pointed toward the conclusion that media attention to the high-profile trials of the 1990s has worked to diminish many citizens' overall confidence in the quality of justice in the United States. This finding, which we elaborate on later, provides tangible evidence that there have been real consequences to this style of legal coverage. Additionally, this finding offers support for our second hypothesis that tabloid-style coverage leads to more negative assessments of the legal system. We now turn to public attitudes about specific actors within the justice system.

JURIES, JUDGES, AND THE POLICE

Moving beyond general assessments, we asked our respondents whether these cases affected their assessment of the performance of particular figures involved in the judicial process. Each of the seven cases we studied tended to highlight the behavior of particular figures within the criminal justice system. Accordingly, in this section we examine the public's reaction to the performance of juries, judges, and the police, all of which have come under intense criticism in the media's analysis of these cases.

Juries

The institution of the jury has been characterized variously as "the most fascinating and the most controversial aspect" and as one of "the most romanticized and the most vilified actors" in the U.S. judicial process.[40] Debates about the role of juries have undoubtedly been heightened by several of the high-profile criminal trials in the 1990s. Controversial jury verdicts in the trials of Lorena Bobbitt, the Menendez brothers, Louise Woodward, the officers who beat Rodney King, and especially in the O.J. Simpson trial have left many wondering if the jury still serves a useful purpose in the modern U.S. justice system.[41] Discussion and debate about the role of juries have increased recently, despite overall decreases in the percentage of criminal trials decided by juries. In fact, today fewer than 5 percent of all cases that enter the criminal justice system are placed before a jury.[42] Yet despite the chorus of recent criticism, most Americans continue to strongly support the fundamental ideal that any citizen accused of a serious crime is entitled to a verdict rendered by a jury drawn from the community in which the crime has occurred.[43] Thus, the jury remains before us today as a powerful symbol of democracy and justice but perhaps less as our chosen means of processing cases in the criminal justice system.

We employed two separate means of examining how our respondents' assessments of the jury system may have been affected by intense media exposure to five of our chosen cases. First, we simply asked our sample whether the outcome of a particular tabloid case had affected their overall confidence in the jury system. Next, we correlated citizens' reactions to the jury performance in each case with their overall assessment of the U.S. system of jury trials (essentially employing the same type of analysis seen in Table 4.5). Predictably, we focused on the King officers and Simpson trials, where jury verdicts were the source of widespread controversy. As previously mentioned, polls show that a majority of the public believes that the juries in the Simpson criminal trial and in the first trial of the Los Angeles Police Department (LAPD) officers reached the wrong conclusions.

We also examined the verdicts in the Menendez and William Kennedy Smith trials. In the first Menendez case, the jury deadlocked along gender lines, and a mistrial was eventually declared. In the William Kennedy Smith case, jurors deliberated for less than one hour before acquitting what many observers believed was a guilty defendant. Finally, the jury verdict in the Louise Woodward case was notable because it was highlighted by the rare action of a judge throwing out the jury's verdict. We did not include the Senate impeachment trial of President Clinton, because a jury composed of 100 senators cannot be compared to one impaneled in a typical criminal trial. The top portion of Table 4.6 reveals the results of the direct-assessment question; the top section of Table 4.7 shows the correlation coefficients.

Table 4.6 reveals that for all of the cases except that of Erik and Lyle Menendez, respondents' trust in the jury system suffered as a result of what they saw. These data were particularly pronounced for the Simpson case, although a loss of confidence was also revealed in the wake of the Rodney King officers and William Kennedy Smith trials. Similarly, Table 4.7 reveals that citizens who reacted negatively to jury behavior in a given case were significantly more likely to possess a generally low level of confidence in the jury system as a whole. Such correlations were statistically significant for all of the cases and were particularly pronounced for the Simpson, King, and Kennedy Smith trials.

Table 4.6   Influence of Tabloid Trials on Citizen Confidence in Juries, Judges, and the Police

	% Less Confident	% More Confident	% No Change
Change in confidence in the jury system as a result of exposure to the following cases:			
Criminal trial of O.J. Simpson	62	5	30
Trial of the officers who beat Rodney King	38	5	31
Trial of William Kennedy Smith	29	2	21
Trial of Louise Woodward	17	7	40
Trials of the Menendez brothers	11	23	33
Change in confidence in judges as a result of exposure to the following cases:			
Criminal trial of O.J. Simpson	57	4	35
Trial of the officers who beat Rodney King	31	5	39
Trial of William Kennedy Smith	26	2	24
Trial of Louise Woodward	23	6	35
Trials of the Menendez brothers	10	21	35
Change in confidence in the police as a result of exposure to the following cases:			
Investigation into the death of JonBenet Ramsey	67	3	19
Criminal trial of O.J. Simpson	57	6	34
Trial of the officers who beat Rodney King	52	3	20
Trials of the Menendez brothers	10	21	43

Note: N = 1,003. Rows do not add to 100 because "don't know" responses are not shown.

Judges

Trial judges possess a great deal of power and discretion in criminal cases. From the point of arrest, or even earlier if warrants are issued, to the final disposition of a case, judges preside over every step in the criminal justice process. They often exert much of their power and discretion in negotiations and meetings with lawyers outside the courtroom.[44] Not surprisingly, this wide latitude allows trial judges to perform their duties in a variety of different styles.[45] Some judges run highly regimented courtrooms, in which they work closely with staff, prosecutors, and defense attorneys, whereas other judges take a more hands-off approach, letting the opposing attorneys dominate trial procedures. Hence, the complex reality of the judge's role confounds the typical public notion that a judge's job consists mainly of presiding over live courtroom trials.[46]

Table 4.7   Correlation Coefficients Between General Confidence in the Jury System, Judges, and the Police and the Tabloid Cases

	Correlation Coefficient
General confidence in the jury system correlated with the confidence in the jury system in the following cases:	
Criminal trial of O.J. Simpson (960)	.17**
Trial of the officers who beat Rodney King (745)	.17**
Trial of William Kennedy Smith (521)	.24**
Trial of Louise Woodward (642)	.15**
Trials of the Menendez brothers (662)	.08*
General confidence in judges correlated with the confidence in judges in the following cases:	
Criminal trial of O.J. Simpson (961)	.20**
Trial of the officers who beat Rodney King (741)	.24**
Trial of Kennedy Smith (519)	.24**
Trial of Louise Woodward (634)	.23**
Trials of the Menendez brothers (660)	.12**
General confidence in the police correlated with confidence in the police in the following cases:	
Investigation into the death of JonBenet Ramsey (881)	.08*
Criminal trial of O.J. Simpson (964)	.18**
Trial of the officers who beat Rodney King (755)	.20**
Trials of the Menendez brothers (656)	.08*

Note: Sample sizes in parentheses. General confidence in the legal system was coded 1 to 5, with 1 representing the most confidence and 5 representing the least confidence. Individual cases were coded 1 to 3, with 1 representing the most confidence and 3 representing the least confidence. Entries are Pearson correlation coefficients with a two-tailed significance test, ** $p < .01$ and * p is $< .05$.

Turning to the judges who have been at the center of our tabloid trials, we can see many of the advantages and disadvantages of judicial discretion. In our selected cases, only two judges truly became public figures (excluding Chief Justice William Rehnquist, who presided over the Senate trial of Bill Clinton). These are Judges Lance Ito of the Simpson criminal trial and Hiller Zobel of the Louise Woodward case. Virtually every media commentator has been highly critical of the manner in which Ito presided over the Simpson trial. Many in the legal profession believe that he did not maintain adequate control of the courtroom, rein in grandstanding lawyers, or move the case along in a timely fashion. In fact, in some legal circles, Ito's name has become synonymous with incompetent and ill-advised judicial behavior.[47]

Zobel also commanded center stage when he threw out a jury's verdict, but his actions received a more mixed response from legal observers. To some, he was a hero for overturning an unjust jury verdict. To others, he exhibited an inexcusable misuse of judicial discretion. Justice John Greaney, who reviewed the appeal of Judge Zobel's decision, wrote in his dissent: "Here it appears that the judge [Zobel] identified himself with Woodward's cause, compromising the public's confidence in the integrity and impartiality of our courts."[48]

We also asked respondents about judges in three other cases. Our goal was to determine whether tabloid proceedings might turn the public against judges simply by their association with a negatively viewed outcome. We asked respondents to rate how the judges in the Rodney King, William Kennedy Smith, and Menendez brothers trials made them feel about the work of judges overall. The results to these questions are presented in Tables 4.6 and 4.7.

The responses to our queries reveal a pattern suggesting that the public rates the performance of the judges (as was the case with juries) in connection with their overall approval of the outcome of the case. The performance of Judge Ito in the Simpson case greatly reduced the confidence of the public in judges undoubtedly because the outcome of the trial received such widespread public disdain. The highly publicized reversal by Judge Zobel in the Woodward case did not meet the same level of scorn, largely because this trial outcome was not viewed as negatively as the Simpson verdict. The other cases mentioned in Table 4.6 follow the same pattern, with some serious reservations revealed about the work of judges in the King officers and Kennedy Smith cases. We would speculate that for those who remember the outcomes of these cases, they generally disagreed with the outcome and have held the judge responsible. True to form, the work of judges was actually more likely to gain the approval of the public in the trial of the Menendez brothers. Again, this finding can most likely be explained by the "favorable" outcome of the case.

▓ The Police

Attorney General Janet Reno admitted in public appearances in 1999 that citizen trust in the police, particularly among racial minorities, has steadily declined in the past several years.[49] For instance, early in the 1990s the Rodney King case gave rise to an intense public debate about police behavior. Television stations throughout the nation repeatedly broadcast the infamous videotape showing members of the LAPD savagely beating King. Since the King incident, the mass media have cast a consistently watchful eye on police conduct. Such conduct was heavily analyzed during the Simpson trials and more recently during the ongoing JonBenet Ramsey investigation.

In 1998 and 1999, two highly publicized New York City incidents called further attention to the behavior of law enforcement officers. The first of these cases involved the torture of Abner Louima, a Haitian immigrant who was arrested in a bar room brawl. Louima later claimed that New York police officers sodomized him with a toilet plunger in a bathroom at the police station, and one officer eventually pled guilty to the charges. The second episode involved West African immigrant Amadou Diallo, an unarmed street vendor who died in a hail of forty-one bullets fired by four undercover New York Police Department officers.[50]

In order to analyze public attitudes about the police, we followed the same approach that we used to examine judges and juries. The bottom portions of Tables 4.6 and 4.7 reveal our sample's assessments of police performance in the Simpson, Ramsey, King, and Menendez cases. The bottom portion of Table 4.6 reveals some very high levels of discontent with the police behavior in the Ramsey, Simpson, and King cases.[51] Public criticism in the King case was largely rooted in the allegedly racist behavior of members of the LAPD (we explore these racial dynamics in more detail in Chapter 5). In the Ramsey investigation, the mass media have focused heavily on supposedly less-than-stellar police work. Numerous journalistic accounts have documented the police's mistakes at the beginning of the investigation,[52] and one critic characterized law enforcement efforts in the case as "utterly inept."[53]

Regardless of the accuracy of such assessments, the public perception in this case is that the police have failed to do their jobs competently. In the Simpson case, many assailed the LAPD as both racist and incompetent. Racial slurs uttered by Officer Mark Furhman, as well as sloppy evidence collection, were frequently cited as explanations for Simpson's acquittal. In contrast, reaction to the Menendez case revealed little criticism of the police, because law enforcement behavior was not an overtly relevant or controversial issue in those proceedings.

In sum, our polling on each of these three specific components of the criminal justice system shows that public faith in the system as a whole has decreased as a result of what citizens know about these specific cases. Thus, media exposure of particular trials can have the result of highlighting, and at times discrediting, particular actors within the system. Further, the results in Tables 4.6 and 4.7 reveal that the public draws conclusions about the behavior of juries, judges, and the police simply by assessing the outcome of a given case. Further, Table 4.7 reveals that respondents who held negative views about the behavior of juries, judges, and the police in the cases themselves also held strongly negative views about these legal actors more generally.

Overall, the results in these tables lend further support for our second hypothesis. We should emphasize again that what troubles us is not that citizens are drawing negative conclusions about the system or its particular components. It is that no single criminal case can illuminate any of these important issues adequately, particularly when it is covered in the tabloid justice style.

▮ TRIAL COVERAGE AND A LOSS OF LEGITIMACY

By means of a final set of questions, we sought to understand how the public's diminished confidence in the criminal justice system might translate into changes in individual citizens' expectations about how they themselves might be treated in an encounter with the system. Prior to asking these questions, we encouraged respondents to think about the trials and investigations that we had been discussing throughout the questionnaire (see Appendix B). We explicitly requested that respondents reflect on the tabloid justice cases while answering these questions. Essentially, we wanted to know whether what the citizens had learned about the cases affected their expectations about what they might personally encounter if they were to come in contact with law enforcement or the judicial system. In these questions, we asked people to assess how they would feel if they or a family member were forced to interact with judges, juries, the police, and prosecuting attorneys. The results of these questions and responses are displayed in Table 4.8.

Table 4.8 reveals that the era of tabloid justice has contributed to a large number of citizens losing faith in how they or someone close to them would be treated in the U.S. criminal justice system. As a result of what citizens have learned through the media's coverage of these criminal cases, roughly 40 percent of our respondents claimed that they now had less confidence that the legal system would protect their rights, that prosecutors would treat them fairly, and that the police

Table 4.8   Personal Impact of Knowledge of Tabloid Cases

	% Less Confident	% More Confident	% No Change
As a result of the criminal trials and investigations we have been discussing, do you have less, more, or the same confidence that:			
the laws surrounding the criminal justice system would protect your rights?	44	14	41
you or a family member would be treated fairly by prosecuting attorneys if arrested as a suspect in a crime?	38	9	51
you or a family member would be treated fairly by the police if arrested as a suspect in a crime?	37	14	48
you or a family member would be treated fairly by a judge if you had been arrested and were standing trial for a crime?	26	13	58
you or a family member would be treated fairly by a jury if you been arrested and were standing trial for a crime?	23	14	61

Notes: N = 1,003. Rows do not add to 100 because "don't know" responses are not shown.

would adequately respect their privacy and due process guarantees. Perceptions of judges and juries suffered somewhat less, with about one quarter of our sample saying that their trust in these legal actors had been diminished by their knowledge of our selected cases. Only a handful of citizens gained confidence in how they would be treated by the various components of the system.

It is clear that exposure to these cases has undermined the confidence of a significant number of citizens. Such increased cynicism may be the most damaging effect of tabloid-style legal coverage. This overall decrease in legitimacy, when combined with low levels of factual knowledge and dismal levels of political and civic participation, is what concerns us most of all. It is not unreasonable for citizens to be dissatisfied with the operation of the justice system, even at a fundamental level. Today, however, such criticism is driven by a sensationalistic, misleading style of legal coverage, which is transmitted to a receptive yet undiscerning audience.

ASSESSING THE EFFECTS OF INCREASED LEVELS OF MEDIA EXPOSURE

Our third and final hypothesis focused on whether an increase in one's level of media exposure would lead to increasingly negative attitudes toward the justice system. In attempting to determine if this was true, we asked respondents in our sample about the frequency with which they watched network national newscasts, read newspapers, and watched the cable news channels such as Fox News Channel, MSNBC, and Court TV.

Our results revealed that there was little or no relationship between a respondent's negative attitudes about the tabloid cases and their media consumption habits. The frequency with which one watched the news appears to have almost no significant effect on one's attitudes about either the individual cases or the overall system of criminal justice. The only clear pattern of differences that emerged was our finding that regular viewers of cable news programs claimed to have significantly higher levels (on average by about 10 percent more) of familiarity with each of the cases. This finding is one we would have expected.

Originally, we were quite surprised when we found that there were few differences in attitudes between high- and low-volume news consumers. Upon further investigation, however, these findings began to make sense. In our sample, 70 percent of the respondents said that they watched a national news program every day, 56 percent read a daily newspaper, and 45 percent said that they tuned in to a cable news station each day. Thus, almost all Americans follow the news in some form or another. Among the respondents, more than 90 percent said that they watched or read the news at least "several times a week." Only 8 percent of the sample said that they "rarely" or "never" paid attention to any of the news outlets that we mentioned. These findings about news habits are consistent with other recent research.[54]

Ultimately, these results offer support for our contention that there is almost total cultural immersion in (and societal awareness of) the tabloid justice cases. Because these events are covered in every media outlet, almost all citizens become aware of them, and consequently most citizens develop opinions about them. People who follow the news at *any* level are well acquainted with JonBenet Ramsey and O.J. Simpson, for example. Even among the 8 percent who indicated that they did not follow the news, over half claimed that they were familiar with the Menendez brothers, and 41 percent with Louise Woodward.

There is no escape from the coverage of these cases, and we thus conclude that news consumption habits have little bearing on one's overall assessment of the criminal justice system. Similarly, in an atmosphere of near total media saturation, it is difficult for any citizen to avoid hearing about the facts and outcomes of high-profile legal cases. What this means is that our poll results do not offer support for our third hypothesis. An increase in one's news consumption did not necessarily lead to more negative assessments of the criminal justice system. In the end, a large number of our respondents, regardless of their level of exposure to the mass media, offered negative assessments of the system.

■ CONCLUSION

We began this chapter by posing a general question about whether the style, volume, or intensity of tabloid-style legal coverage has influenced how people think about the justice system. We operationalized this question by advancing three hypotheses. Our first hypothesis—that citizens possess substantial knowledge of and familiarity with the tabloid cases—is supported by the findings displayed in Tables 4.1 and 4.2. This is important, because no other hypothesis about media effects would be particularly plausible if citizens did not maintain some strong recollection of the facts surrounding the tabloid cases.

Our second hypothesis involved the premise that the public's faith in the criminal justice system has been eroded by the media's coverage of the judicial process. This decreased public confidence can be seen in opinions about individual actors and aspects within the criminal justice process, as well about the system as a whole. The findings presented in this chapter support such contentions. Our conclusions are most noteworthy in the sense that poll respondents are quite explicit about how the tabloid justice cases have affected their views of justice in the United States. Thus, there is strong evidence supporting our second hypothesis.

There turned out to be little support for our third hypothesis, however, that a greater level of negativity toward the system would accompany greater exposure to news coverage. On the contrary, we found that given the nearly complete saturation of the public consciousness with tabloid justice information, all groups of citizens voiced similar, very dismal levels of confidence in the criminal justice process as a result of their reaction to the media coverage of these events.

We conclude here by once again noting two important points. The public has become fairly knowledgeable about the basic facts of these cases and has reacted to the media presentation of these dramas on the one hand with morbid fascination, and on the other by drawing increasingly negative conclusions about the general state of criminal justice in the United States. Contrary to the wider public benefits hypothesized by some, increased public exposure to the workings of the judicial system has not led to more confidence on the part of citizens.[55] Lacking both a responsible press and an engaged and civic-minded public, these cases have not provided the much-needed forum for a meaningful civic discussion of important criminal justice issues.

▩ NOTES

1. Christy Casey, "Majority of Callers Disagree: Au Pair Found Guilty," *Boston Globe*, October 31, 1997, p. A16.

2. Karen Abbott, "Verdict Is the Talk of Denver: News Brings Reactions Ranging from Sadness to Prayerful Gratitude," *Denver Rocky Mountain News*, October 4, 1995, p. 30A.

3. Kate Folmar and Pamela J. Johnson, "Many Residents Glad Senate Trial Is History," *Los Angeles Times*, Ventura County Edition, February 13, 1999, p. B1.

4. Andrew Kohut, "TV Trials Captivate Public," *Times Mirror Center for the People and the Press*, February 4, 1994.

5. See Appendix B for a copy of the survey and a description of the survey methods that were employed.

6. See C. Danielle Vinson and John S. Ertter, "Entertainment or Education: How Do Media Cover the Courts?" (paper presented at the Midwestern Political Science Association in Chicago, Ill., April 15–18, 1999). There has been some work examining the impact of trial coverage in terms of its effects on the victims of crime in both trials and pretrial publicity. See Debra Gersh, "Crime Victims and the Media: Press Coverage Has a Lasting Impact on Their Lives," *Editor and Publisher* 125, September 26, 1992, pp. 12–14; and Dorothy J. Imrich, Charles Mullin, and Daniel Linz, "Measuring the Extent of Prejudicial Pretrial Publicity in Major American Newspapers: A Content Analysis," *Journal of Communication* 45 (summer 1995): 94–117.

7. Kohut, "TV Trials Captivate Public," p. 10.

8. These responses represent the combined percentages of those who said they were "highly" and "fairly" confident about the legal system.

9. Frank Newport, "Small Business and Military Generate Most Confidence in Americans," *The Gallup Poll Monthly*, August 15, 1997, pp. 3–5.

10. John M. Scheb and William Lyons, "Public Perception of the Supreme Court in the 1990s," in Eliot E. Slotnick, ed., *Judicial Politics: Readings from Judicature* (Chicago: American Judicature Society, 2000), pp. 466–469.

11. The most comprehensive study of this subject is Richard Davis, *Decisions and Images: The Supreme Court and the Press* (Englewood Cliffs, N.J.: Prentice-Hall, 1994), especially at pp. 10–19 and 132. Also see Walter F. Murphy and Joseph Tanenhaus, "Public Opinion and the Supreme Court," *Law and Society Review* 2 (February 1968): 357–382; Valerie Hoekstra and Jeffrey A. Segal, "The Shepherding of Local Public Opinion: The Supreme Court and Lamb's Chapel," *Journal of Politics* 58 (1996): 1079–1102; Charles Franklin and Liane Kosacki, "Media, Knowledge, and Public Evaluations of the Supreme Court," in Lee Epstein, ed., *Contemplating Courts* (Washington, D.C.: Congressional Quarterly Press, 1995); Gregory Caldeira, "Neither the Purse Nor the Sword," *American Political Science Review* 80 (1986): 1209–1226; and John P. Robinson and Dennis K. Davis, "Television News and the Informed Public: An Information-Processing Approach," *Journal of Communication* 40 (1982): 106–119.

12. Scheb and Lyons, "Public Perception of the Supreme Court," p. 466.

13. Joseph S. Nye, Jr., "The Media and Declining Confidence in Government," *Journal of Press and Politics* (summer 1997): 4–9.

14. See, for instance, E. J. Dionne, *Why Americans Hate Politics* (New York: Simon and Schuster, 1991); Joseph Nye, Philip Zelikow, and David C. King, *Why People Don't Trust Government* (Cambridge, Mass.: Harvard University Press, 1997); and Stephen Earl Bennett, *Apathy in America* (Dobbs Ferry, New York: Transnational Publishers, 1986).

15. Such trends are noted in Richard Davis and Diana Owen, *New Media and American Politics* (New York: Oxford University Press, 1998); and David L. Paletz, *The Media in American Politics* (New York: Longman, 1999).

16. See Richard Krajicek, *Scooped* (New York: Columbia University Press, 1998), p. 60.

17. Krajicek, *Scooped*, p. 64.

18. Angelique Paul, "Turning the Camera on Court TV: Does Televising Trials Teach Us Anything About the Real Law?" *Ohio State Law Journal* 58 (1997): 666.

19. Ibid., pp. 693–694.

20. David A. Harris, "The Appearance of Justice: Court TV, Conventional Television, and Public Understanding of the Criminal Justice System," *Arizona Law Review* 35 (1993): 822.

21. This question was asked by the authors at a public lecture given by Darden at Indiana University–Purdue University, Indianapolis, in March 1997.

22. David Shaw, "The Simpson Legacy," *Los Angeles Times*, October 9, 1995, p. S5.

23. Ibid.

24. Frank Macchiarola, "Finding the Truth in an American Criminal Trial: Some Observations," *Cardozo Journal of International Comparative Law* (spring 1997), online without pagination.

25. These percentages are based on respondents who said that they followed the trial "very" or "fairly" closely. See Andrew Kohut, "The Pew Research Center News Interest Index," *Pew Research Center for the People and the Press*, June 1997, p. 4.

26. Kohut, "TV Trials Captivate Public," p. 4.

27. More precisely, 47 percent responded that they were more knowledgeable, 10 percent said that they were less knowledgeable, and 43 percent said that there was no change in their knowledge of the criminal justice system.

28. For a review of four of these books, see Joyce Carol Oates, "The Mystery of JonBenet Ramsey," *New York Review of Books*, June 24, 1999, pp. 31–37.

29. Kohut, "TV Trials Captivate Public," p. 4.

30. See generally Dionne, *Why Americans Hate Politics;* and Nye, Zelikow, and King, *Why People Don't Trust Government.*

31. Gallup poll annual survey questions about public confidence in the criminal justice system show a confidence level hovering around 20 percent. An archive of Gallup poll releases showing these responses can be found online at http://www.gallup.com/.

32. See, for instance, Doris Graber, *Mass Media and American Politics,* 5th ed. (Washington, D.C.: Congressional Quarterly Press, 1997); Thomas R. Dye, L. Harmon Zeigler, and S. Robert Lichter, *American Politics in the Media Age,* 4th ed. (Fort Worth, Tex.: Harcourt Brace, 1992), p. 106; Maxwell McCombs, "News Influence on Our Pictures of the World," in Jennings Bryant and Dolf Zimmerman, eds., *Media Effects: Advances in Theory and Research* (Hillsdale, N.J.: Lawrence Erlbaum, 1994), pp. 1–16; and Roy Edward Lotz, *Crime and the American Press* (Westport, Conn.: Praeger, 1991).

33. For a complete discussion of our methods, see Appendix B.

34. See Schmuel T. Lock, Robert Y. Shapiro, and Lawrence R. Jacobs, "The Impact of Political Debate on Government Trust: Reminding the Public What the Federal Government Does," *Political Behavior* 21 (1999): 239–264.

35. John Zaller, *The Nature and Origins of Mass Opinion* (New York: Cambridge University Press, 1992), pp. 79–80.

36. Zaller, *The Nature and Origins of Mass Opinion*, especially chapters 4 and 5. Also see John Zaller and Stanley Feldman, "A Simple Theory of the Survey Response: Answering Questions Versus Revealing Preferences," *American Journal of Political Science* 36 (1992): 579–616.

37. Frank Newport, "Fifth Anniversary of Nicole Brown Simpson and Ron Goldman Murders Finds Americans Still Pointing at O.J. Simpson," *The Gallup Poll Monthly,* June 14, 1999. This report can be accessed at http://www.gallup.com/.

38. Oates, "The Mystery of JonBenet Ramsey," p. 32.

39. See *The Gallup Poll Monthly*, June 1998.

40. See Henry Abraham, *The Judicial Process*, 7th ed. (New York: Oxford University Press, 1998), p. 109; and Eliot E. Slotnick, ed., *Judicial Politics: Readings from Judicature* (Chicago: American Judicature Society, 1992), p. 235.

41. The trials of the 1990s have led many in the legal community to suggest a host of reforms of the system. For a good review of such proposals, see Douglas Smith, "Structural and Functional Aspects of the Jury: Comparative Analysis and Proposals for Reform," *Alabama Law Review* 48 (winter 1997): 441–581.

42. Barbara Boland, Paul Hahanna, and Ronald Stones, *The Prosecution of Felony Arrests* (Washington, D.C.: U.S. Department of Justice, Bureau of Justice Statistics, Feb. 1992). This study shows that only three out of every 100 felony arrests go to trial, and only about a third of those are tried before a jury.

43. Polls conducted after the Simpson trial show that almost 60 percent of Americans view a jury trial as an essential provision of the Constitution. See *The Gallup Poll Monthly*, April 1995. In addition, polling shows that a clear majority of the electorate views jury duty as a basic duty in a democracy (which may be ironic, given the lengths to which some citizens go to *avoid* jury service).

44. See, for instance, John Paul Ryan, Allan Ahman, Bruce Sales, and Sandra Shane Dubow, *American Trial Judges* (New York: Free Press, 1980).

45. For an outstanding review of the literature concerning judicial roles and decisionmaking, see Gregory Sisk, Michael Heise, and Andrew P. Morriss, "Charting the Influences on the Judicial Mind: An Empirical Study of Judicial Reasoning," *New York University Law Review* 73 (November 1998): 1377–1500.

46. David W. Neubauer, *America's Courts and the Criminal Justice System*, 6th ed. (Belmont, Calif.: Wadsworth Publishing, 1999), pp. 183–186.

47. Paul Jacobs, "Matt Did Not Get the Title," *Los Angeles Times*, June 19, 1996, p. A3.

48. Judge Zobel's ruling was upheld, but Justice Greaney dissented from that decision. See Jack Sullivan, "Nanny Goes Free; Dissenters Rip Zobel for Compromising System," *Boston Herald*, June 17, 1998, p. 3.

49. Kevin Johnson, "'Too Many' Believe They Can't Trust Police, Reno says," *USA Today*, April 16, 1999, p. 8A.

50. This case ultimately concluded in early 2000 with the full acquittal of all four officers in a trial in Albany, New York.

51. Victoria Pope and Annik Stahl, "The All-Too-Typical JonBenet Case," *U.S. News and World Report*, December 1, 1997, pp. 32–36.

52. For instance, see Daniel Glick, Sherry Keene-Osborn, and Andrew Murr, "The Door that Never Opened," *Newsweek*, July 13, 1998, p. 32.

53. Oates, "The Mystery of JonBenet Ramsey," p. 32.

54. See Stephen Ansolabehere, Roy Behr, and Shanto Iyengar, *The Media Game* (New York: Macmillan, 1993), pp. 12–15.

55. Susanna Barber summarizes this research in *News Cameras in the Courtroom: A Free Press–Fair Trial Debate* (Norwood, N.J.: Ablex, 1987), especially at pp. 54 and 94. Also see Ronald L. Goldfarb, *TV or Not TV: Television, Justice, and the Courts* (New York: New York University Press, 1998), pp. 160–166; Alan M. Dershowitz, *Reasonable Doubts: The Criminal Justice System and the O.J. Simpson Case* (New York: Simon and Schuster,

1997), pp. 129–134, 146–148, 203–204; Anna Quindlen, "Order in the Court," *New York Times*, July 25, 1994; Eileen Libby, "Court TV: Are We Being Fed a Steady Diet of Tabloid Television?" *ABA Journal* (May 1994): 47; and Ruth Ann Strickland and Richter H. Moore, Jr., "Cameras in State Courts: A Historical Perspective," *Judicature* 78 (November/December 1994): 128–135.

5

Race, Gender, Class, and Tabloid Justice

I find it tragically ironic that women are encouraged to press charges when they are the victims of sexual harassment or violence. Why should they? It's just an opportunity to be called an emotionally unstable liar in a court of law. Detailed, wrenching memories of harassment and rape mean nothing to rich, powerful men and a society that does not want to acknowledge that there is anything wrong. This country is unsafe for women.

> —Dayton, Ohio, woman responding to the
> verdict in the William Kennedy Smith rape trial[1]

There is no humanly possible way a jury could sit there and hear the testimony and see the tape and come up with the verdict they had. Some of the police officers that were on the scene were admitting that the officers were wrong. In that verdict, there was no concern for Rodney King or the wrong that was done.

> —Ventura, California, resident responding to the verdict
> in the first trial of the officers who beat Rodney King[2]

A poor man would be swinging by now . . . the race issue was a pretty big smoke screen. It's an amazing verdict with the mountain of evidence against him.

> —Seattle, Washington, man responding to the Simpson verdict[3]

In this chapter, we focus on the social divisions that the press has consistently highlighted in its coverage of the tabloid justice cases. The media style of presentation for these cases has often focused on race, class, and gender cleavages as a means of marketing these criminal dramas.[4] When a trial is portrayed as a symbol of the current state of race or gender relations, the story becomes much bigger than a mere exposition of the criminal conduct of the participants. A case presented as a battle between blacks and whites or women and men or rich and poor becomes a story that calls for widespread public attention.

As we have argued elsewhere in this book, none of these cases, with the possible exception of the first Rodney King beating trial, warranted the volume of media attention that they received. However, once they received such high levels of coverage, citizens responded to the presentation of those cases and formed judgments accordingly. Further, with so much of the coverage focusing on race, gender, and class issues, many citizens have used these cases as a means of assessing the fairness and effectiveness of the system. In the course of presenting important social issues in these cases, the media had an opportunity to help educate and inform citizens about the inequities of the justice system. However, the overall tenor of the coverage was often inflammatory rather than educational and informative in nature.

A brief review of some of our high-profile trials reveals the extent to which race, gender, and social class dynamics were presented as central elements in the cases. For instance, in the King and Simpson cases, the media heavily emphasized race, whereas in presenting the Kennedy Smith and Clinton dramas, the coverage frequently focused on gender issues. Unfortunately, it would appear that the opportunity for civil and thoughtful reflection about the serious social issues emanating from these cases was, more often than not, lost in a blur of tabloid-style coverage.

Our goal in this chapter is to assess whether there have been significant consequences of the extensive media coverage that has focused specifically on the aforementioned social cleavages. We are concerned here with two related questions: First, do members of distinct social and demographic groups have different views of the criminal justice system and the tabloid justice cases? Second, do blacks and whites, men and women, and affluent and less affluent groups actually develop different attitudes about the criminal justice system based partly on how the media covers tabloid justice cases? This second question is more difficult to answer, for the effects of coverage are undoubtedly among many factors that help to shape a person's views about the legal system.

Because of the difficulty of measuring something as complex as public attitudes on questions of race, gender, and class, our goals in this chapter are modest. Primarily, we will compare how members of different demographic groups view the legal system and the tabloid cases of the 1990s. We will then speculate on the effect sensationalized and tabloid media coverage has had on different groups of citizens.

We have divided this analysis into two parts. Part one begins by briefly discussing existing opinion and legal theory regarding the role of the law in the United States. In this section we also describe numerous examples of the types of polarizing coverage that we have been referring to. Part two returns to the results of our national survey and examines how members of different demographic groups assess the legal system and the tabloid justice cases. Here we will focus largely on race and gender cleavages.

TABLOID JUSTICE MEDIA COVERAGE: SENSATIONALIZING DIFFERENCES

The claim that the legal system has serious shortcomings in terms of how minorities, women, and the poor are treated was certainly not introduced by tabloid justice media coverage. Public perceptions of the legal system have shown for years that citizens believe minorities receive harsher treatment by the system and that the wealthy receive more favorable treatment.[5] The public view of how women have been treated in the legal system has been examined less frequently and the findings have been somewhat more mixed.[6] Beyond these long-standing public perceptions about fairness, scholars and legal historians have developed a number of theoretical and philosophical critiques analyzing U.S. law by focusing on issues of race, gender, and social class.

Many of these critiques are metatheoretical works that seek to uncover and lay bare the fundamental contradictions and inequities in the legal system. The Critical Legal Studies (CLS) movement, which began in the mid-1960s, yields most of the contemporary critiques of this nature.[7] For adherents of the CLS movement, law is believed to be structured in such a way that workers, ethnic and racial minorities, women, and the poor are placed at a distinct disadvantage. The law is seen as a tool for the wealthy and for those already in power. The CLS movement has strongly influenced the development of theoretical approaches concerned explicitly with sexual and racial inequality in the law. Feminist legal theory is one such movement, and it has been quite influential, at least in academic settings, since the early 1970s.[8] Feminist legal thinking is highly diverse but begins with the premise that women continue to occupy a subordinate place in society and that the law tends to reflect and reinforce that position.[9] Finally, drawing insights from both CLS and feminist jurisprudence, critical race theory emerged in the early 1990s as an explicitly race-based critique of U.S. law.[10] This perspective examines legal concepts, categories, and doctrines from the point of view of people of color (mainly African Americans) and, like the CLS movement and feminist jurisprudence, is concerned with questions of difference, discrimination, oppression, and inequality.[11]

The tradition of such criticism has helped to further an understanding of how the system has at times not treated citizens of different backgrounds, races, and genders fairly. Accordingly, in this chapter we focus on how, in covering the tabloid justice cases, the media have chosen to present issues of race, gender, and class in such a way that they are oversimplified and trivialized. As we have noted previously, race, gender, and class issues are often the central elements that help a legal or criminal case reach the "national stage." A great deal of the coverage that we discussed in earlier chapters has been focused on these social divisions. The media coverage surrounding these legal events often pits blacks and whites and men and women against one another. And, although these cases have occasionally raised serious and important social issues, we would contend that the larger media spectacle of the tabloid justice era generally has not allowed for a thoughtful discussion of issues such as racism and sexism in the criminal justice system. What would appear to occur in the media presentation of many of these issues is a way of discussing these issues that exploits differences in people to create a more dramatic story line and better entertainment. A brief overview of some of this coverage will illustrate the media atmosphere surrounding many of these cases.

In both the King and Simpson cases, the mass media seized almost every opportunity to raise the issue of race. In the wake of the riots that were triggered by the acquittals of the officers who beat Rodney King, news coverage focused heavily on the racial dynamics of the case. The coverage of the King beating began with reflective tones, as the *Los Angeles Times* ran an editorial within a few days of the Rodney King video titled "Shocking Incident Leads to Worrisome Questions About L.A. Police."[12] The editorial raised questions about police brutality first and possible racism second. Much of the media coverage preceding the trials of the officers who were accused of beating King explored the current state of racial dynamics in the United States. Well-known columnists such as Anna Quindlen and Art Buchwald wrote columns lamenting the deep divide between white and black Americans.[13] ABC's late night news program *Nightline* used a subtle approach in a postriot program titled "The Two Facets of the Los Angeles Riots." This program focused on police work during the riots and on tensions between African Americans and Korean Americans.[14] However, another *Nightline* program, which had been aired immediately after the first verdicts were announced, involved a dramatic confrontation between a white juror from the Rodney King case and black Los Angeles city councilman Mark Ridley-Thomas.[15]

Overall, though, these examples highlight a relatively more reserved tone in the media coverage of the King trials. However, the television media's repetitive usage of the King beating videotape often undercut any truly reasoned public discussion of the story. The imagery from the King videotape, consisting of a short edit of white officers beating a black man, was played so many times on television that many of the more complex issues in the King case were effectively pushed aside.

Mass media coverage in the Simpson case was far more exploitative of racial tensions, and it highlights the increasing tabloid fervor that emerged during the mid-1990s. From the very morning after the murders, coverage around the country pointed to the racial undercurrents of the case. Within two weeks of the crime, and long before the trial itself was under way, the New York City daily *Newsday* ran an editorial titled "O.J. Triggers a Racist Quake That's Off the Richter Scale."[16] Other headlines also predicted a racial showdown. One front-page newspaper story, which appeared within a week of Simpson's arrest, trumpeted, "O.J. Case Haunted by Racial Undertone, Black Community Faces Wrenching Test."[17] Throughout the course of the trial, there was extensive and growing coverage focusing on the racial dynamics of the case.

Outlets in both the traditional and new media had been covering the racial angle throughout the trial. ABC's *Nightline* and CNBC's *Rivera Live* had devoted numerous programs specifically to this issue. By its conclusion, the trial was being discussed in the news media almost exclusively in racial terms. On the day that the trial ended, NBC's *Dateline* newsmagazine titled its program "The Verdict, in Black and White." Each of the three nightly network news programs discussed race relations at the top of their broadcasts. All three networks contrasted pictures of crowd reactions that showed jubilant black citizens and distressed white citizens. In the wake of the trial, almost all of the cable talk shows devoted some of their programming to discussing the racial implications of the Simpson trial.

Cable programs such as *Rivera Live*, *Cal Thomas*, and *Charles Grodin* discussed the racial fallout of the trial for weeks. Following the verdict, the weekend political programs *Face the Nation*, *Meet the Press*, and *This Week* all welcomed prominent guests to discuss the state of race relations in the country. Significantly, in almost all of these televised venues, black and white guests were shown disagreeing about the verdict and its impact on race relations. CBS News commentator Andy Rooney characterized the Simpson verdict as "the worst thing that's happened to race relations in 40 years."[18] Further, newspapers and magazines throughout the nation ran literally thousands of stories and editorials that addressed the racial implications of the trial. *Time* magazine's cover story, released within hours of the verdict, focused largely on the racial dynamics of the case.[19]

In covering the Simpson trial, the media had not suddenly discovered the issue of race in the United States, nor did this coverage necessarily create the gap in public opinion between blacks and whites regarding Simpson's guilt or innocence (see Table 5.3). But with their intense coverage of the case, the mass media were undoubtedly taking their cues from the activities that had unfolded in the courtroom. The defense team relied heavily on a racial explanation for the supposed police framing of Simpson, and the media were eager to deliver this story to the nation. In fact, one lasting impact of the Simpson case would appear to be the imprint it left on how race relations are discussed in the United States. But whether any single event, particularly one that is so highly charged and sensationalized, should be presented in the news media as the defining moment of race relations is an important question. Whether it was justifiable for the media to take a double murder trial with a celebrity African American defendant and two white victims and turn it into a national referendum on race relations is another. In an attempt to maintain ratings and create interest in the story, the case was covered as the most important development in race relations in decades. The racially focused coverage in the Simpson case demonstrates how the media's agenda-setting power can be corrupted by ratings-driven sensationalism, as well as the public's ready acceptance of the media-dictated terms of public debate.

As with the use of race as a dominant feature of the news coverage in some of the tabloid stories, gender dynamics were also a frequent focus of the reporting in the 1990s. Specifically, the news media discussed gender relations in regard to the rape trial of William Kennedy Smith, the genital mutilation trial of Lorena Bobbitt, the first verdicts in the trials of the Menendez brothers, and the Clinton-Lewinsky scandal. This focus on gender was most prominent in the first three of these cases. For instance, the outcome of the Kennedy Smith trial became a springboard for media speculation about the prevalence of rape and the status of gender relations. In the wake of the trial, news programs across the nation discussed the verdict in terms of men versus women. ABC News ran a lengthy special program (hosted by top news anchor Peter Jennings) entitled "Men, Sex and Rape," which was filmed in Palm Beach County, the site of the trial. Using strong rhetoric, Jennings opened the program by stating that "the William Kennedy Smith case [and others] . . . have been at the center of a pained debate among men and women." Jennings went on to state that while "there have been no bricks or bullets exchanged on this subject yet . . . the anger and fear of some women is such that perhaps men should not be surprised when they are."[20]

Some news reports hypothesized that the Kennedy Smith verdict would cause date rape to become more common while others speculated that the prosecution's treatment of Patricia Bowman (the alleged rape victim) would hinder other women from coming forward in future cases.[21] Paralleling the evolution of race-based coverage, the initial use of the gender angle in the Kennedy Smith case was also more reserved and reflective than some of the coverage that would come with later cases. Regardless, the nature of some of the coverage clearly tried to make the Kennedy Smith case seem emblematic of more general relations between the sexes.

Media coverage of the genital mutilation trial of Lorena Bobbitt in 1994 much more strongly conjured up images of men and women getting ready to battle each other. A search of national media outlets revealed that almost 500 news stories used the phrase "war of the sexes" in analyzing the Bobbitt case.[22] Geraldo Rivera titled one program on the Bobbitt trial "Women Slash Back." CNN analyst William Schneider casually concluded on the air that "a war between the sexes was evident in . . . the verdict in the Bobbitt emasculation trial. More women . . . sympathized with Lorena Bobbitt, and said John deserved what he got."[23] Reporters and news programs focused on the case to turn up the heat on the idea that men and women were gravely and fundamentally at odds. Articles and news stories abounded asking if a new "war between the sexes was under way."[24] The Bobbitt case, which is not one we have focused on extensively in our analysis, is a good example of the media exploiting a lurid yet largely unimportant criminal case to create a national sensation. Columnist Ellen Goodman acerbically commented that "a sleeping man had his penis amputated. It's not a media event. It's a criminal case."[25] Goodman went on to describe with bewilderment how this case had escalated into a referendum on sexual equality.[26]

Gender dynamics were also emphasized in the media coverage of the first Menendez trial. After the jury in the trial of Erik Menendez had deadlocked along gender lines, the press immediately seized on this story angle. The Associated Press wire service released a story using the phrase "war of sexes" to describe the jury's deliberations.[27] Other headlines characterized the jury dynamics in an only slightly less incendiary manner, including "Women Say Gender War Split Jury," and "Menendez Jurors Split Between Men, Women."[28] In a final example, ABC's newsmagazine *Primetime Live* devoted a segment to the Menendez case titled "Three Angry Men." The program included several of the male jurors from the Menendez case making derogatory comments about the performance of several of the women jurors on the panel.[29]

And finally, the Clinton impeachment ordeal gave rise to numerous gender questions. The entire saga began with Paula Jones's allegation that then-Arkansas governor Bill Clinton had sexually harassed her in a Little Rock hotel room. A number of these alleged relationships were discussed in great detail on television news programs. Charges leveled against Clinton ranged from adultery to sexual harassment to rape. These charges received considerable attention in the top television news venues. An interview with Kathleen Willey, a former Democratic Party activist who alleged that the president had made a forceful and unwanted sexual advance, was aired on *60 Minutes*. Within a few weeks of the U.S. Senate's vote not to remove the president from office, NBC's *Dateline* ran an interview with Juanita Broderick, who alleged that in 1978, twenty years previously, then attorney general of Arkansas Bill Clinton had raped her in a hotel room. Clinton's ultimate

Senate acquittal led many media commentators to conclude that the system did not adequately protect the interests of women.[30]

The last social division we consider is wealth and social class. In most of the cases that we have discussed in this book, the issue of wealth became an important feature of the media's coverage. More specifically, the idea that wealthy defendants are able to "buy justice" in the U.S. legal system was widely raised in the coverage of these cases. Literally thousands of newspaper articles and editorials were written in the 1990s that associated one or more of these cases with the role of wealth in the legal system.[31] In the William Kennedy Smith trial, there was widespread speculation that high-priced lawyers and jury consultants had unfairly stacked the deck in favor of Kennedy Smith. One headline proclaimed that "Jury Consultants Buy 'Justice' for the Rich."[32] Similar analyses followed the hung jury that produced a mistrial in the Menendez case. In both of these cases, much of the media analysis portrayed wealthy defendants as the beneficiaries of special treatment by the police, prosecutors, and judges. This analysis was nowhere more obvious than in the Simpson criminal trial, in which headlines such as "Justice for Sale; High-priced Defenses Mock the System" were common.[33]

In the most recent example, a focus on wealth and class surfaced repeatedly in the investigation into the murder of JonBenet Ramsey. Speculation about the role played by the slain child's parents has been widespread since the case began. The Ramseys, a very wealthy family, have been accused of receiving special treatment from the police and prosecutors. *Denver Post* columnist Chuck Green characterized the investigation this way: "Justice is for sale in America . . . you get the level of justice you can afford."[34] This type of assertion has come on the heels of widespread reporting that the Ramseys have spent millions on lawyers and publicists, despite the fact that they have never been either formally named as suspects or formally charged with the crime.[35] In a final example, the impeachment drama involving President Clinton has also received considerable attention for what many in the media viewed as special treatment given the president.[36]

The message presented throughout all of these cases was that wealth buys better treatment in our criminal justice system. Numerous television programs ran segments using these trials as a means of exposing class bias in the legal system. Geraldo Rivera hosted a program in 1998 titled "Justice for Sale: Why the Rich Get Away with Murder." Rivera began the program by stating that "murder and mayhem done by the rich and famous is often treated differently than crimes committed by the poor. That's a fact of life. . . . Justice is for sale and . . . the rich and famous are buying it."[37]

In sum, the media have utilized issues of race, gender, and class as a means of promoting tabloid cases for entertainment purposes. Again, our point is not that these cases do not present serious or alarming developments pertaining to social cleavages, because some of the cases did raise important issues. Rather, we would maintain that when phrases such as "war of the sexes," "gender battle," "racist quake," "bullets exchanged," "worst in 40 years," or "justice for sale" are employed, they are used as a means of sensationalizing the cases and making them historical and substantial news stories. When otherwise relatively unimportant criminal trials become the avenue for assessing social dynamics, the national agenda is being driven by tabloid journalism— something that is not conducive to the thoughtful and civil engagement of important issues.

GENERAL LEVELS OF CONFIDENCE IN THE CRIMINAL JUSTICE SYSTEM

Given the manner in which race and gender have played a role in recent trial coverage, it is important to understand how citizens have reacted to the emphasis placed on these issues by the media. Recall that the public's overall trust in the criminal justice system is quite low. Accordingly, Table 5.1 examines whether confidence in the criminal justice system differs based on age, education, political party identification, family income, race, and sex.

In our discussion of race we limit our analysis to black/white dynamics, as this distinction was notably featured in several of the tabloid trials. Also, in our national poll, aside from the white respondents, the sample size of the black respondents was the only other ethnic or racial group large enough to be statistically representative.[38]

Turning first to race, Table 5.1 reveals no significant disparity between blacks and whites in terms of overall confidence in the criminal justice system. Most U.S. citizens have a dismal view of the system in general. When we examine three other specific actors within the system, however, we see that African Americans demonstrate significantly lower levels of trust in the police, judges, and juries. Particularly regarding assessments of the police, these findings confirm what other

Table 5.1   Confidence in Several Aspects of the Criminal Justice System Among Demographic Groups

	% Having High Levels of Confidence in:			
	Criminal Justice System	Jury System	Police	Judges
Race				
Black	18	21	13**	17*
White	20	30	33	29
Sex				
Women	17ᵗ	27	30	25ᵗ
Men	22	31	34	30
Age				
18–29	24	26	29	34
30–49	16	29	29	28
50–59	24	27	31	24
Over 60	20	32	36	25
Education				
Some high school	13**	19**	17**	28
High school grad	13	24	29	23
Some college	19	28	32	24
College grad	26	36	36	35
Family Income				
Less than $15,000	12**	26	25	18**
$15,000–29,999	18	29	31	25
$30,000–49,999	14	24	28	24
$50,000–75,000	26	35	37	34
Over $75,000	28	35	32	34
Party Identification				
Democrat	20	30	28**	28
Republican	18	27	37	26
Independent	24	26	24	27

Note: N = 1,003. "High levels of confidence" include those with "complete" or "quite a lot of confidence." Chi-square test performed within each category, ** $p < .01$, * $p < .05$, and ᵗ $p < .10$.

researchers have found in previous studies. Blacks consistently voice their lowest levels of confidence in the police.[39]

When we turn to the gender variable, disparities between the attitudes of men and women are much smaller than those based on race. Women demonstrate slightly lower levels of confidence in several of the categories. At a general level, it appears that men and women hold fairly similar views about the criminal justice system. But even the existence of small differences draws attention to the gender gap, which continues to be the subject of considerable academic investigation and media speculation.[40]

The other variables we tested produced a few additional noteworthy differences. Citizens with higher incomes tend to have higher levels of trust in the criminal justice system and in its specific components than do citizens with lower incomes. Whether such a finding relates to the fact that most of our selected cases involved wealthy protagonists who were acquitted is open to speculation. The education variable produced results in the same direction as income, with citizens possessing lower levels of education tending to have less confidence in the legal system than those with higher levels of education. The political party identification variable also yielded one significant finding, in that self-described Democrats indicated significantly less confidence in the police than did Republicans. This is not particularly surprising, as the ideologies of the two major parties differ, with Democrats tending to emphasize due process and civil rights, whereas the Republicans tend to emphasize crime control. Finally, the age variable did not yield any clear patterns in assessments of either the overall system or its components.

Going beyond general attitudes toward criminal justice in the United States and the various actors in the system, we sought to answer the question of whether different groups of citizens had changed their views of the legal system based on what they know about the tabloid justice cases. We present five cases in Table 5.2, including those involving O.J. Simpson, JonBenet Ramsey, the Rodney King officers, President Clinton, and William Kennedy Smith. We compare the percentages of people in each category who said they had less confidence in the legal system as a result of what they had learned about each of these cases.

The results in Table 5.2 reveal a wide disparity in the manner in which white and black Americans view the criminal justice system, as significant racial differences exist in three of these five cases. Consistent with previous polls, white respondents are more likely than black respondents to assert that the Simpson and Clinton cases undermined their faith in the system. Public reaction to both the criminal and civil trials of Simpson revealed deep racial differences in perspective. African Americans have tended to view the Simpson saga as the story of a black man wrongly accused; whites have viewed it largely as the story of a wealthy celebrity purchasing his freedom.

The racial differences in the Clinton case are likely linked to President Clinton's high degree of popularity among African Americans

Table 5.2 Confidence in Criminal Justice System Among Demographic Groups as a Result of Exposure to Five Tabloid Trials

	% Having Less Confidence in the Criminal Justice System As a Result of the:				
	Criminal Trial of O.J. Simpson	JonBenet Ramsey Investigation	First Rodney King Trial	Clinton Impeachment Trial	William Kennedy Smith Trial
Race					
Black	53**	79	76*	43*	66
White	80	78	61	62	60
Sex					
Women	79	82**	66	62	69
Men	76	74	62	59	62
Age					
18–29	67**	65**	60	48**	48*
30–49	77	76	63	58	64
50–59	78	80	64	61	63
Over 60	83	86	67	69	75
Education					
Some high school	73	67**	61*	52	74**
High school grad	76	81	68	62	73
Some college	81	80	65	64	70
College grad	77	71	59	55	56
Family Income					
Less than $15,000	83	82	75	69*	81
$15,000–29,999	74	76	68	52	67
$30,000–49,999	77	79	62	62	68
$50,000–75,000	80	78	63	65	69
Over $75,000	81	76	61	51	57
Party Identification					
Democrat	74**	76*	69*	52**	68
Republican	84	83	60	70	66
Independent	77	79	61	64	67

Note: N = 1,003. Chi-square test performed within each category, ** $p < .01$ and * $p < .05$.

in realms apart from the scandal.[41] Further, the Clinton impeachment drama, as we have previously suggested, may have caused both ends of the ideological spectrum to lose some faith in the system. Those on the political right have viewed the impeachment and Senate trial as a case of the president skillfully evading serious legal charges, while the political left has interpreted these events as a partisan witch hunt orchestrated by an overly zealous and politically ambitious prosecutor. Neither side gained any confidence in the legal system as a result of the House impeachment and Senate trial. The racial disparities in the Rodney King case are noteworthy as well, with black citizens more likely than whites to state that the King case contributed to their decreased trust in the system.

When we turn to gender disparities in reactions to these cases, we see somewhat smaller differences. Women are more likely than men to have less faith in the legal system as a result of each of the cases, though the result was statistically significant only in the JonBenet Ramsey murder investigation.[42]

In terms of our other variables, age was important in four of the cases, with older respondents exhibiting greater declines in confidence as a result of these proceedings. A comparison of the eighteen- to twenty-nine-year-old category with the over-sixty category reveals a sharp contrast in the Simpson, Ramsey, and Clinton cases. The discrepancy in the age variable may be a result of young people growing up in a time when sordid or scandalous events are less shocking and more common. In the time of tabloid justice, sensational and scandalous stories are reported with such regularity that younger citizens may regard them as normal events.[43] In contrast, older Americans might be reacting negatively to what has been perceived as a loss of dignity and civility in our national discourse. Regarding political party identification, Republicans hold a dimmer view of the Simpson and Ramsey proceedings than do Democrats. As expected, Republicans' trust in the legal system was more severely shaken by the proceedings in the impeachment trial. It is important to note, however, that more than 50 percent of Democrats also state that the case undermined their confidence in the system.

When we assess the important social divisions that emerge in this analysis of confidence in the criminal justice system and the tabloid justice cases, we see some important differences. Race and gender (although gender to a lesser extent) have surfaced as important divisions. We now turn to a more focused examination of how tabloid coverage might affect these groups' attitudes.

AFRICAN AMERICANS AND THE CRIMINAL JUSTICE SYSTEM

The two cases that most clearly raise questions involving race are those of the Rodney King officers and O.J. Simpson. In Chapter 1, we recounted the facts of these well-known cases. Both the Simpson case and the trials of the Los Angeles Police Department officers fueled discussions of race and the criminal justice system. But, unlike the officers' trials, in which both blacks and whites lamented the excessive treatment of a black suspect, the Simpson trial produced a sharp divergence of opinion along racial lines from the very beginning. Despite the importance of the Rodney King story, the Simpson drama remains the touchstone for any discussion of race and criminal law in contemporary America. Table 5.3 shows a timeline of racial differences in reaction to the Simpson criminal trial over a period of five years.

What can account for the continuing wide disparity of racial attitudes about O.J. Simpson? Any answer to this question is necessarily multifaceted. However, one possible explanation is the polarizing media coverage that surrounded the trial. For instance, as noted previously in this chapter, all prominent television news outlets broadcast numerous programs focusing on the role of race in the criminal justice system. A great deal of the coverage presented public opinion as blacks versus whites, often employing black and white pundits to argue opposing perspectives. Several commentators complained that this type of coverage was a caricature of the public's more complex attitudes and that it served merely to foment an already tense situation.[44] The style of this media coverage, which frequently highlighted racial differences, certainly conveyed the sense that there was widespread and mounting tension between blacks and whites. One postverdict poll found that

Table 5.3 Racial Differences in Assessing the Guilt of O.J. Simpson

	Those Who Believed Charges Against Simpson Were True	
	Whites (%)	Blacks (%)
July 1994	68	24
August 1994	61	29
March 1995	66	24
July 1995	75	25
October 1995 (after criminal verdict)	73	25
April/May 1996	66	16
February 1997 (after civil verdict)	74	26
February 1999	79	35

Source: The Gallup Poll Monthly, February 1997, 1999.

more than 74 percent of all Americans believed that the Simpson trial had "hurt" race relations in the United States.[45] Indeed, many commentators cited the media exposure of racial tensions and racially charged public opinion as the chief legacy of the case.[46]

Turning now to the results of our survey, we first asked respondents how the Rodney King and O.J. Simpson cases made them feel about the treatment that African Americans receive from the U.S. criminal justice system. Table 5.4 shows the results of these questions. The Rodney King trial raised the highest level of concern about the treatment of African Americans. More than 40 percent of our respondents indicated that the case gave them less confidence in the legal system's ability to treat African Americans fairly, whereas only 4 percent said it bolstered their trust in the system. Roughly the same number of people said that the Simpson *and* King cases had given them less confidence in the system. Yet nearly one-sixth of our respondents asserted that the Simpson ordeal had given them more confidence that the system would treat blacks fairly. More than 95 percent of those who gave this response were white, indicating that perhaps they believed Simpson's race garnered him the benefit of the doubt and that this might possibly be granted to other African Americans as well.

The preceding findings become more revealing when we compare the attitudes of black and white citizens concerning these two cases. Table 5.5 presents the responses by race of those who felt these two proceedings decreased their confidence in the criminal justice system's fair treatment of African Americans. Table 5.5 reveals a sharp disparity in how blacks and whites view the cases involving King and Simpson. Once again, this is consistent with our previous discussion of black attitudes toward the police, judges, and juries. It becomes increasingly clear that white and black Americans view the criminal justice system differ-

Table 5.4   Influence of Two Tabloid Trials on Citizen Beliefs That the Criminal Justice System Treats African Americans Fairly

	% Less Confident	% More Confident	% No Change
Change in confidence that the legal system treats African Americans fairly as a result of:			
Trial of the officers who beat Rodney King	42	4	30
Criminal trial of O.J. Simpson	38	16	43

Note: N = 1,003. Rows do not total 100 because "don't know" responses are not shown.

Table 5.5   Influence of Two Tabloid Trials on Citizen Beliefs That the Criminal Justice System Treats African Americans Fairly by Race

	Blacks (%)	Whites (%)
Possess less confidence that the legal system treats African Americans fairly as a result of:		
Trial of the officers who beat Rodney King	69**	41
Criminal trial of O.J. Simpson	61**	36
N	87	832

Note: Chi-square test, ** $p < .01$.

ently, and these cases, in particular, in quite different ways. The more interesting question for our analysis is whether the mass media's presentation of these cases actually caused or deepened such differences, or if this coverage merely reflects and reinforces preexisting views. This is perhaps the most difficult dynamic to understand, as causation simply cannot be firmly determined.

In an attempt to determine whether the media's coverage of the Simpson case had any lasting impact on attitudes, the Gallup Organization conducted extensive public opinion polls both during and after the Simpson criminal trial. Table 5.6 includes several questions about race asked in Gallup polls in the years before, during, and after the trial. The first three questions in Table 5.6 focus on general attitudes regarding the criminal justice system. The most striking transformation of opinion appears in the first question listed in Table 5.6. In 1993, blacks and whites were about equally likely to say they would be more willing to believe the testimony of a police officer over another witness. However, when asked the same question in March 1995, after the initial testimony of Detective Mark Fuhrman and several other police officers was completed, African Americans' trust in the police fell by more than half, whereas trust by whites fell only slightly. The initial Fuhrman testimony, covered extensively in the news media, may have had substantial effects on African American attitudes toward the police. Stories discussing Fuhrman's reportedly racist past dominated coverage of the trial at several different junctures. A typical headline released by the Scripps Howard News Service stated, "O.J. Defense Set to Pounce on Fuhrman; Calls Tapes' Racial Slur 'Chilling.'"[47] Numerous stories put the contents of the Fuhrman tapes on the front page of newspapers

Table 5.6   Gallup Poll Questioning on Impact of Simpson Verdict on Racial Attitudes

	Blacks (%)	Whites (%)
If you were on a jury in a trial would you be more willing to believe the testimony of a police officer than another witness who is not a police officer? Yes		
February 1993	43	45
March 1995	18	37
Do you think the American justice system is biased against black people? Yes		
April 1993	68	33
March 1995	66	37
October 1995	54	33
Who do you think is treated more harshly in this country's criminal justice system—blacks or whites—or are they treated about the same? Blacks more harshly		
October 1993	74	35
July 1995	77	45
In general, how do you think people in the United States feel about people of other races? Do you think only a few white people dislike blacks, many dislike blacks, or almost all white people dislike blacks? Many and almost all combined		
May 1992	32	36
October 1995	30	33
Do you think only a few black people dislike whites, many dislike whites, or almost all black people dislike whites? Many and almost all combined		
May 1992	35	48
October 1995	31	46

Source: The Gallup Poll Monthly, March and October 1995.

throughout the United States. The CBS *Evening News* with Dan Rather and NBC's *Nightly News* with Tom Brokaw led their newscasts several times with the Fuhrman story.[48] By this point, the press had turned almost completely to a racial focus in its coverage of the trial.

The second and third questions in Table 5.6 reveal some minor changes in outlook toward the system for both blacks and whites. The responses to these questions show that, following the Simpson criminal trial verdict, the percentage of African Americans perceiving an antiblack bias in the criminal justice system declined by more than 10 percent. By the same token, during the trial, there was a 10 percent increase in the number of whites who believed that the system treats blacks more harshly. These shifts suggest that this highly anomalous case and the previously unparalleled level of media coverage actually changed the public's views about the criminal justice system.

Finally, a major concern in the wake of the Simpson drama involved whether these events and the sensationalizing media coverage worsened tensions between black and white Americans. Although this is an extremely difficult question to answer, public opinion polling has not revealed many significant or lasting changes. The last two questions displayed in Table 5.6 asked blacks and whites to assess the level of racism in the United States. Comparing the responses from 1992 and 1995 reveals that perceived levels of racism in society were unchanged as a result of the Simpson case. Overall, about a third of Americans consistently perceive a deep-seated racism on the part of most of their fellow citizens. Thus, despite the fact that press coverage sent the message that the United States was on the verge of a race war in the wake of the Simpson trial, most direct measures have shown that public opinion regarding race was changed very little as a result of that case.[49]

WOMEN AND THE CRIMINAL JUSTICE SYSTEM

In addition to the above racial aspects, several of our chosen cases raise questions involving gender and whether the legal system treats women fairly. The Kennedy Smith, Simpson, and Clinton cases contained issues variously related to sexual assault, sexual harassment, and domestic abuse. In the Kennedy Smith case, defense attorney Roy Black pursued the controversial strategy of exposing and attacking the past sexual behavior of the woman accuser. This was thought by some observers to highlight the pervasive sexism present in a system unable or unwilling to protect the rights and reputations of women who bring sexual assault and harassment charges.[50] In the Clinton-Lewinsky proceedings, many critics, mostly Republicans in Congress, argued for the impeachment of President Clinton on the grounds that it was necessary to protect women against sexual harassment.

The Simpson criminal trial also briefly became a media vehicle for exploring gender dynamics, although the outcome of the trial did not turn on this issue. The ten-year history of domestic violence involving

O.J. and Nicole Brown Simpson, in which Simpson had never been fully prosecuted, raised questions about the ability of the legal system to adequately address domestic violence. Further, the television media focused on the issue by constantly displaying old photographs of the bruised and battered face of Nicole Simpson and describing the history of abuse she had undergone. These photos were another example of images that the media displayed repeatedly as a means of developing interest in the trial. In the end, the domestic violence angle was overshadowed both in the trial and in the media when Simpson's defense team began to push charges of police racism.

We asked respondents to our national poll to assess how these three cases made them view the legal system's treatment of women. Table 5.7 reveals that, based on their knowledge of each of these three cases, our respondents expressed high levels of concern about the treatment of women. Half of our sample responded that the Simpson case gave them less confidence in the system's treatment of women, and more than a third felt the same way about the William Kennedy Smith trial and the Clinton-Lewinsky scandal.

We now turn to a consideration of whether men and women view the treatment of women in these cases differently. Did the media coverage that often identified these cases as representative of larger problems between men and women affect how they were received? Table 5.8 compares the percentages of men and women who contend that each case decreased their confidence in the criminal justice system's ability to treat women fairly. In each of the three cases, we found women less likely than men to have confidence in the ability of the legal system to treat women fairly. Both men and women view the Kennedy Smith case as the most troubling for gender relations, with

Table 5.7   Influence of Three Tabloid Trials on Citizen Beliefs That the Criminal Justice System Treats Women Fairly

	% Less Confident	% More Confident	% No Change
Change in confidence that the legal system treats women fairly as a result of:			
Criminal trial of O.J. Simpson	50	3	42
Trial of William Kennedy Smith	36	1	17
Senate impeachment trial of Bill Clinton	42	3	51

Note: N = 1,003. Rows do not total 100 because "don't know" responses are not shown.

Table 5.8   Influence of Three Tabloid Trials on Citizen Beliefs That the Criminal Justice System Treats Women Fairly by Sex

	Men (%)	Women (%)
Possess less confidence that the legal system treats women fairly as a result of:		
Trial of William Kennedy Smith	60**	73
Criminal trial of O.J. Simpson	46**	57
Senate impeachment trial of Bill Clinton	38*	48
N	440	548

Note: Chi-square test, ** $p < .01$ and * $p < .05$.

almost 75 percent of women familiar with the case saying that it had made them less confident in the possibility of gender fairness in the law.

Importantly, our broader search of polling data did not reveal any evidence that general views of gender equality or gender fairness have shifted significantly in the wake of the tabloid justice cases. The decade of the 1990s did not reveal many shifts in public opinion about the role of women in the family, sex discrimination, or passage of the Equal Rights Amendment.[51] Questions in these areas have been the indicators used historically by pollsters and survey researchers to assess gender dynamics in society. Nevertheless, a small but significant gender gap clearly exists, with more women viewing the system as unfair. Perhaps, as with the issue of race, tabloid justice media coverage simply reinforces people's existing views about the criminal justice system. If the coverage of these anomalous cases has solidified women's unwillingness to come forward in cases of sexual harassment, domestic violence, and rape, however, this reinforcement is particularly unfortunate, and is a serious indictment of the type of coverage that has arisen with these cases.

PERSONAL WEALTH AND THE CRIMINAL JUSTICE SYSTEM

While the inscription above the entrance to the U.S. Supreme Court reads "Equal Justice Under Law," most Americans seem to believe that in courts of law, as elsewhere in society, the wealthy are simply "more equal."[52] Significant discussion in the media and by the public about whether, and in what ways, wealth allows one to manipulate the criminal justice system accompanied many of the tabloid justice cases.[53] With the exception of the Rodney King officers and Louise Woodward, all of our selected cases featured participants who could afford high-priced legal representation. This fact alone highlights the phenomenally unrepresentative nature of these trials and investigations.

The substantial wealth of the Kennedy family, the Menendez brothers, O.J. Simpson, and the Ramsey family has been well documented and warrants no further discussion. Even Louise Woodward, who was not wealthy, managed to attract some extremely high-powered legal assistance, including that of Barry Scheck, the renowned DNA expert and former member of the O.J. Simpson legal team. Further, widespread international recognition of Woodward's plight resulted in a considerable defense fund set up to help defray her legal bills.[54] And finally, President Clinton's ability to assemble a team of topflight lawyers and other defense personnel is evident, and various reports estimate his total legal debts to have reached into the range of several million dollars, although he needed a defense fund for which contributors were sought.

We asked our survey sample how each of our seven selected cases made them feel in terms of equal treatment for rich and poor defendants in the criminal justice process. Table 5.9 illustrates perhaps the strongest and most unambiguous results in our poll. In every case, respondents claimed that the trial or investigation gave them substantially less faith in the criminal justice system's ability to treat people fairly, regardless of their economic status. A particularly high percentage of citizens

Table 5.9   Influence of Seven Tabloid Trials on Citizen Beliefs That the Criminal Justice System Treats People Fairly Regardless of Economic Status

	% Less Confident	% More Confident	% No Change
Change in confidence that the legal system treats people fairly regardless of whether they are rich or poor.			
Criminal trial of O.J. Simpson	76	2	19
Investigation into the death of JonBenet Ramsey	69	2	18
Senate impeachment trial of Bill Clinton	63	1	32
Trial of the officers who beat Rodney King	46	3	27
Trial of William Kennedy Smith	44	1	10
Trial of Louise Woodward	27	3	35
Trials of the Menendez brothers	23	12	32

Note: Rows do not total 100 because "don't know" responses are not shown.

expressed this sentiment for the Simpson, Clinton, and Ramsey stories, although more than 40 percent of all respondents had the same reaction to the Kennedy Smith and Rodney King cases, too.

When we attempted to determine whether a respondent's *own* wealth or education had an impact on how he or she viewed the system's class fairness, we found no significant differences. Citizens from every income and education level drew the same set of conclusions about the selected tabloid cases. Large majorities believe that the wealthy fare better in the criminal justice system than do the less affluent. The vast majority of Americans has long considered the criminal justice system to favor the wealthy.

Thus, the tabloid justice coverage of the 1990s may simply have reinforced this belief. Such coverage about the "rich buying justice" or the class bias of the system may reflect accurate and understandable observations about the basic nature of law in the United States. However, stories focusing on how "the rich get away with murder" rarely consider the fundamental contradictions in the criminal justice system or what reforms might make the system more equitable. Rather than reporting on budget cuts to the federal Legal Services Corporation or local public defender's offices, for instance, the press is more likely to offer reporting that simply foments a visceral resentment of the entire system.

SOCIAL CLEAVAGES AND PERSONAL EXPECTATIONS ABOUT THE CRIMINAL JUSTICE SYSTEM

As in Chapter 4, we conclude the presentation of our findings by turning to the question of how people expect that they themselves would be treated by the criminal justice system based on what they learned from the tabloid cases. In Table 5.10, we compare the answers of blacks and whites, and men and women. (Again, we found no significant differences associated with income and education.) Table 5.10 confirms several of the differing attitudes of black and white Americans that we have previously described. As a result of what they have learned about the tabloid justice cases, blacks are significantly more likely than whites to believe that they would be treated unfairly by the police and by judges. Fully six in ten African Americans feel they would be mistreated by police officers based on what they have learned in the tabloid justice cases, a troubling comment on the overall legitimacy of con-

Table 5.10   Personal Impact of Knowledge of Tabloid Cases by Race and Sex

	Blacks (%)	Whites (%)	Men (%)	Women (%)
Percentage of people who, as a result of the criminal trials and investigations in the 1990s, have less confidence that:				
the laws surrounding the criminal justice system would protect their rights.	46	41	37*	45
they or a family member would be treated fairly by prosecuting attorneys if arrested as a suspect in a crime.	45	39	41	38
they or a family member would be treated fairly by the police if arrested as a suspect in a crime.	60**	36	36	40
they or a family member would be treated fairly by a judge if they had been arrested and were standing trial for a crime.	45**	24	24^t	29
they or a family member would be treated fairly by a jury if they had been arrested and were standing trial for a crime.	26	23	21^t	26
N	86	831	440	541

Note: Chi-square test, ** $p < .01$, * $p < .05$, and ^{t} $p < .10$.

temporary law enforcement. Given our extensive questioning about the tabloid justice cases, the mass media coverage of these events has served to reinforce and perhaps even strengthen African Americans' distrust of the justice system.

The differences between men and women, once again, are modest. Women feel somewhat less confident in judges, juries, and the system in general. These lower levels of confidence could be related to women's greater concerns about how other women were treated and how the media exploited gender issues in the Kennedy Smith, Simpson, and Clinton cases. However, the small differences do not allow for much grounded speculation.

CONCLUSION

We began this chapter by presenting two related questions. The first was whether members of different social and demographic groups have differing views of the criminal justice system and the tabloid justice cases. The second was whether blacks and whites, men and women, and affluent and less affluent groups actually developed differing attitudes about the criminal justice system based, at least in part, on how the media have covered tabloid justice cases. Because of the complexity in answering the second question, most of our data are directed at answering the first.

Clearly, most Americans have very low levels of trust in the criminal justice system. Our poll has provided further evidence that race is the most pronounced indicator of attitudes toward the justice system. Not only do blacks and whites hold significantly different views about the criminal justice system, but they also react to our selected criminal cases differently. African Americans demonstrate lower levels of confidence in juries, judges, and the police. Racial disparities, especially in evaluating the police, pose a serious challenge for the creation of a criminal justice system that is perceived as fair and just. However, we would argue that the anomalous nature of these trials and investigations does not make them useful vehicles for any clear-eyed and reflective dialogue about the legal system or police behavior in the United States.

The views of men and women are far less disparate than those of blacks and whites. The findings we have reported point to a small but significant and consistent gender gap in how citizens assess the legal system, both generally and in response to the individual cases. Although men's and women's reactions to the cases are slightly different in the aggregate, it is not entirely clear what role tabloid justice media coverage has played in shaping these opinions.

Turning to social class, apart from the fact that the wealthiest of Americans have a somewhat higher level of confidence in the criminal justice system, we uncovered no particularly pronounced differences based on income, education, community type, or political party affiliation. All groups of Americans generally agree that those with money have an advantage in the legal system. Perhaps this is because the contemporary mass media have so uniformly saturated public consciousness that people of every station in society are now exposed to essentially the same images of current events.

In the end, we find that large portions of all subgroups believe that these tabloid justice cases have raised their concerns that the criminal justice system is not capable of treating blacks, women, or the poor fairly. In spite of the different reactions of different groups to the particular trials and investigations, the nature of the mass media presentation has caused, or at least strongly contributed to, a situation in which nearly all Americans now question the basic equity of the system. Thus, perhaps we can conclude that the tabloid-style coverage we have highlighted throughout this book may have ironically brought citizens together in recognizing the need for deep reform of criminal justice in the United States.

Unfortunately, the media presentation of these admittedly important issues is often superficial, purposely graphic and titillating, and based on a less-than-random selection of highly unusual cases which in no way represent the everyday workings of the system. In other words, although this coverage draws attention to many critical issues of race, gender, class, due process, and substantive justice, its effect is weakened by its emphasis on *entertainment*. Essentially, the era of tabloid justice has undermined the dispassionate and detail-oriented discussion required to develop meaningful and workable public policy solutions to the many intractable criminal justice problems that virtually everyone agrees exist.

NOTES

1. "Letters from Readers," *Minneapolis Star Tribune*, December 19, 1991, p. 26A.

2. "The Rodney King Verdict: Aftermath Verdicts Wrong, Most Ventura Residents Say in Poll: 68% Angry Over Acquittals," *Atlanta Journal and Constitution*, May 7, 1992, p. 14A.

3. Haya El Nasser, "Reaction Illustrates Racial Divide: Verdict Called 'A Message,'" *USA Today*, October 4, 1995, p. 6A.

4. See George Lipsitz, "The Greatest Story Ever Sold: Marketing and the O.J. Simpson Trial" in Toni Morrison and Claudia Brosky Lacour, eds., *Birth of a Nation'hood*. (New York: Pantheon Books, 1997), pp. 3–29.

5. The Gallup Organization has asked many question about race and the criminal justice system over the years. These polls consistently reveal that the general public believes that African Americans are treated less fairly in the criminal justice system.

6. Polling on public attitudes about how women are treated in the legal system is almost nonexistent. There have been some independent polls exploring attitudes about how particular women were treated in the legal system, but these have failed to produce any clear patterns.

7. The CLS had its intellectual origins in the tradition of legal realism, an academic movement of the 1920s and 1930s that argued against the earlier belief that law was supreme, objective, and neutral. The realists contended that

because good lawyers and judges could argue either side of any given case, the outcome of legal encounters depended more on the attitudes, goals, and skills of legal professionals than on the letter of the law itself. Thus, law was in no way related to science but rather was deeply embedded in the realms of politics, economics, and culture. Legal *reasoning*, therefore, was not a detached or objective mode of inquiry; it was a complicated function of the biases and social context in which legal questions were answered. In sum, "the law" was indeterminate and value laden, tending to reinforce existing social relations (including existing inequalities).

The major difference between the two movements is that the CLS was, in large part, explicitly leftist, tending to view law as protective of society's dominant interests. The major focus of CLS theorists was attacking existing legal categories and doctrines and, simultaneously, constructing new theories and doctrines that would be more sympathetic to, and reflective of, class, gender, and racial differences. For good overviews of legal realism and critical legal studies, see Steven Vago, *Law and Society,* 6th ed. (Upper Saddle River, N.J.: Prentice-Hall, 2000); Bailey Kuklin and Jeffrey W. Stempel, *Foundations of Law: A Jurisprudential Primer* (St. Paul, Minn.: West Publishing, 1994); Walter E. Murphy and C. Herman Pritchett, *Courts, Judges, and Politics,* 4th ed. (New York: McGraw-Hill, 1986); Lawrence Friedman, *A History of American Law,* 2d ed. (New York: Simon and Schuster, 1986); and David Kairys, *The Politics of Law: A Progressive Critique,* 3d ed. (New York: Basic Books, 1998).

8. The feminist approach to law is fundamentally oppositional in that it is, by definition, highly suspicious of current legal arrangements, whether they take the form of sex-based legal categories or formal gender neutrality. For instance, Suzanna Sherry and others have asserted that the U.S. Constitution, although neutral in its explicit language, strongly embodies values that are distinctly male. Feminist approaches to the law involve three main themes: (1) the difference between men and women in life experience (for example, it is impossible to treat pregnancy in a gender-neutral manner); (2) the different voice of women's moral and legal reasoning (as when a woman judge is thought to understand the balance between rights and responsibilities necessary to decide child custody cases better than a man can); and (3) the dominance of the male legal and social hierarchy (in which the vast majority of lawyers, judges, and legislators are male, who by definition give primacy to male concerns and perspectives).

For good overviews of feminist approaches to the law, see Martha Chamallas, *Introduction to Feminist Jurisprudence* (New York: Aspen Law and Business, 1999); Patricia Smith, ed., *Feminist Jurisprudence* (New York: Oxford University Press, 1994); Leslie F. Goldstein, *The Difference Debate: Feminist Jurisprudence* (Lanham, Md.: Rowman and Littlefield, 1992); Katharine R. Bartlett and Rosanne Kennedy, eds., *Feminist Legal Theory: Readings in Law and Gender* (Boulder, Colo.: Westview, 1992); Gayle Binion, "The Nature of Feminist Jurisprudence," *Judicature* (November/December 1993): 140–143; Suzanna Sherry, "Civic Virtue and the Feminine Voice in Constitutional Adjudication," *Virginia Law Review* 72, (1986): 543–591; and

Cass Sunstein, "Feminism and Legal Theory," *Harvard Law Review* 101 (1988): 826–848.

9. The theoretical underpinnings of feminist legal scholars have been supported by some recent empirical examinations. For instance, to address the question of gender bias in courtrooms, thirty-six states have created task forces to investigate the problem. Although these bodies have varied in both size and scope of responsibility, one academic review of the findings of these task forces concluded that there exists a nationwide pattern of gender bias in the areas of domestic violence, sexual assault, divorce, and behavior directed toward women in the legal profession. See Craig Hemmens, Kristin Strom, and Elicia Schlegel, "Gender Bias in the Courts: A Review" (paper presented at the Academy of Criminal Justice Sciences, Louisville, Ky., 1997), cited in David W. Neubauer, *America's Courts and the Criminal Justice System,* 6th ed. (Belmont, Calif.: Wadsworth Publishing, 1998), p. 194.

Similarly, various studies examining the experiences of women judges, lawyers, and law enforcement and correctional officers have generally concluded that informal, institutional sexism continues to inhibit women's professional prospects in the system, as well as the quality of justice available to women defendants and victims in criminal cases. For a discussion of the gendered atmosphere in the criminal justice system, see Joanne Belknap, "Women in Conflict: An Analysis of Women Correctional Officers," *Women and Criminal Justice* 2 (1991): 89–116; Elaine Martin, "Women on the Bench: A Different Voice?" *Judicature* 77 (1993): 126–128; Susan Ehrlich Martin and Nancy C. Jurik, *Doing Justice, Doing Gender: Women in Law and Criminal Justice Occupations* (Thousand Oaks, Calif.: Sage, 1996); and Clarice Feinman, *Women in the Criminal Justice System* (Westport, Conn.: Praeger, 1994).

10. Critical race theory aims to expose the legal domination of the white majority, whether through explicit racism on the part of legal professionals, a legally supported economic system that inhibits minority economic progress, or various less easily visible historical artifacts of slavery. The major collections in the field include Kimberle Crenshaw, ed., *Critical Race Theory: The Key Writings That Formed the Movement* (New York: New Press, 1996); and Richard Delgado, ed., *Critical Race Theory: The Cutting Edge* (Philadelphia, Pa.: Temple University Press, 1995). Also useful is Kuklin and Stempel, *Foundations of Law*, pp.181–182.

11. Theorists in this area would point to racially discriminatory practices in policing techniques and sentencing as evidence to support their claims. For instance, a recent report by the United Nations asserted that race remains a strong indicator in sentencing disparities of prisoners on death row in the United States, with blacks significantly more likely to be sentenced to death. In addition, a recent study of homicides in Philadelphia concluded that blacks were four times more likely than whites to receive capital sentences. The study also reported that 98 percent of prosecutors with death-penalty authority were white (see David Rovella, "Race Pervades the Death Penalty," *National Law Journal*, June 8, 1998, p. A200). This piece provides an update to the now famed "Baldus Study," which found that blacks were more likely to be sentenced to death in Georgia. The evidence from the Baldus Study was of central

importance in *McCleskey* v. *Kemp*, 481 U.S. 279 (1987), in which the U.S. Supreme Court ruled that defendants must demonstrate the existence of racial discrimination in their own specific cases and could not rely on general or institutional studies.

More recently, the issue of "racial profiling" has called the practices of law enforcement professionals into question. See Paul Zielbauer, "Racial Profiling Tops N.A.A.C.P. Agenda 25," *New York Times*, July 11, 1999, Section 1, p. 23; Thomas J. Lueck, "Bias in State Police Protested in Atlantic City," *New York Times*, July 4, 1999, Section 1, p. 22. Several studies have demonstrated that race is widely used as a tool by police officers in establishing probable cause to stop motorists. Researchers at Carnegie Mellon and Temple Universities have found black motorists 4.8 times more likely than white drivers to be pulled over on the New Jersey Turnpike. See Jim Dwyer, "N.J. Cops Hide Race Profiling," *Daily News*, February 21, 1999, p. 8. A more elaborate study of twenty-three states showed that law enforcement officials have explicitly targeted minority travelers ("An End to Racial Profiling," *St. Louis Post-Dispatch*, June 14, 1999, p. D14).

12. "The Investigation of a Videotaped Beating; Shocking Incident Leads to Worrisome Questions About L.A. Police," *Los Angeles Times*, March 7, 1991, p. B6.

13. Anna Quindlen, "Will Blacks, Whites Ever Meet Across the Divide?" *Seattle-Post Intelligencer*, May 5, 1992, p. A15; and Art Buchwald, "Solving America's Racial Puzzle: Black and White Pieces Don't Connect for Whites," *Atlanta Journal and Constitution*, May 5, 1992, p. A29.

14. "Two Facets of the Los Angeles Riots," *Nightline* transcript from May 6, 1992.

15. "Rioting Follows King Verdict," *Nightline* transcript from April 30, 1992.

16. Ben Stein, "O.J. Triggers a Racist Quake That's Off the Richter Scale," *Newsday*, June 26, 1994, p. A32.

17. Shante Morgan, "O.J. Case Haunted by Racial Undertone, Black Community Faces Wrenching Test," *San Diego Union-Tribune*, June 27, 1994, p. A1.

18. Joe Urschel, "Poll: A Nation More Divided," *USA Today*, October 9, 1995, p. 5A.

19. Richard Lacayo, "An Ugly End to It All; Escalating Racial Rhetoric, Inside and Outside the Courtroom, Dominates the Trial's Final Days and Sets the State for a Divisive Verdict," *Time*, October 9, 1995, cover and p. 30.

20. "ABC News Forum: Men, Sex, and Rape," ABC News program hosted by Peter Jennings, May 5, 1992.

21. For typical examples of this coverage, see Steve Wick, "Rape Experts Look to Future Trials," *Newsday*, December 12, 1991, p. 7; and Susannah Vesey, "Smith Trial May Educate on Date Rape; But Women May Be Scared Into Silence," *Atlanta Journal and Constitution*, December 12, 1991, p. F1.

22. This figure is based on a Lexis-Nexis search of national news sources, conducted in the summer of 1999, using the key words "Bobbitt" and "war of the sexes." This search turned up 478 sources.

23. "CNN Poll Shows Gender Split on Issues of Bobbitt Trial," CNN News transcript, reported by William Schneider, January 23, 1994.

24. See, for example, Rudy Abramson, "Has the Bobbitt Case Escalated the War Between the Sexes?" *Los Angeles Times*, November 22, 1993, p. E1.

25. Ellen Goodman, "Bobbitts Represent 'Two Pathetic People,' Not Latest War Between Sexes," *Fresno Bee*, January 14, 1994, p. B5.

26. Ibid.

27. Seth Mydans, "Menendez Trials' Collapse Discourages Both Sides," *New York Times*, January 30, 1994, p. 16.

28. "Women Say Gender War Split Jury," *The Courier Journal* (Louisville, Ky.), January 30, 1994, p. 8A; and "Menendez Jurors Split Between Men, Women," *Chicago Tribune*, January 30, 1994, p. 20C.

29. "Three Angry Men," *Primetime Live*, transcript of program that aired February 3, 1994.

30. Thomas B. Edsall and Terry M. Neal, "Response to Dismissal Has Partisan Flavor," *Washington Post*, April 2, 1999, p. A16.

31. A series of internet searches using Lexis-Nexis where the names of the cases were combined with terms such as "wealth," "privilege," and "buy justice" revealed that there have been literally thousands of articles that have referred to the role of wealth in relation to the legal system.

32. Peter J. Riga, "Jury Consultants Buy 'Justice' for the Rich," *USA Today*, October 13, 1994, p. 12A.

33. For another example, see Martin Dyckman, "Justice for Sale," *St. Petersburg Times*, October 5, 1995, p. 17A.

34. Jean Sonmor, "JonBenet's Quiet City in Torment; Child Beauty Queen's Brutal Murder Cast a Dark Shadow Over Her Parents," *Toronto Sun*, October 12, 1997, p. 36.

35. Charlie Brennan, "The Ramsey Team: Parents of Slain Girl Have at Least 9 Professionals Working on Case," *Denver Rocky Mountain News*, January 19, 1997, p. 20A.

36. For one account of how the president may have received special treatment, see William Glaberson, "Testing of a President: Legal Issues; In Truth, Even Those Little Lies Are Prosecuted Once in a While," *New York Times*, November 17, 1998, p. A1.

37. "Justice for Sale: Why the Rich Get Away with Murder," *Rivera Live*, transcript from August 14, 1998.

38. See Appendix B for a description of the sample.

39. The Pew Research Center for the People and the Press, "Trust and Citizen Engagement in Metropolitan Philadelphia: A Case Study." The findings in this study were based on a survey of 2,517 Philadelphia residents, conducted in November and December of 1996.

40. The gender gap has been the subject of extensive academic inquiry. For a brief overview, see M. Margaret Conway, Gertrude A. Steuernagel, and David W. Ahern, *Women and Political Participation* (Washington, D.C.: Congressional Quarterly Press, 1997), pp. 33–34, 138–139.

41. For a list of possible reasons for black support of Clinton during the impeachment proceedings, see Julianne Malveaux, "Why Blacks Stand by Clinton," *USA Today*, August 21, 1998, p. 17A.

42. Several studies of men and women public officials and studies of the gender gap have found that women place a higher priority on children's issues. For instance, see Sue Thomas, *How Women Legislate* (New York: Oxford University Press, 1994).

43. As mentioned in Chapter 4, William Haltom refers to a process of "dramatized normality," which might be particularly strong for younger citizens who have grown up seeing abnormal cases presented as if they were normal; *Reporting on the Courts: How the Mass Media Cover Judicial Actions* (Chicago: Nelson-Hall, 1998), p. 186.

44. For instance, see Michael Gartner, "O.J. Circus? Blame TV," *USA Today*, October 3, 1995, p. 11A; Alexandra Marks, "O.J. Simpson Case Puts Courtroom Cameras On Trial," *Christian Science Monitor*, September 19, 1995, p. 10; Joanne Ostrow, "Camera Equally Beholds Circus, Serious Media Fulfill Best and Worst Expectations," *Denver Post*, October 4, 1995, p. A14; and David Shaw, "The Simpson Legacy; Obsession: Did the Media Overfeed a Starving Public?" *Los Angeles Times*, October 9, 1995, p. S4.

45. *The Gallup Poll Monthly*, October 1995, p. 5.

46. A good example of this type of analysis is found in Christo Lassiter, "The O.J. Simpson Verdict: A Lesson in Black and White," *Michigan Journal of Race and Law* (winter 1996), online without pagination.

47. "O.J. Defense Set to Pounce on Fuhrman: Calls Tapes' Racial Slur 'Chilling,'" *Arizona Republic*, August 13, 1995, p. A2.

48. See the Television News Archive, maintained by Vanderbilt University, available online at http://tvnews.vanderbilt.edu/index.html.

49. The extensive polls conducted by Gallup after the trial, beyond those questions mentioned in Table 5.6, consistently revealed that the trial did not significantly change the way blacks felt about whites or whites felt about blacks. The only attitudes that appeared to be altered in terms of race were attitudes toward the justice system itself. See *The Gallup Poll Monthly*, all months during 1995.

50. For further discussion of these dynamics, see Helen Boritch, "Gender and Criminal Court Outcomes: An Historical Analysis," *Criminology* 30 (1992): 293–325; and Eve S. Buzawa, *Women As Victims* (Thousand Oaks, Calif.: Sage, 1996).

51. Unlike poll questions about race and the O. J. Simpson trial, no polling organization has attempted to measure whether general indicators about gender roles and gender equality have been changed as a result of the tabloid justice cases. There are questions frequently asked about support for women political candidates and the proper role of women in the family structure, but there is no evidence that any of these measures have changed as a result of the tabloid cases that involved gender issues. For a summary of some of this polling, see Nancy E. McGlen and Karen O'Connor, *Women, Politics, and American Society* (New York: Prentice-Hall, 1998), chapter 4.

52. Perceptions that the poor do not fare as well in the criminal justice system have been supported by compelling evidence that suggests that the public may be correct in viewing the system as favoring the elite. See Jeffrey Reiman, *The Rich Get Richer and the Poor Get Prison: Ideology, Class, and Criminal Justice* (Boston: Allyn and Bacon, 1995). For a brief review of the literature

assessing treatment of defendants by economic class, see Neubauer, *America's Courts and the Criminal Justice System*, pp. 408–409.

53. For instance, the Ramsey investigation generated a great deal of discussion about the wealth of defendants. See Karen Auge, "Boulder Readies for Grand Jury Media Scrutiny: County Panel May Be Charged with Hearing JonBenet Case," *Denver Post*, April 22, 1998, p. B1. The role of wealth in the Ramsey case itself was even deemed worthy of an editorial in the *New York Times*, "New Look at an Unsolved Murder," editorial desk, March 14, 1998, p. A16.

54. Woodward's defense fund has variously been reported to have reached an amount somewhere between $300,000 and $500,000. See Patricia Nealon, "Eappens, Woodward Settle Suit," *Boston Globe*, January 30, 1999, p. A1.

PART 3

Conclusion

6

Is There Any Escape from Tabloid Justice?

The Simpson trial was the media's Chernobyl; we [in the media] headed over the edge of a precipice and I am not sure that there is any going back.

—Robert Kovacik, news anchor,
KCOP Channel 13, Los Angeles[1]

The preceding quotation is compelling, in that the Simpson case clearly stands as the defining moment in the modern mass media era, at least with regard to the criminal justice system. But if the media indeed "headed over the edge of a precipice" with the Simpson story, they were speeding out of control toward the cliff at least four years prior to that trial. In fact, the Simpson case was in some ways an inevitable explosion of numerous volatile trends that had begun several years prior to the violent murders in Brentwood.

In the past dozen or so years, Americans have witnessed an exponential increase in the mass media's coverage of crime, criminal trials, and criminal investigations. Stories about crime now regularly surpass the media attention paid to issues such as Medicare, social security, welfare reform, environmental protection, public education, and campaign finance reform, even though the incidence of violent crime has been dropping nationwide since the early 1990s. Subsequently, citizens are now exposed to the inner workings of the criminal justice system in a way that would have been nearly unimaginable just twenty years ago. Evidence of exposure to these proceedings abounds, as polls indicate that Americans are more familiar with JonBenet Ramsey, Monica Lewinsky, Rodney King, and of course O.J. Simpson than with most of the highest-ranking officials in the U.S. government. This is particularly striking given that the judicial system has historically been by far the least-covered branch of government at all levels of the political system.[2]

Traditionally, many journalists and scholars have argued that there would be a number of benefits to opening the judicial system up to more scrutiny by the electronic media. Indeed, numerous contemporary commentators, such as Court TV founder Steven Brill and Harvard law professor Alan Dershowitz, continue to assert that the increasing media coverage of the courts is highly desirable and contributes to a more democratic society.[3] One of the predicted benefits is said to be an increase in civic education, as citizens supposedly become more knowledgeable about the realities of the judicial system. This is thought, in turn, to improve the behavior of juries and to prompt citizens to participate more willingly in other public proceedings. Second, casting a more public eye on the courts is believed to make the professional actors within the system more accountable. There are fewer opportunities for due process violations of all kinds, for corruption, deal making, railroading of uneducated defendants, and jury tampering. In short, increasing media access to the courts would force them to conform more closely to the ideals of the Bill of Rights and less to the imperatives of bureaucratic efficiency and political expediency. And finally, it was thought that because of the greater degree of both public knowledge and accountability that would be present, public confidence in the system would increase as well. Overall, it is held that the legitimacy of the criminal justice system would be greatly enhanced if citizens understood the system better and could see that officials exercised their power in fair, just, and efficient ways.

For years, the preceding discussion focused largely on the issue of cameras in the courtroom. Nevertheless, the argument holds that these same benefits might result from a generally heightened attention to the criminal justice system on the part of all the mass media. In fact, much of the increased attention to criminal trial proceedings in the media is a result of courtroom cameras providing dramatic footage that can be used in newscasts. Would the trials of William Kennedy Smith, the Menendez brothers, O.J. Simpson, or Louise Woodward have been such media sensations without live and constant television coverage? Cameras in the courtroom have led to more exposure to the system for all citizens. Thus, we are left with the question of whether the predicted benefits have come to pass.

In a sense, this is the question that led us to undertake our study. More specifically, we have sought to answer two closely related questions. First, how have high-profile legal proceedings been covered in the present media culture? That is, have the amount and style of criminal justice news fundamentally changed in the 1990s? And second, what impact has this coverage had on the public's knowledge of and attitudes about the justice system? In other words, have the previously outlined civic benefits, which are held to accompany an increased exposure of the system, actually been realized? In the preceding five chapters, we have presented a wealth of both primary and secondary data that now allow us to address these questions with some level of confidence.

THE TABLOID JUSTICE ERA: A BRIEF SUMMARY OF FINDINGS

Ultimately, there are five broad findings that emerge in this analysis that help us to address the preceding questions. First, the mass media's increasing focus on criminal trials and investigations, which we have documented in Chapters 2 and 3, has largely been motivated by commercial interests. As news organizations have been forced to compete ever more fiercely for an audience, criminal cases (and especially trials) have become "commodified" much like other dramatic television shows. The use of trials as the subject for intensive news investigation has perhaps changed the standards of newsworthiness that are employed by media outlets. Further, the fact that it is television that exposes most Americans to these events holds enormous importance for how citizens develop attitudes about law, crime, and politics. Television possesses its own set of imperatives, which encourage the repetitive showing of striking images and the presentation of news in short and dramatic segments. Neither of these television-specific attributes leads to the presentation of legal proceedings in a manner that is conducive to meaningful civic education.[4]

A second crucial finding is that the mainstream media are increasingly moving in the direction of the tabloid press. We have termed this, as regards the coverage of criminal trials and investigations, "tabloid justice" coverage. This phrase refers to the adoption by the mainstream press of a mode of coverage that has previously been the exclusive domain of the tabloid newspapers and magazines and is related to what Neal Gabler has called the culture of "celebrity journalism."[5] This change is, once again, mostly likely the result of a more competitive news environment that forces the old bastions of journalism to turn to topics that they normally would have ignored. The importance of this transformation is that many news outlets take their cues from the national news organizations. When the most respected venues of both broadcast and print journalism embrace tabloid trials as a legitimate subject for extensive inquiry, then there is nothing that prevents complete cultural saturation by these stories.

Third, it has become clear that a critical element in promoting the environment of tabloid justice is the role played by new and emerging media such as cable television, the Internet, and talk radio. The round-the-clock drumbeat of cable news stations serves to keep tabloid justice cases in the forefront of the news environment. There are several all-news stations that continually cover these stories, suggesting to the public that they are very important news events. And although the audiences for these stations are relatively small, they include many important public opinion makers and other journalists. Further, the wealth of information on the Internet has also served to promote the tabloid justice era. The new media outlets have in many ways made the entire media market more diverse, which has encouraged some of the commercial competitiveness that is clearly degrading the quality of news coverage.

The preceding developments—an enormous growth in the media's focus on criminal cases and trials, a more competitive commercial environment due to the proliferation of new and emerging media forms, and the subsequent "tabloidization" of criminal justice coverage—have actually contributed to an unprecedented level of public exposure to the workings of the criminal system. However, contrary to the idealized prediction that greater public exposure would bring about the range of public benefits outlined previously, we believe that citizens are simply being more misinformed. The tabloid style of contemporary criminal justice coverage has actually resulted in less knowledge of other important political issues and more distrust in the system as a whole. In short, more coverage has translated into less democratic legitimacy.

Accordingly, our fourth central finding is that although public knowledge of and familiarity with high-profile trial proceedings have increased, faith in the system has actually decreased. Although causation is extremely difficult to establish, the data from our national survey repeatedly point toward negative effects caused by the current mode of mass media coverage of the justice system. These data permit us to conclude that, given the extremely high degree of public familiarity with these cases, and the corresponding apathy and lack of media coverage of arguably more important political and social topics, this anticipated negative effect has, indeed, come to pass. Further, we have described the essentially misleading nature of tabloid justice–style coverage. Here again, it seems clear that when citizens are fed a steady diet of legal information emanating from highly anomalous trials and investigations, they receive a distorted picture that does not comport with the everyday realities of the criminal justice system. As we have written previously, an important opportunity for civic education is squandered by such dynamics. Our most important finding in this regard concerns the public's loss of faith in the U.S. criminal justice system generally, as well as in many of the specific components within that system.

In addition, we found that people's attitudes about the system indicated a disconcerting lack of faith on the part of citizens that they themselves would be treated fairly by the system. As a result of what citizens have learned from the coverage of these tabloid justice trials, roughly 40 percent of our respondents claimed that they had less confidence that the laws would protect their rights, that prosecutors would treat them fairly, and that police would be respectful of their privacy and due process protections. Thus, we strongly believe that the evidence we provide supports the notion that tabloid-style coverage of the law does work to reduce people's faith in the criminal justice system. And as we repeatedly point out, the public may have legitimate reasons to distrust the system. Our point is simply that it is unfortunate that the citizenry is basing its attitudes largely on the distorted presentation of highly anomalous legal events.

Fifth, we noted some additional interesting attitudinal patterns based on our respondents' race and gender. Americans of all stripes have very low levels of trust in the criminal justice system. In fact, one of our most striking findings is the basic lack of faith that all citizens hold in the police, the first line of contact with the legal system for most people. Still, we found that racial differences are by far the most pronounced indicators of attitudes toward the justice system. Not only do blacks and whites hold significantly different views about the criminal justice system in general, but they also react to our selected criminal cases in different ways. African Americans have lower levels of confidence in juries, judges, and the police. Clearly, this poses serious challenges for creating a criminal justice system that is perceived as legitimate, fair, and equitable.

The disparate views of men and women are considerably less pronounced than those of blacks and whites. The findings we reported point to a small but significant and consistent gender gap in how citizens assess the legal system, both generally and in response to these particular cases. But although men's and women's reactions to the cases are slightly different in the aggregate, we are unable to conclusively state that the mass media coverage of the cases has either caused or intensified this gender gap. Finally, we should briefly note that Americans of all economic levels strongly believe that the justice system favors the wealthy over those with fewer financial resources. Our survey suggests that such a view has increased as a result of what citizens have learned by following the tabloid justice trials of the 1990s.

Thus, tabloid justice–style media coverage, which often sensationalizes the sexual, racial, and economic dynamics of criminal cases, has served to reinforce existing public attitudes about these social cleavages. Although our data do not allow us to assert that this coverage has caused or even necessarily worsened such divisions, it is clear that it has solidified preexisting attitudes, often based on the mistaken impression that the tabloid cases represent the real everyday workings of the criminal justice system.

The preceding findings force us to conclude that the scholars who see great social benefits in greater public exposure to the judicial process have been mistaken. They did not anticipate the evolution of the mass media that occurred in the 1990s. They have failed to take into account the changed nature of crime coverage and have thus underestimated the power of the "tabloid imperative" in the presentation of such stories. We do not condemn the increase in coverage itself, but we lament the detrimental consequences of the tabloidization of that coverage.

A TIME OF TABLOID JUSTICE: THE BROADER IMPLICATIONS

Our key findings and central argument are by now quite clear, but the data we have presented raise several broader concerns. Most notably, this study exposes the dangerous nexus between the agenda-setting function of the media and the commodification of criminal trials and investigations. Media scholars such as Shanto Iyengar and Donald Kinder have convincingly shown that news organizations set the public agenda, in effect dictating what the news is.[6] Thus, it is disingenuous for journalists to claim that their coverage of criminal justice is merely driven by consumer demand. The endless drumbeat, graphic nature, and purposeful controversy of such coverage give tabloid trials a public prominence that most of them do not deserve. Such coverage appears to be driven by simple commercial imperatives rather than true newsworthiness, which lead to the serialization, personalization, and commodification of crime stories.

As we have noted, criminal trials readily lend themselves to *serialization*, or the presentation of news as a series of short dramatic events (involving a relatively small number of recurring characters with specific roles) over an extended period of time. Further, we have noted the *personification* of the presentation of events through a focus on the emotional, personal, and human aspects of a story, which are often presented at the expense of context, background, structure, and analysis. This is the manner in which television presents virtually all news, but it is particularly problematic when this style of coverage is used to present images of the judicial process. After all, in theory the law embodies objectivity, procedure, stability, predictability, and equality. The emotional states, biases, and personal backgrounds of the participants are not intended to influence the outcome of criminal investigations and trials. All of these media strategies embody attempts to draw in viewers and increase ratings shares with the hope of maximizing profit. Most media organizations have abandoned their idealized roles as public watchdogs and the signifiers of important events in favor of the pursuit of commercial success. We may ultimately end up with a world of legal news in which the agenda is driven not by the presence of important issues or social phenomena but by marketability. Again, we are not so naïve as to believe that such imperatives are anything new. Rather, as we attempted to show in Chapters 2 and 3, the changing dynamics of the news business, including the emergence of cable television and the Internet, have exponentially increased the ever-present pressure for a share of the finite audience.

Another broader concern that emerges from our study is the need to better understand the role of the mass public in encouraging the tabloid justice environment. In this analysis we have focused on the tactics of the media, and often condemned them, but certainly the public's role in driving tabloid coverage is crucial. However, the public's interest in tabloid cases is often paradoxical. In some surveys, citizens claim that they have no interest in these trials and investigations and that they believe the press gives them far too much attention. Yet, as we have demonstrated in Chapters 2 and 3, the ratings of many newscasts have significantly increased at key points in particular trials. Additionally, the respondents in our survey had a high level of familiarity with these cases, even those involving events that had occurred several years prior to our poll. This seems to undermine the notion that there is no public demand for tabloid justice information. And of course, the media themselves point to the aforementioned ratings increases as a justification for pursuing an increasing number of tabloid justice stories.

And yet, recalling our previous discussions of the agenda-setting function of the press, it is still possible that the internal imperatives of the media lead them to decide unilaterally to cover these stories rather than others that could plausibly be deemed more newsworthy. We seem left with an incomprehensible and vicious cycle similar to that identified by Robert Entman in his excellent book *Democracy Without Citizens*. Entman asserts that we cannot expect the media to produce and market high-quality and thoughtful journalism to a citizenry that is intellectually ill equipped to comprehend and digest it and is not particularly interested anyway.[7] In the end, it is clear that much more scholarly inquiry is needed if we are to determine the true public role in encouraging the tabloid trends in the mass media.

A third issue arising from our findings is whether there are any *benefits* to be derived from the type of coverage we have described. Some observers might conclude that tabloid-style coverage, which we have deplored throughout our book, has actually brought citizens together in recognizing the need for deep reform of criminal justice in the United States. We would respond that this is not the case, as the presentation of many potentially important social issues contained in at least a few of these stories tends to be superficial and based on a selection of highly anomalous cases that do not represent the everyday workings of the system. In other words, while this coverage does draw attention to many critical issues of race, sex, class, due process, and substantive justice, its style—that is, its focus on *entertainment*—undermines the possibility of restrained, measured, and empirically based policy discussion.

The media now simply shift the same "machinery" and approach among their coverage of stories as disparate in nature as the Columbine High School shootings in Colorado, the murder of JonBenet Ramsey, the deaths of Princess Diana and John F. Kennedy, Jr., the trial of Jack Kevorkian, and the impeachment of the president of the United States.[8] When the same panels of pundits and reporters discuss such stories in a nearly identical fashion, with little indication as to the relative importance of each and with little context or institutional background, the era of tabloid justice can be seen to seriously undermine the dispassionate discussion required to develop meaningful and workable public-policy solutions to the many intractable criminal justice problems that virtually everyone agrees exist.

Finally, one is left to consider whether there are any broad reforms that could curtail the negative effects of the tabloid justice era. It is not immediately clear that legal or structural reforms emanating from the federal government could counteract any of the trends described in our book. Given the First Amendment and the United States' historic commitment to a free press, most explicit restraints on the mass media would shoulder a heavy burden of constitutional suspicion. Further, the Internet has not even begun to be fully understood in terms of its political, legal, commercial ramifications.

Thus, attempts by Congress, such as the ill-fated Communications Decency Act of 1998, are at best politically problematic and at worse may exacerbate the problems they are intended to address. In the wake of a number these trials, there have been calls to ban cameras in the courtroom and to prevent lawyers and other trial participants from speaking with the media. These types of reforms are not likely to result in any significant change in the public's understanding of the criminal justice system. Again, it is not the *amount* of coverage that is harmful but rather the style in which these stories are presented. As long as the media pay as much attention to Marcia Clark's hairstyle or Monica's breakfast as they do the finer points of evidence, the proper role of judges, and the nature of due process, the few structural reforms that have been proposed will likely be futile.

The only potentially effective long-term reform or solutions may lie in the realms of civic education, a greater public awareness of the problem, and a new sense of propriety on the part of both the citizenry and the media. But given the phenomenal popularity of *Jerry Springer*, the *World Wrestling Federation*, and *South Park*, a renewed sense of public modesty seems unlikely. For the time being, the U.S. public seems woefully disconnected to its own civic life. That said, the more pressing concern might be how the media can continue to top themselves. The Menendez brothers trial may have been interesting and provocative in the early 1990s, but now that the network evening news programs have discussed the president's semen in prime time, would the mere saga of two rich boys killing their parents have the same level of public appeal?

Any reform efforts that are aimed simply at regulating media behavior or restricting press access to the courts and to police activities undoubtedly would have little impact on the tabloid justice environment. Many of the dynamics of the situation are far more complicated than the irresponsible conduct of the news media. Popular culture, commercial imperatives, and a complacent and unengaged citizenry have all converged to produce this set of problems. As news anchor Robert Kovacik's statement that opened this chapter suggests, it is difficult to imagine how we can move toward a relationship between the public and the mass media that is characterized by truly serious news reporting and thoughtful analysis by citizens. In the meantime, we will likely just collectively sit back and await the next "trial of the century."

▓ NOTES

1. Richard Fox interview with Robert Kovacik, January 12, 1999.

2. See Doris Graber, *Mass Media and American Politics,* 5th edition (Washington, D.C.: Congressional Quarterly Press, 1997), pp. 306–313.

3. Brill's comments are cited in "The Simpson Legacy," *Los Angeles Times Report,* October 8, 1995, p. F5. Also see Alan M. Dershowitz, *Reasonable Doubts: The Criminal Justice System and the O.J. Simpson Case* (New York: Simon and Schuster, 1997).

4. In support of this argument, see Barry Brummett, "Mediating the Laws: Popular Trials and the Mass Media," in Robert Hariman, ed., *Popular Trials: Rhetoric, Mass Media, and the Law* (Tuscaloosa: University of Alabama Press, 1990), pp. 179–193.

5. Neil Gabler, "The People's Prince: What JFK Jr. Meant to America," *The New Republic,* August 9, 1999, pp. 13–15.

6. Shanto Iyengar and Donald Kinder, *News That Matters* (Chicago: University of Chicago Press, 1987).

7. Robert Entman, *Democracy Without Citizens: Media and the Decay of American Politics* (New York: Oxford University Press, 1989), chapter 7.

8. Gabler, "The People's Prince," pp. 13–15.

Appendix A

This appendix identifies the exact search terms employed to produce the results in Tables 2.3, 2.5, 2.6, 2.9, and 3.8. The searches were originally conducted in November 1998, and they were reconfirmed on the specific dates listed below for each table. Results may vary slightly for Lexis-Nexis searches, as this search engine alters publication accessibility. Also, general searches using Yahoo! and Netscape, as in Table 3.8, will vary, as the presence of Internet websites often changes. Further, Internet searches of almost any type can be imperfect, as they may underestimate the number of references for a particular topic. For instance, an article discussing the O.J. Simpson trial might not employ the usage of "O.J." and therefore would not be included in our total figures in Table 2.3. For each of the searches listed below, we experimented extensively to determine which search phrases produced the most comprehensive findings.

SEARCH TERMS BY TABLE

Table 2.3

Source: Lexis-Nexis. Separate searches were conducted using the categories "major newspapers" and "all magazines" for all of the following terms. For magazines, only articles in *Time, Newsweek,* and *U.S. News and World Report* were counted.

Date Searched	Search Term(s)
7/19/99	menendez and brothers
7/19/99	kennedy and smith
7/19/99	rodney and king
6/23/99	bobbitt
6/23/99	paula and jones
6/23/99	o.j. and simpson
7/19/99	jonbenet and ramsey
6/23/99	louise and woodward
7/19/99	monica and lewinsky

▓   Table 2.5

Source: Vanderbilt University TV News Archives, which may be accessed online at http://tvnews.vanderbilt.edu/index.html. Searches on this website must be conducted by year. Searches for O.J. Simpson and the presidential scandal utilized several search instructions to more fully identify the types of trial coverage in that year. For each year, all trial segments were examined to make certain they were legal trials. Story segments that employed the term "trial" but were not about legal cases or issues were dropped from the analysis (see also Chapter 2, note 51).

Year(s) Searched	Search Term(s)
1968 through 1993	trial
1994	trial not simpson; simpson and murder
1995	trial
1996	trial
1997	trial
1998	paula and jones not trial; lewinsky not trial; trial

▓   Table 2.6

Source: Vanderbilt University TV News Archives.

Years Searched	Search Terms
1969 through 1971	manson and cbs; manson and nbc; manson and abc
1980 through 1985	bulow and cbs; bulow and nbc; bulow and abc
1994 through 1997	simpson and murder and nbc; simpson and murder and cbs; simpson and murder and abc not carole

For Tables 2.5 and 2.6, we were careful not to include articles that mentioned ABC news anchor Carole Simpson as opposed to O.J. Simpson.

■ Table 2.8

Source: Vanderbilt University TV News Archives. All searches were conducted for the year 1997. Each search phrase was conducted for each of the three networks. Thus, each search used the primary search phrase along with "and abc," "and cbs," and "and nbc."

Year Searched	Search Terms
1997	simpson and civil; jonbenet; cunanan [for Versace murder investigation]; paula and jones; louise and woodward; cosby and murder; marv and albert; timothy and mcveigh; death and princess and diana; ups and strike; septuplets; heaven's and gate; hamburger and recall; china; bosnia; yeltsin; un [United Nations] and inspectors and iraq; medicare; abortion; affirmative and action; welfare; health and care; social and security; hmo

■ Table 3.8

Source: Yahoo! and Netscape. These search engines can be accessed at Yahoo.com and Netscape.com. Each search term was employed for each search engine.

Date Searched	Search Terms
November 1998	marv albert; menendez brothers; lorena and john bobbitt; o.j. simpson; louise woodward; jonbenet ramsey; monica lewinsky; paula jones

Appendix B

METHODS AND DEMOGRAPHICS OF THE SAMPLE

The national poll described in Chapters 4 and 5 was conducted between April 1 and June 15, 1999. All respondents were contacted by phone and were selected through a random sampling of listed residential telephone numbers for the United States. We recognize that a sample of listed numbers is not as reliable as a telephone poll conducted through random digit dialing. Thus, in our sample we did not have access to people without listed phone numbers. This may have excluded certain types of occupations that are less likely to list their home phone numbers (such as doctors or police officers). Nevertheless, we note that there is no research that suggests random digit dialing produces drastically different poll results, particularly for a general audience survey such as that used in this book. We chose to utilize only listed numbers primarily as a cost-saving measure, as this increases the chances of calling a willing respondent and thus reduces the overall number of calls necessary. We conducted our survey on a somewhat limited budget.

The poll was administered by the Brentwood Group, a national polling firm located in Albany, New York. This firm's callers are professionally trained in carrying out survey research. They were also given a set of instructions on how to handle respondents who asked questions concerning the survey items so as to ensure consistent interaction with those in our survey pool. The total sample for the poll was 1,003. What follows is a brief listing of the general demographics of the sample, which enables our pool of respondents to be compared with other national samples. The sample size for each category of demographic characteristics does not add up to 1,003, as a number of the respondents (as is often the case) were unwilling to answer questions about race, education, and income.

Demographic Group	Sample Size	% of Responses
Race		
White	832	83
Black	87	9
Hispanic	21	2
Asian	6	1
Other	16	2
Refused to state	41	4
Gender		
Men	448	45
Women	555	55
Age		
18–29	115	12
30–39	193	19
40–49	221	22
50–59	170	17
Over 60	293	29
Refused to state	7	1
Education Level		
Did not complete high school	47	5
High school diploma	270	27
Some college	354	35
Four-year college grad	317	32
Refused to state	15	2
Household Income		
0–$14,999	79	8
$15,000–29,999	180	18
$30,000–49,999	275	27
$50,000–74,999	204	20
Over $75,000	145	15
Refused to state	120	12
Party Identification		
Democrats, including "leaners"	412	41
Republicans, including "leaners"	366	37
Independents	132	13
Other/refused to state	93	9

ASSESSING THE QUALITY OF THE SAMPLE

In many ways, the sample does a good job of mirroring the U.S. public, although there are a few areas where the sample does not quite capture an accurate demographic breakdown. The sample slightly over-represents women, older citizens, more highly educated citizens, and white citizens. Overall, although our sample slightly over- and under-estimates some demographic groups, we believe it is adequate for evaluating public attitudes toward the tabloid justice trials. As is shown in the data presented in Chapters 4 and 5, for a number of the demographic factors, there is no significant impact on views of the justice system. Further, for the variables we wanted to make comparisons with, the sample sizes were sufficient.

VARIATIONS IN THE SURVEY INSTRUMENT

There were a total of four versions of the survey instrument used. We moved some of the questions around to determine whether topic order altered how respondents answered. For half of the surveys (two of the versions), we put the general questions about confidence in the criminal justice system and other various parts of the system at the beginning. For the other half, we placed these questions toward the end. This was done in an attempt to determine if first recalling the specific cases made the respondents think of the criminal justice system more negatively. The results of this experiment were discussed in Chapter 4.

In another experiment, we placed the questions about the O.J. Simpson case at the beginning of half of the surveys. In the other half of the surveys, Simpson was the final case that we asked about. We moved this case around to see if reaction to the Simpson events would in any way change how people responded to the other questions. We found that the placement of the Simpson questions had no influence on how the respondents answered the questions, and we thus ignored this aspect of the survey in presenting the results. What follows is one version of the questionnaire that we used.

Tabloid Justice Survey (referred to as the "citizen survey")

Hello, may I speak to _____? Hello, I am _____. I am working on a national poll being conducted by the Brentwood Group for Union College, and I would like very much to get your opinion on a number of current events from the past few years. We are surveying a large number of Americans to assess their attitudes about various issues that have been in the news. Your opinions are very important to us and the survey will take about eight to ten minutes. Is that okay?

Question 1: How much confidence do you have in the following aspects of the criminal justice system in the United States? Would you say you have complete confidence, a great deal of confidence, some confidence, little confidence, or no confidence at all in:

	Complete	A Great Deal	Some	Little	No
The police	1	2	3	4	5
The jury system	1	2	3	4	5
Judges	1	2	3	4	5
Defense attorneys	1	2	3	4	5
Prosecuting attorneys	1	2	3	4	5

When you learn of the verdict in a criminal case, whether in the news or through talking with friends and family, how confident are you that the criminal justice system made the correct verdict?

Complete confidence	A great deal of confidence	Some confidence	Little confidence	No confidence

Question 2: How familiar are you with the facts surrounding the following criminal cases? Would you say you are very familiar, somewhat familiar, somewhat unfamiliar, or very unfamiliar with:

	Very Familiar	Somewhat Familiar	Somewhat Unfamiliar	Very Unfamiliar
The trial of Louise Woodward (also called the nanny trial)	1	2	3	4
The criminal trial of O.J. Simpson	1	2	3	4
The investigation into the death of JonBenet Ramsey	1	2	3	4
The first trial of the officers who beat Rodney King	1	2	3	4

The trials of the Menendez brothers	1	2	3	4
The rape trial of William Kennedy Smith	1	2	3	4
The Senate impeachment trial of Bill Clinton	1	2	3	4

Question 3: First, I would like you to think about the criminal trial of O.J. Simpson. Does the O.J. Simpson trial make you feel more, the same, or less confident in the criminal justice system, generally?

	More	Same	Less	Don't Know the Trial
The criminal justice system	1	2	3	4
As a result of this trial are you more, the same, or less confident:				
In the work of police	1	2	3	4
In the jury system	1	2	3	4
In the work of judges	1	2	3	4
That the criminal justice system treats women fairly	1	2	3	4
That the criminal justice system treats African Americans fairly	1	2	3	4
That the criminal justice system treats people fairly regardless of whether they are rich or poor	1	2	3	4

Question 4: Now I would like you to think about the Louise Woodward trial, also known as the "nanny trial" or the "au pair trial." Does the Louise Woodward trial make you feel more, the same, or less confident in the criminal justice system, generally?

	More	Same	Less	Don't Know the Trial
The criminal justice system	1	2	3	4
As a result of this trial, are you more, the same, or less confident:				
In the jury system	1	2	3	4
In the work of judges	1	2	3	4

That the criminal justice system treats women fairly	1	2	3	4
That the criminal justice system treats people fairly regardless of whether they are rich or poor	1	2	3	4

Question 5: Now I would like you to think about the investigation into the murder of JonBenet Ramsey. Does the JonBenet Ramsey murder investigation make you feel more, the same, or less confident in the criminal justice system, generally?

	More	Same	Less	Don't Know the Trial
The criminal justice system	1	2	3	4
As a result of this investigation, are you more, the same, or less confident:				
In the work of police	1	2	3	4
That the criminal justice system treats people fairly regardless of whether they are rich or poor	1	2	3	4

Question 6: Now I would like you to think about the rape trial of William Kennedy Smith. Does the William Kennedy Smith trial make you feel more, the same, or less confident in the criminal justice system, generally?

	More	Same	Less	Don't Know the Trial
The criminal justice system	1	2	3	4
As a result of this trial, are you more, the same, or less confident:				
In the jury system	1	2	3	4
In the work of judges	1	2	3	4
That the criminal justice system treats women fairly	1	2	3	4
That the criminal justice system treats people fairly regardless of whether they are rich or poor	1	2	3	4

Question 7: Now I would like you to think about the trials of Erik and Lyle Menendez. Do the trials of the Menendez brothers make you feel more, the same, or less confident in the criminal justice system?

	More	Same	Less	Don't Know the Trials
The criminal justice system	1	2	3	4
As a result of these trials, are you more, the same, or less confident:				
In the work of police	1	2	3	4
In the jury system	1	2	3	4
In the work of judges	1	2	3	4
That the criminal justice system treats people fairly regardless of whether they are rich or poor	1	2	3	4

Question 8: Now I would like you to think about the first trial of the officers charged with beating Rodney King. Does the Rodney King trial make you feel more, the same, or less confident in the criminal justice system?

	More	Same	Less	Don't Know the trial
The criminal justice system	1	2	3	4
As a result of this trial are you more, the same, or less confident:				
In the work of police	1	2	3	4
In the jury system	1	2	3	4
In the work of judges	1	2	3	4
That the criminal justice system treats African Americans fairly	1	2	3	4
That the criminal justice system treats people fairly regardless of whether they are rich or poor	1	2	3	4

Question 9: Now I would like you to think about the Senate impeachment trial of Bill Clinton. Does the Senate trial of Bill Clinton make you feel more, the same, or less confident in the criminal justice system?

	More	Same	Less	Don't Know the Trial
The criminal justice system	1	2	3	4
As a result of this trial, are you more, the same, or less confident:				
In the work of prosecutors	1	2	3	4
That the criminal justice system treats women fairly	1	2	3	4
That the criminal justice system treats African Americans fairly	1	2	3	4
That the criminal justice system treats people fairly regardless of whether they are rich or poor	1	2	3	4

We have only a few questions left and the survey will be completed. Thank you for your patience.

Question 10: As a result of the criminal trials and investigations that we have been discussing, we are interested in knowing whether these cases have changed your personal feelings about the criminal justice system.

    a. As a result of these cases, how interested are you in serving as a juror?

        More interested   Less interested   No change in interest

    b. As a result of these cases, how knowledgeable do you feel about the criminal justice system?

   More knowledgeable   Less knowledgeable   No change in knowledge

    c. As a result of these cases, are you more or less confident that you or a family member would be treated fairly by the police if arrested as a suspect for a crime?

        More confident   Less confident   No change in confidence

    d. As a result of these cases, are you more or less confident that you or a family member would be treated fairly by prosecuting attorneys if arrested as a suspect for a crime?

        More confident   Less confident   No change in confidence

e. As a result of these cases, are you more or less confident that you or a family member would be treated fairly by a judge if you had been arrested and were standing trial for a crime?

    More confident   Less confident   No change in confidence

f. As a result of these cases, are you more or less confident that you or a family member would be treated fairly by a jury if you had been arrested and were standing trial for a crime?

    More confident   Less confident   No change in confidence

g. As a result of these cases, are you more or less confident that the laws surrounding the criminal justice system would protect your rights?

    More confident   Less confident   No change in confidence

---

Question 11: News habits. How often do you:

	Every Day	Several Times a Week	Several Times a Month	Rarely	Never
Read the newspaper?	1	2	3	4	5
Watch world/national news programs?	1	2	3	4	5
Watch the channel MSNBC?	1	2	3	4	5
Watch the Fox News Channel?	1	2	3	4	5
Watch the channel CNN?	1	2	3	4	5
Watch the channel Court TV?	1	2	3	4	5

Question 12: Background questions.

a. Sex: interviewee identification   ___ Male   ___ Female
b. State of respondent   ____   ___Rural/urban
c. Would you tell me your age bracket?   18–24   25–29   30–39   40–49   50–59   Over 60
d. What race do you consider yourself? RECORD VERBATIM

e. What is your religious preference? Is it Protestant, Catholic, Jewish, some other religion, or no religion?

___Protestant   ___Catholic   ___Jewish
___Other   ___None

f. Which of the following describes your own educational background?

___ Did not complete high school
___ High school graduate
___ Some college
___ Graduate of a two-year college
___ Graduate of a four-year college
___ Attended postgraduate or professional school but did not graduate
___ Completed a postgraduate or professional school degree

g. Additionally, we need to know which one of the following broad categories covers your total expected family income for this year—that is, 1999.

____ 0–$14,999   ____ $50,000–$74,999
____ $15,000–$29,999   ____ Over $75,000
____ $30,000–$49,999

h. Generally speaking, do you usually think of yourself as a Republican, Democrat, Independent, or what?

___Republican   ___Democrat   ___Independent   ___Other

If a Republican or Democrat: Would you consider yourself a strong (Republican/Democrat) or not a very strong (Republican/Democrat)?

Strong   Not strong

If Independent or no preference: Do you think of yourself as closer to the Republican or Democratic Party?

___Republican   ___Democratic   ___Neither

Thank you for your participation and have a good day.

Bibliography

Abraham, Henry (1998). *The Judicial Process*. 7th ed. New York: Oxford University Press.

Altheide, David L. (1984). "TV News and the Social Construction of Justice." In Ray Surette, ed., *Justice and the Media*. Springfield, Ill.: Charles C. Thomas, pp. 292–304.

Ansolabehere, Stephen, Roy Behr, and Shanto Iyengar (1993). *The Media Game*. New York: Macmillan.

Bagdikian, Ben (1997). *The Media Monopoly*. 5th ed. Boston: Beacon Press.

Bailey, F. Lee, with Harvey Aronson (1971). *The Defense Never Rests*. New York: Stein and Day Publishers.

Bandura, Albert (1994). "Social Cognitive Theory of Mass Communication." In Jennings Bryant and Dolf Zimmerman, eds., *Media Effects: Advances in Theory and Research*. Hillsdale, N.J.: Lawrence Erlbaum, pp. 61–90.

Barak, Gregg, ed. (1994). *Media, Process, and the Social Construction of Crime: Studies in Newsmaking Criminology*. New York: Garland.

Barber, Susanna (1987). *News Cameras in the Courtroom: A Free Press–Fair Trial Debate*. Norwood, N.J.: Ablex.

Bartlett, Katharine R., and Rosanne Kennedy, eds. (1992). *Feminist Legal Theory: Readings in Law and Gender*. Boulder, Colo.: Westview.

Belknap, Joanne (1991). "Women in Conflict: An Analysis of Women Correctional Officers." *Women and Criminal Justice* 2: 89–116.

Bennett, Lance W., and David L. Paletz, eds. (1994). *Taken by Storm*. Chicago: University of Chicago Press.

Bennett, Stephen Earl (1986). *Apathy in America*. Dobbs Ferry, N.Y.: Transnational Publishers.

Berger, Arthur Asa (1996). *Manufacturing Desire*. New Brunswick, N.J.: Transaction Publishers.

Binion, Gayle (1993). "The Nature of Feminist Jurisprudence." *Judicature* (November/December): 140–143.

Boland, Barbara, Paul Hahanna, and Ronald Stones (1992). *The Prosecution of Felony Arrests.* Washington, D.C.: U.S. Department of Justice, Bureau of Justice Statistics (February).

Boritch, Helen (1992). "Gender and Criminal Court Outcomes: An Historical Analysis." *Criminology* 30: 293–325.

Brummett, Barry (1990). "Mediating the Laws: Popular Trials and the Mass Media." In Robert Hariman, ed., *Popular Trials: Rhetoric, Mass Media, and the Law.* Tuscaloosa: University of Alabama Press, pp. 179–193.

Bryant, Jennings, and Dolf Zimmerman, eds. (1994). *Media Effects: Advances in Theory and Research.* Hillsdale, N.J.: Lawrence Erlbaum.

Bugliosi, Vincent, with Curt Gentry (1974). *Helter Skelter: The True Story of the Manson Murders.* New York: W. W. Norton.

Buzawa, Eve S. (1996). *Women As Victims.* Thousand Oaks, Calif.: Sage.

Caldeira, Gregory (1986). "Neither the Purse Nor the Sword." *American Political Science Review* 80: 1209–1226.

Cannon, Lou (1997). *Official Negligence: How Rodney King and the Riots Changed Los Angeles and the LAPD.* New York: Times Books.

Cantril, Albert H. (1991). *The Opinion Connection.* Washington, D.C.: Congressional Quarterly Press.

Chamallas, Martha (1999). *Introduction to Feminist Jurisprudence.* New York: Aspen Law and Business.

Chiasson, Lloyd, Jr., ed. (1997). *The Press on Trial.* Westport, Conn.: Praeger.

Christian, John, and William Turner (1978). *The Assassination of Robert Kennedy.* New York: Random House.

Cohn, Majorie, and David Dow (1998). *Cameras in the Courtroom: Television and the Pursuit of Justice.* Jefferson, N.C.: McFarland.

Conway, M. Margaret, Gertrude A. Steuernagel, and David W. Ahern. *Women and Political Participation* (Washington, D.C.: Congressional Quarterly Press, 1997).

Crenshaw, Kimberle, ed. (1996). *Critical Race Theory: The Key Writings That Formed the Movement.* New York: New Press.

Darden, Christopher A., with Jess Walter (1996). *In Contempt.* New York: ReganBooks.

Dautrich, Kenneth, and Thomas H. Hartley (1999). *How the News Media Fail American Voters: Causes, Consequences, and Remedies.* New York: Columbia University Press.

Davis, Dennis K., and John P. Robinson (1990). "Television News and the Informed Public: An Information-Processing Approach." *Journal of Communication* 40: 106–119.

Davis, Richard (1996). *The Press and American Politics.* 2d ed. Upper Saddle River, N.J.: Prentice-Hall.

——— (1998). *The Web of Politics: The Internet's Impact on the American Political System.* New York: Oxford University Press.

Davis, Richard, and Diana Owen (1998). *New Media and American Politics.* New York: Oxford University Press.

Davison, W. Phillips (1983). "The Third-Person Effect in Communication." *Public Opinion Quarterly* 47 (spring): 1–15.

Delgado, Richard, ed. (1995). *Critical Race Theory: The Cutting Edge.* Philadelphia: Temple University Press.

Dershowitz, Alan M. (1997). *Reasonable Doubts: The Criminal Justice System and the O.J. Simpson Case.* New York: Simon and Schuster.

——— (1986). *Reversal of Fortune.* New York: Random House.

Dionne, E. J. (1991). *Why Americans Hate Politics.* New York: Simon and Schuster.

Dominick, Joseph (1978). "Crime and Law Enforcement in Mass Media." In Charles Winick, ed., *Deviance and Mass Media.* Thousand Oaks, Calif.: Sage, pp. 105–128.

Dye, Thomas R., L. Harmon Zeigler, and S. Robert Lichter (1992). *American Politics in the Media Age.* 4th ed. Fort Worth, Tex.: Harcourt Brace.

Entman, Robert (1989). *Democracy Without Citizens: Media and the Decay of American Politics.* New York: Oxford University Press, chapters 5 and 6.

——— (1997). "Modern Racism and Images of Blacks in Local Television News." In Shanto Iyengar and Richard Reeves, eds., *Do the Media Govern?* Thousand Oaks, Calif.: Sage, pp. 283–286.

Epstein, Lee (1998). *Contemplating Courts.* 2d ed. Washington, D.C.: Congressional Quarterly Press.

Feinman, Clarice (1994). *Women in the Criminal Justice System.* Westport, Conn.: Praeger.

Franklin, Charles, and Liane Kosacki (1995). "Media, Knowledge, and Public Evaluations of the Supreme Court." In Lee Epstein, ed., *Contemplating Courts* (Washington, D.C.: Congressional Quarterly Press), pp. 352–375.

Friedman, Lawrence (1986). *A History of American Law.* 2d ed. New York: Simon and Schuster.

Gabler, Neil (1998). *Life: The Movie.* New York: Alfred Knopf.

Gans, Herbert J. (1979). *Deciding What's News: A Study of CBS Evening News, NBC Nightly News, Newsweek, and Time.* New York: Vintage Books.

Garrison, Jim (1988). *On the Trail of Assassins.* New York: Sheridan Press.

Geis, Gilbert, and Leigh B. Bienen (1998). *Crimes of the Century.* Boston: Northeastern University Press.

Gilliam, Franklin D., Jr., Shanto Iyengar, Adam Simon, and Oliver Wright (1997). "Crime in Black and White: The Violent, Scary World of Local News." In Shanto Iyengar and Richard Reeves, eds., *Do the Media Govern?* Thousand Oaks, Calif.: Sage, pp. 287–295.

Goldfarb, Ronald L. (1998). *TV or Not TV: Television, Justice, and the Courts.* New York: New York University Press.

Goldstein, Leslie F. (1992). *The Difference Debate: Feminist Jurisprudence.* Lanham, Md.: Rowman and Littlefield..

Goode, Stephen (1979). *Assassination! Kennedy, King, Kennedy.* New York: Watts.

Graber, Doris (1980). *Crime News and the Public.* Westport, Conn.: Praeger.

———— (1997). *Mass Media and American Politics.* 5th ed. Washington, D.C.: Congressional Quarterly Press.

Graysmith, Robert (1997). *Unabomber: A Desire to Kill.* Washington, D.C.: Regnery Publishing.

Greek, Cecil (1996). "Crime and the Media Course Syllabus and Lectures," online without pagination, at www.fsu.edu/~crimdo/grade&m.html#lectures.

Hallin, Daniel C. (1986). *The "Uncensored War": The Media and Vietnam.* New York: Oxford University Press.

Haltom, William (1998). *Reporting on the Courts: How the Mass Media Cover Judicial Actions.* Chicago: Nelson-Hall.

Harris, David A. (1993). "The Appearance of Justice: Court TV, Conventional Television, and Public Understanding of the Criminal Justice System." *Arizona Law Review* 35: 785–827.

Harwood, Richard (1999). "Searching for Facts in a Sea of Speculation." *Nieman Report* 53 (summer): 61.

Hemmens, Craig, Kristin Strom, and Elicia Schlegel (1997). "Gender Bias in the Courts: A Review." Paper presented at the Academy of Criminal Justice Sciences, Louisville, Ky.

Hill, Kevin (1998). *Cyberpolitics: Citizen Activism in the Age of the Internet.* Lanham, Md.: Rowman and Littlefield.

Hoekstra, Valerie, and Jeffrey A. Segal (1996). "The Shepherding of Local Public Opinion: The Supreme Court and Lamb's Chapel." *Journal of Politics* 58: 1079–1102.

Imrich, Dorothy J., Charles Mullin, and Daniel Linz (1995). "Measuring the Extent of Prejudicial Pretrial Publicity in Major American Newspapers: A Content Analysis." *Journal of Communication* 45 (summer): 94–117.

Iyengar, Shanto (1991). *Is Anyone Responsible? How Television Frames Political Issues.* Chicago: University of Chicago Press.

Iyengar, Shanto, and Donald Kinder (1987). *News That Matters.* Chicago: University of Chicago Press.

Iyengar, Shanto, and Richard Reeves, eds. (1997). *Do the Media Govern?* Thousand Oaks, Calif.: Sage.

Jacoby, Jacob, and Wayne D. Hoyer (1982). "Viewer Miscomprehension of Televised Communications: Selected Findings." *Journal of Marketing* 46 (fall): 12–26.

Jamieson, Kathleen Hall, and Karlyn Kohrs Campbell (1998). *Interplay of Influence: News, Advertising, Politics, and the Mass Media.* 4th ed. Belmont, Calif.: Wadsworth Publishing.

Jordan, Tim (1999). *Cyberpower: The Culture and Politics of Cyberspace and the Internet.* New York: Routledge.

Kairys, David (1998). *The Politics of Law: A Progressive Critique.* 3d ed. New York: Basic Books.

Kappeler, Victor, Mark Blumberg, and Gary W. Potter (1996). *The Mythology of Crime and Criminal Justice.* 2d ed. Prospect Heights, Ill.: Waveland Press.

Katz, Burton S. (1998). *Justice Overruled: Unmasking the Criminal Justice System.* New York: Warner Books.

Kerbel, Matthew Robert (1995). *Remote and Controlled.* Boulder, Colo.: Westview Press.

——— (1994). *Edited for Television.* Boulder, CO: Westview Press.

Knappman, Edward W., ed. (1995). *American Trials of the 20th Century.* Detroit, Mich.: Visible Ink Press.

Knight, Alfred H. (1996). *The Life of the Law: The People and the Cases That Have Shaped Our Society, from King Alfred to Rodney King.* New York: Oxford University Press.

Kovach, Bill, and Tom Rosenstiel (1999). *Warp Speed: America in the Age of Mixed Media.* New York: The Century Foundation Press.

Krajicek, Richard (1998). *Scooped.* New York: Columbia University Press.

Kuklin, Bailey, and Jeffrey W. Stempel (1994). *Foundations of Law: A Jurisprudential Primer.* St. Paul, Minn.: West Publishing.

Kurtz, Howard (1995). *Hot Air.* New York: Basic Books.

Lanoue, David J., and Peter Schrott (1991). *The History, Impact, and Prospects of American Presidential Debates.* Westport, Conn.: Greenwood Press.

Lassiter, Christo (1996). "The O.J. Simpson Verdict: A Lesson in Black and White." *Michigan Journal of Race and Law* 1 (winter): 69–118.

Laufer, Peter (1995). *Inside Talk Radio.* New York: Birch Lane Press.

Lehrer, Jim (1999). "Blurring the Lines Hurts Journalism." *Nieman Report* 53 (summer): 65.

Lipsitz, George (1997). "The Greatest Story Ever Sold: Marketing and the O.J. Simpson Trial." In Toni Morrison and Claudia Brosky Lacour, eds., *Birth of a Nation' hood: Gaze, Script, and Spectacle in the O.J. Simpson Case.* New York: Pantheon Books, pp. 3–29.

Littleton, Cynthia (1995). "Verdict Propels Tabloid Ratings." *Broadcasting and Cable,* October 1, p. 8.

Lock, Schmuel T., Robert Y. Shapiro, and Lawrence R. Jacobs (1999). "The Impact of Political Debate on Government Trust: Reminding the Public What the Federal Government Does," *Political Behavior* 21: 239–264.

Lotz, Roy Edward (1991). *Crime and the American Press.* Westport, Conn.: Praeger.

Macchiarola, Frank (1997). "Finding the Truth in an American Criminal Trial: Some Observations." *Cardozo Journal of International Comparative Law* 5 (spring): 97–113.

Mandrese, Joe, and Thomas Tyler (1995). "Simpson Shakes New TV Season." *Advertising Age,* October 16, p. 8.

Martin, Elaine (1993). "Women on the Bench: A Different Voice?" *Judicature* 77: 126–128.

Martin, Susan Ehrlich, and Nancy C. Jurik (1996). *Doing Justice, Doing Gender: Women in Law and Criminal Justice Occupations.* Thousand Oaks, Calif.: Sage.

McCombs, Maxwell (1994). "News Influence on Our Pictures of the World." In Jennings Bryant and Dolf Zimmerman, eds., *Media Effects: Advances in Theory and Research.* Hillsdale, N.J.: Lawrence Erlbaum, pp. 1–16.

McGlen, Nancy E., and Karen O'Connor (1998). *Women, Politics, and American Society.* New York: Prentice-Hall.

Miller, Joanne, and Jon A. Krosnick (1997). "Anatomy of News Media Priming." In Shanto Iyengar and Richard Reeves, eds., *Do the Media Govern?* Thousand Oaks, Calif.: Sage, pp. 258–275.

Morgan, David (1978). *The Capitol Press Corps: Newsmen and the Governing of New York State.* Westport, Conn.: Greenwood Press.

Morrison, Toni, and Claudia Brodsky Lacour, eds. (1997). *Birth of a Nation'hood: Gaze, Script, and Spectacle in the O.J. Simpson Case.* New York: Pantheon Books.

Murphy, Walter E., and C. Herman Pritchett (1986). *Courts, Judges, and Politics.* 4th ed. New York: McGraw-Hill.

Murphy, Walter F., and Joseph Tanenhaus (1968). "Public Opinion and the Supreme Court." *Law and Society Review* 2 (February): 357–382.

Neubauer, David W. (1998). *America's Courts and the Criminal Justice System.* 6th ed. Belmont, Calif.: Wadsworth Publishing.

Neuman, Russell W. (1991). *The Future of the Mass Audience.* New York: Cambridge University Press.

Nye, Joseph S., Jr. (1997). "The Media and Declining Confidence in Government." *Journal of Press and Politics* 2 (summer): 4–9.

Nye, Joseph, Philip Zelikow, and David C. King (1997). *Why People Don't Trust Government.* Cambridge, Mass.: Harvard University Press.

Oates, Joyce Carol (1999). "The Mystery of JonBenet Ramsey." *New York Review of Books,* June 24, pp. 31–37.

Page, Benjamin I., Robert Y. Shapiro, and Glenn R. Dempsey (1987). "What Moves Public Opinion." *American Political Science Review* 81 (March): 23–43.

Paletz, David L. (1999). *The Media in American Politics.* New York: Longman.

Parenti, Michael (1986). *Inventing Reality.* New York: St. Martin's Press.

Patterson, Thomas (1993). *Out of Order.* New York: Knopf.

——— (1988). *The Mass Media Election: How Americans Choose Their President.* 3d ed. Westport, Conn.: Praeger.

Paul, Angelique (1997). "Turning the Camera on Court TV: Does Televising Trials Teach Us Anything About the Real Law?" *Ohio State Law Journal* 58: 655–694.

Postman, Neil (1986). *Amusing Ourselves to Death: Public Discourse in the Age of Show Business.* New York: Viking Penguin.

Protess, David L., and Maxwell E. McCombs, eds. (1991). *Agenda Setting.* Hillsdale, N.J.: Lawrence Erlbaum.

Reiman, Jeffrey (1995). *The Rich Get Richer and the Poor Get Prison: Ideology, Class, and Criminal Justice.* Boston: Allyn and Bacon.

Robinson, John P., and Dennis K. Davis (1990). "Television News and the Informed Public: An Information-Processing Approach." *Journal of Communication* 40: 106–119.

Robinson, Michael (1976). "Public Affairs Television and the Growth of Malaise." *American Political Science Review* 70: 409–432.

Rogers, Everett M., William B. Hart, and James W. Dearing (1997). "A Paradigmatic History of Agenda-Setting Research." In Shanto Iyengar and Richard Reeves, eds., *Do the Media Govern?* Thousand Oaks, Calif.: Sage, pp. 225–236.

Ryan, John Paul, Allan Ahman, Bruce Sales, and Sandra Shane Dubow (1980). *American Trial Judges.* New York: Free Press.

Sabato, Larry J. (1993). *Feeding Frenzy.* New York: Free Press.

Schlessinger, Philip, and Howard Tumber (1994). *Reporting Crime: The Media Politics of Criminal Justice.* Oxford: Clarendon Press.

Selnow, Gary (1998). *Electronic Whistle-Stops: The Impact of the Internet on American Politics.* Westport, Conn.: Praeger.

Shaw, Donald, and Maxwell McCombs (1977). *The Emergence of American Political Issues.* St. Paul, Minn.: West Publishing.

Scheb, John M., and William Lyons (2000). "Public Perception of the Supreme Court in the 1990s." In Eliot E. Slotnick, ed., *Judicial Politics: Readings from Judicature* (Chicago: American Judicature Society).

Shenk, David (1998). *Data Smog: Surviving the Information Glut.* San Francisco: Harper.

Sherry, Suzanna (1986). "Civic Virtue and the Feminine Voice in Constitutional Adjudication." *Virginia Law Review* 72: 543–591.

Sisk, Gregory, Michael Heise, and Andrew P. Morriss (1998). "Charting the Influences on the Judicial Mind: An Empirical Study of Judicial Reasoning," *New York University Law Review* 73: 1377–1500.

Slotnick, Elliot E., ed. (1992). *Judicial Politics: Readings from Judicature.* Chicago: American Judicature Society.

Smith, Eric R. A. N. (1989). *The Unchanging American Voter.* Berkeley: University of California Press.

Smith, Douglas (1997). "Structural and Functional Aspects of the Jury: Comparative Analysis and Proposals for Reform." *Alabama Law Review* 48 (winter): 441–581.

Smith, Patricia, ed. (1994). *Feminist Jurisprudence.* New York: Oxford University Press.

Stempel, Guido, III, and John Windhauser (1991). *The Media and the 1984 and 1988 Elections.* Westport, Conn.: Greenwood Press

Strickland, Ruth Ann, and Richter H. Moore Jr. (1994). "Cameras in State Courts: A Historical Perspective," *Judicature* 78 (November/December): 128–135.

Sunstein, Cass (1988). "Feminism and Legal Theory." *Harvard Law Review* 101: 826–848.

Surette, Ray (1989). "Media Trials." *Journal of Criminal Justice* 17: 293–308.

———— (1998). *Media, Crime, and Criminal Justice: Images and Realities.* 2d ed. Belmont, Calif.: Wadsworth Publishing.

———— (1991). "Methodological Problems in Determining Media Effects on Criminal Justice: A Review and Suggestions for the Future." *Criminal Justice Policy Review* 6: 291–310.

Thaler, Paul (1994). *The Watchful Eye: American Justice in the Age of the Television Trial.* Westport, Conn.: Praeger.

Thomas, Sue (1994). *How Women Legislate.* New York: Oxford University Press.

Tolchin, Susan J. (1995). *The Angry American.* Boulder, Colo.: Westview Press.

Toobin, Jeffrey (1997). *The Run of His Life: The People v. O.J. Simpson.* New York: Touchstone.

Vago, Steven (2000). *Law and Society.* 6th ed. Upper Saddle River, N.J.: Prentice-Hall.

Vinson, C. Danielle, and John S. Ertter (1999). "Entertainment or Education: How Do Media Cover the Courts?" Paper presented at the Midwest Political Science Association, Chicago, April 15–18.

Watson, Tex (1978). *Will You Die for Me?* Old Tappan, N.J.: Fleming Revell.

Wattenberg, Martin P. (1990). *The Decline of American Political Parties: 1952–1988.* Cambridge, Mass.: Harvard University Press.

Wilson, Barbara, et al. (1997). *National Television Violence Study.* Vol. 1. Thousand Oaks, Calif.: Sage.

Wilson, Theo (1997). *Headline Justice.* New York: Thunder's Mouth Press.

Wright, William (1983). *The Von Bulow Affair.* New York: Delacorte Press.

Zaller, John (1992). *The Nature and Origins of Mass Opinion.* New York: Cambridge University Press.

Zaller, John, and Stanley Feldman (1992). "A Simple Theory of the Survey Response: Answering Questions Versus Revealing Preferences." *American Journal of Political Science* 36: 579–616.

Zeigler, L. Harmon, and William Haltom (1989). "More Bad News About the News." *Public Opinion* (May/June): 50–52.

Index

23, 73, 77, 156, 168. *See also* Television news

Charles Grodin show, 88, 97, 101, 156

Civic education, legal system coverage as, 11, 81, 187, 189

Clinton-Lewinsky scandal, 42–43; cable news coverage of, 105–106; coverage perceived as legitimate, 103–104; gender focus in, 157, 158–159; national issues in, 46–47; public knowledge of, 129; public trust in legal system affected by, 134, 162–164; tabloid-style coverage of, 2, 4, 27, 28, 43–44, 55

CNBC, 10, 61; ratings, 104, 105

CNN network, 23, 32, 92, 93, 95, 97, 157; Gulf War coverage, 90; ratings, 104, 105

Commodification of criminal trials, 28, 47, 78; agenda-setting function and, 97, 191

Communications Decency Act, 193

Court system: media coverage impacts, 186–187, 193; public perceptions of, 123, 124. *See also* Criminal justice system

Court TV, 32, 36, 41, 93–94

Criminal justice system: exposure, as civic education, 11, 81, 187, 189; historical coverage of, 24–25; increased coverage of, 1–3; new media's exposure of, 114–115; perceptions of judges in, 139–140; perceptions of jury system in, 136–137; personal wealth and fairness in, 171–173; public assessment of, 160–164; social/racial cleavages in, 153–154; trustworthiness and

fairness in, 126, 142–143, 153, 175–176, 189

Criminal trial coverage. *See* Legal proceedings; Tabloid justice coverage

Critical Legal Studies (CLS) movement, 153–154, 176–177n7

Critical race theory, 154

Curtis, James, 97, 99–100

Dahmer, Jeffrey, 67–68

Darden, Christopher, 126

Dateline, 3, 59, 77, 78–79, 156

Davis, Richard, 9

Deciding What's News (study), 9

Denver Post, 46

Denver Rocky Mountain News, 46

Dershowitz, Alan, 73, 186

Diallo, Amadou, 141

Domestic violence: Simpson trial and, 170

Donaldson, Sam, 43

Drudge, Matt, 10

Dunne, Dominick, 36–37

E! Entertainment Television, 28

Early Show, The, 59

Entertainment: crime and legal proceedings presented as, 4, 5, 29, 35, 37, 47, 54–56, 57–58, 192; and news, melding of, 101–102, 103–104; news media's transition toward, 59; value, newsworthiness and, 9–10

Entman, Robert, 192

Equal Time, 97

ESPN/ESPN2, 23

Expert commentators, in news media, 95, 107–110

About the Book

Few would disagree that we have entered an era of "tabloid justice"—one in which the sensationalistic and often tawdry details of criminal cases have become the centerpiece of news coverage. Richard L. Fox and Robert W. Van Sickel show just how far this situation has progressed, and with what results.

Drawing on a wealth of primary data, the authors find that the mass media's excessive attention to high-profile trials has highlighted, and at times aggravated, many of the deepest social divisions in U.S. society, especially those associated with race, gender, ethnicity, and social class. Their results also show that a distorted presentation of the justice system has reduced the legitimacy and authority of the law in the eyes of the public.

This groundbreaking book focuses on the cases of Rodney King, William Kennedy Smith, the Menendez brothers, Louise Woodward, O.J. Simpson, JonBenet Ramsey, and Bill Clinton to document the tactics of a media driven by profit to the detriment of important political and legal principles.

Richard L. Fox is assistant professor of political science at Union College. He is author of *Gender Dynamics in Congressional Elections*. **Robert W. Van Sickel** is assistant professor of political science at Purdue University, Calumet. His publications include *Not a Particularly Different Voice: The Jurisprudence of Sandra Day O'Connor*.

DATE DUE

APR 0 5 2005			
			Printed in USA